MANHATTAN GMAT

GMAT Roadmap:
Expert Advice Through Test Day

GMAT Strategy Guide

This guide provides a comprehensive look at preparing to face the GMAT outside the scope of Quant or Verbal preparation. You'll learn about pacing, time management, and how to deal with test anxiety.

guide **0**

GMAT Roadmap: Expert Advice Through Test Day, Fifth Edition

10-digit International Standard Book Number: 1-935707-69-8
13-digit International Standard Book Number: 978-1-935707-69-1
eISBN: 978-0-974806-99-0

Note: *GMAT, Graduate Management Admission Test, Graduate Management Admission Council,* and *GMAC* are all registered trademarks of the Graduate Management Admission Council, which neither sponsors nor is affiliated in any way with this product.

Layout Design: Dan McNaney and Cathy Huang
Cover Design: Evyn Williams and Dan McNaney
Cover Photography: Adrian Buckmaster

SUSTAINABLE FORESTRY INITIATIVE

Certified Chain of Custody
Promoting Sustainable Forestry
www.sfiprogram.org
SFI-00756

INSTRUCTIONAL GUIDE SERIES

0   **GMAT Roadmap**
(ISBN: 978-1-935707-69-1)

1   **Fractions, Decimals, & Percents**
(ISBN: 978-1-935707-63-9)

2   **Algebra**
(ISBN: 978-1-935707-62-2)

3   **Word Problems**
(ISBN: 978-1-935707-68-4)

4   **Geometry**
(ISBN: 978-1-935707-64-6)

5   **Number Properties**
(ISBN: 978-1-935707-65-3)

6   **Critical Reasoning**
(ISBN: 978-1-935707-61-5)

7   **Reading Comprehension**
(ISBN: 978-1-935707-66-0)

8   **Sentence Correction**
(ISBN: 978-1-935707-67-7)

9   **Integrated Reasoning & Essay**
(ISBN: 978-1-935707-83-7)

SUPPLEMENTAL GUIDE SERIES

Math GMAT Supplement Guides

Foundations of GMAT Math
(ISBN: 978-1-935707-59-2)

Advanced GMAT Quant
(ISBN: 978-1-935707-15-8)

Official Guide Companion
(ISBN: 978-0-984178-01-8)

Verbal GMAT Supplement Guides

Foundations of GMAT Verbal
(ISBN: 978-1-935707-01-9)

MANHATTAN
GMAT

April 24th, 2012

Dear Student,

Thank you for picking up a copy of *GMAT Roadmap*. We hope this book provides just the guidance you need to get the most out of your GMAT studies.

As with most accomplishments, there were many people involved in the creation of the book you're holding. First and foremost is Zeke Vanderhoek, the founder of Manhattan GMAT. Zeke was a lone tutor in New York when he started the company in 2000. Now, 12 years later, the company has instructors and offices nationwide and contributes to the studies and successes of thousands of students each year.

Our Manhattan GMAT Strategy Guides are based on the continuing experiences of our instructors and students. For this *GMAT Roadmap*, we are particularly indebted to Liz Ghini Moliski and Abby Pelcyger, who drove the development of this book from start to finish. Many other instructors, including Eric Caballero, Jennifer Dziura, Dmitry Farber, Whitney Garner, Ian Jorgeson, Stacey Koprince, Jamie Nelson, Ron Purewal, Tom Rose, Jon Schneider, and Tommy Wallach, made valuable contributions along the way. Dan McNaney and Cathy Huang provided their design expertise to make the books as user-friendly as possible, and Liz Krisher made sure all the moving pieces came together at just the right time. And there's Chris Ryan. Beyond providing additions and edits for this book, Chris continues to be the driving force behind all of our curriculum efforts. His leadership is invaluable. Finally, thank you to all of the Manhattan GMAT students who provided testimonials and advice for this *Roadmap*. It wouldn't be half of what it is without your voice.

At Manhattan GMAT, we continually aspire to provide the best instructors and resources possible. We hope that you'll find our commitment manifest in this book. If you have any questions or comments, please email me at dgonzalez@manhattangmat.com. I'll look forward to reading your comments, and I'll be sure to pass them along to our curriculum team.

Thanks again, and best of luck preparing for the GMAT!

Sincerely,

Dan Gonzalez
President
Manhattan GMAT

HOW TO ACCESS YOUR ONLINE RESOURCES

If you…

⊳ **are a registered Manhattan GMAT student**

and have received this book as part of your course materials, you have AUTOMATIC access to ALL of our online resources. This includes all practice exams, question banks, and online updates to this book. To access these resources, follow the instructions in the Welcome Guide provided to you at the start of your program. Do NOT follow the instructions below.

⊳ **purchased this book from the Manhattan GMAT online store or at one of our centers**

1. Go to: http://www.manhattangmat.com/practicecenter.cfm.

2. Log in using the username and password used when your account was set up.

⊳ **purchased this book at a retail location**

1. Create an account with Manhattan GMAT at the website: https://www.manhattangmat.com/createaccount.cfm.

2. Go to: http://www.manhattangmat.com/access.cfm.

3. Follow the instructions on the screen.

Your one year of online access begins on the day that you register your book at the above URL.

You only need to register your product ONCE at the above URL. To use your online resources any time AFTER you have completed the registration process, log in to the following URL: http://www.manhattangmat.com/practicecenter.cfm.

Please note that online access is nontransferable. This means that only NEW and UNREGISTERED copies of the book will grant you online access. Previously used books will NOT provide any online resources.

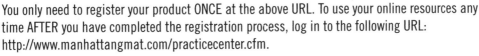

⊳ **purchased an eBook version of this book**

1. Create an account with Manhattan GMAT at the website: https://www.manhattangmat.com/createaccount.cfm.

2. Email a copy of your purchase receipt to books@manhattangmat.com to activate your resources. Please be sure to use the same email address to create an account that you used to purchase the eBook.

For any technical issues, email books@manhattangmat.com or call 800-576-4628.

Please refer to the following page for a description of the online resources that come with this book.

YOUR ONLINE RESOURCES

Your purchase includes ONLINE ACCESS to the following:

⊙ 6 Computer-Adaptive Online Practice Exams

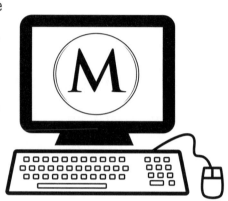

The 6 full-length computer-adaptive practice exams included with the purchase of this book are delivered online using Manhattan GMAT's proprietary computer-adaptive test engine. The exams adapt to your ability level by drawing from a bank of more than 1,200 unique questions of varying difficulty levels written by Manhattan GMAT's expert instructors, all of whom have scored in the 99th percentile on the Official GMAT. At the end of each exam you will receive a score, an analysis of your results, and the opportunity to review detailed explanations for each question. You may choose to take the exams timed or untimed.

The content presented in this book is updated periodically to ensure that it reflects the GMAT's most current trends and is as accurate as possible. You may view any known errors or minor changes upon registering for online access.

Important Note: The 6 computer adaptive online exams included with the purchase of this book are the SAME exams that you receive upon purchasing ANY book in the Manhattan GMAT Complete Strategy Guide Set.

⊙ *OG Archer* Official Guide Tracker

The OG Archer is an online interface for answering OG problems and measuring your performance. Time yourself on individual questions, mark the problems you guessed on, and note those you'd like to do again later. Then, view performance statistics and review answer explanations written by Manhattan GMAT Instructors (OG 12 quant questions only).

⊙ Online Updates to the Contents in this Book

The content presented in this book is updated periodically to ensure that it reflects the GMAT's most current trends. You may view all updates, including any known errors or changes, upon registering for online access.

TABLE *of* CONTENTS

guide **0**

Introduction

You're ambitious and motivated. Otherwise you wouldn't even be considering an MBA. You also know that the GMAT is the real deal. Consider this:

- Every year, over 40,000 people take the GMAT more than once.
- To achieve a 700 score, you must outperform 93% of test-takers.
- High SAT scores do not necessarily correlate to high GMAT scores.
- Many GMAT test-takers study for 2–3 hours per day for 3–4 months, while working 70+ hours per week.

So how do you prepare to face the GMAT? The *GMAT Roadmap* will show you the way, whether you are enrolled in one of our classes or working through our materials on your own.

Every article in this book was written by a veteran instructor with years of experience and success in both classroom teaching and private tutoring, so these pages are overflowing with expert advice. Looking for guidance on time management? Tips for improving reading comprehension? Advice on handling test anxiety? You'll find it all here.

How to Use This Book

Chapter 1: What Is the GMAT?
Read this first if you are unfamiliar with the GMAT.

Chapters 2 & 3: Getting Organized & How to Learn Content
If you've signed up for a Manhattan GMAT course, read *before* your course starts but after you take a Manhattan GMAT practice exam. These chapters will help you interpret your practice test results and chart your game plan.

Chapters 4–12:
These chapters are designed to guide you through our course or through nine weeks of self-study, so read one per week. Focus more on the parts of the book that seem the most relevant for you. For example, if you are struggling in Quant but doing very well in Verbal, you may want to devote extra time to Chapter 4: The Big Picture of GMAT Quant, and just skim through Chapter 5: The Big Picture of GMAT Verbal.

We hope that you will find this book both encouraging and informative. We wish you all the best as you begin your GMAT preparation!

— The instructors of Manhattan GMAT

Chapter 1 of GMAT Roadmap

GMAT Roadmap

What Is the GMAT?

In This Chapter...

Chapter 1:
What Is the GMAT?

The Graduate Management Admission Test (GMAT) is required by most business schools. The test is designed to assess the overall reasoning skills required for success in business school; it is not a test of knowledge or achievement in any particular subject area. Therefore, the GMAT requires only a bare minimum of business-related knowledge—generally limited to basic accounting concepts, such as revenue and profit, that are fundamental enough to be considered general knowledge.

The GMAT does, of course, require some foundational knowledge, but none of that knowledge is particularly advanced. The objective content of the exam is generally limited to high-school algebra and geometry, logical reasoning, and college-level reading comprehension. When GMAT problems are difficult, the challenge does not stem from the use of obscure facts, rules, or procedures; rather, difficult GMAT problems are like puzzles, in that they combine relatively basic concepts in unusual and often ingenious ways. In other words, the test cannot be mastered with linear thinking and memorized routines alone; it depends heavily on intuitive insights and lateral thinking.

The GMAT consists of three separate sections: two 30-minute essays, a 75-minute Quantitative section, and a 75-minute Verbal section, separated by optional 8-minute breaks. The total length of the actual test, then, is just under four hours—and the miscellaneous formalities that precede the test can add up to another hour. The GMAT is thus not only a test of reasoning, it's also a test of endurance.

In June 2012, one of the GMAT's two essays will be replaced by a new section known as Integrated Reasoning (IR). This section, which will consist of 12–15 questions, combines both math and Verbal tasks. It will require test-takers to sort through larger quantities of information; for instance, students will have to extract relevant information from a full page of tables or determine relationships among multiple short passages.

GMAT Structure

TEST FORMAT	# OF QUESTIONS	TIME
The Essays		
Analysis of an Argument	1	30 min
Analysis of an Issue	1	30 min
Optional Break		8 min
Quantitative	37	75 min
Problem Solving (~22)	~22	
Data Sufficiency (~15)	~15	
Optional Break		8 min
Verbal	41	75 min
Sentence Correction	14–15	
Critical Reasoning	13–14	
Reading Comprehension	12–14	
		3 hrs 30 min (+ breaks)

Note: The various question types within each section are randomly distributed throughout that section.

GMAT Test Registration

The GMAT, which costs $250, is administered on most days of the year; only major holidays are completely excluded, although some testing centers do not offer the test on Sundays. Generally, appointments on weekends and during peak application periods are in high demand, so if you live in a large metropolitan area and plan to schedule a weekend appointment, especially during the busy season of August through December, be sure to do so a month or two in advance!

If you need a test date on short notice, try checking your local test center's schedule several times per day. If another test-taker cancels his or her appointment, that time will be made available immediately.

For more information about test scheduling and fees, special accommodations, and available appointment times at your local testing center, see GMAC's official website at **www.mba.com**.

You can't take the GMAT more than once within 31 days, and you can't take it more than five times in 12 months. However, within those restrictions, you may take the test as many times as you wish. In general, business schools only take into account the applicant's *highest* overall score. Considering the fact that most students score higher on the second administration, there is a clear advantage to taking the test twice. Therefore, be sure to plan an application timeline that allows you to schedule two administrations of the test, with at least 31 days in between.

TRIVIA

If you happen to score an 800, you won't be allowed to take the test again until your score expires five years later!

1

Some schools will give you a few extra weeks after the application deadline to take or retake the GMAT, but not all schools are so generous. If you think this extra time might help, call your schools and check their policies.

Canceling & Rescheduling

Once you've scheduled a testing appointment, you do have the option to cancel or reschedule it. If you reschedule your appointment at any time up until seven days before the scheduled administration, GMAC will charge you an additional fee of $50. After that date, if you make any changes, you will forfeit the full $250 fee (and will have to pay another $250 if and when you reschedule).

When you sit for the exam, you will also have the option to cancel your scores immediately after finishing the test (again with no refund). Unlike an advance cancellation, though, this retroactive cancellation *will* appear on your official score report—that is, business schools will see that you were scheduled for the test but did not submit a score. Your report will be similarly affected if you don't show up for your appointment. In either of these two cases, you will also have to wait 31 days to take the test again.

GMAC reserves the right to change any of these policies or fees without notice, so be sure to check the current terms posted at **www.mba.com** when you schedule your appointment.

Scoring

The Verbal and Quantitative sections of the GMAT are scored separately, each on a 51-point scale; the combination of the two scores is then converted into an overall GMAT score on the familiar scale of 200–800. The essays receive a separate score from 1 to 6 (or 0 if an essay fails to address the prompt); this score does not factor into the overall 200–800 score.

The above scores represent your objective performance on the exam, and are independent of other test-takers' performance. However, the GMAC also reports you scores as percentiles, which *do* indicate your performance relative to other test-takers. For instance, a Verbal percentile of 87 indicates that, on the Verbal section, you scored higher than 87 percent of the test-taking population.

In general, a much larger proportion of GMAT test-takers are highly competitive on the Quant section than on the Verbal section. As a result, the numerical scores on the two sections will not translate into percentiles in the same way. A score of 46, for instance, is in the 99th percentile on the Verbal section, but in only the 78th percentile on the Quant section. (Even a Quant score of 51—the highest possible score on that section—is only in the 98th percentile!)

It is important to note that business school admissions are far from formulaic, and that no GMAT score, however high or low, will absolutely guarantee your admission to (or rejection by) any particular school. Still, the published median scores of top schools can be helpful as a general reference. For the top 20 American full-

> **TIP**
>
> Most business schools are not particularly concerned about unbalanced Quant and Verbal scores. However, some schools—most notably international schools—will sometimes state an explicit preference for certain percentile scores, such as 80th or higher percentile on each section. Note that such preferences are much more demanding in Quant than in Verbal!

1

time MBA programs, those median scores range from 670–720. Programs at schools with a more regional influence, as well as part-time and executive MBA programs, generally have slightly lower median scores. In any case, you should research the statistics for each program in which you are interested.

The 0–6 score for the essays is universally considered less important than the 200–800 score. (In fact, this lesser importance is the reason why the essays are not integrated into the overall GMAT score.) Most business schools will have no qualms about an essay score of 4 or higher; even lower essay scores will not necessarily weaken an otherwise strong application.

> **TIP**
>
> Most business schools ask applicants to provide only one GMAT score; however, be sure to check the requirements of each individual application, as some schools may ask for your complete five-year GMAT history. Don't let the latter case worry you! Remember that all schools will ultimately receive the same five-year score history, and that all of them will place primary emphasis on your best scores.

Score Reports

Immediately upon completing the GMAT (unless, of course, you cancel your scores), you will receive an *unofficial score report*, which includes your overall 200–800 score as well as your Quantitative and Verbal subscores and percentile rankings. "Unofficial" does *not* mean that your scores might change— your official scores will be the same, unless they are canceled because of misconduct or irregularities discovered after the test administration. Your *official score report* is different only in that it includes your essay score.

You may select recipient schools for your score reports either before the exam or at any time in the following 5 years. If you choose schools before the test, you are allowed to send up to five reports free of charge; at any later time, each report sent will incur a fee of $28. (GMAT scores officially expire after 5 years, but if you have not taken the GMAT within the past five years, you may send reports for test administrations up to 10 years ago. However, business schools will generally have reservations about accepting such submissions.) It is always best to use your free score reports, as schools will see your entire GMAT history for the past five years—including cancellations—regardless of when you submit your score report. In other words, it is impossible to "game" the score reporting so that schools will only see certain administrations of the test.

How Important Is It Really? How Is the GMAT Used by Schools? – mbaMission

Each admissions committee ("AdCom") assesses applicants across several different dimensions, one of which is academic work, including GPA and GMAT score. (Other dimensions include leadership potential, career progression, and engagement with the world outside of work.) Together, all the dimensions that the AdCom considers create a holistic picture of the candidate.

Viewed in conjunction with your GPA, your GMAT score serves as an important indicator to the AdCom as to whether you will be able to handle the coursework at business school. The AdCom will explore your aggregate score, as well as your Quantitative score and Verbal score, which together make up your overall score. As you determine which schools to target, one straightforward approach is to look at the mean GMAT score of each potential school's incoming class and the range of the middle 80% of enrolled students' scores (both can typically be found on the schools' websites as well as on various independent ranking lists). If your overall GMAT score is near or higher than the mean, you can feel confident that the AdCom will not view this dimension of your application as an issue. Although a high GMAT score can enhance your overall competitiveness at top-tier schools, it alone cannot secure your admission. Meanwhile, a low or average GMAT score by no means precludes your admission.

Your GPA can also affect the relative importance of your GMAT score. If you have a solid GPA in a rigorous analytical field—for example, a 3.5 or higher in accounting or finance—then the AdCom will look at your GMAT score primarily to validate what your GPA already indicates: that you can manage the MBA workload. If, however, your GPA is low or you have not taken any analytical courses, you would need to really perform on test day to prove that despite this apparent shortcoming, you do indeed have the intellectual horsepower to succeed in your MBA studies.

Another notable reason AdComs consider an applicant's GMAT score is that it provides a common assessment tool. Undergraduate GPAs can vary tremendously across colleges and disciplines, and international universities use a variety of grading scales that render "apples to apples" comparisons difficult, if not impossible. The GMAT, however, is a standardized test and thus allows AdComs to compare applicants along the same assessment scale.

GMAT vs. GRE

You may have heard that some business schools are now accepting the GRE in addition to the GMAT. As a result, many students have begun to consider taking the GRE in place of the GMAT. If this is something you are mulling over, there are a couple of things you should keep in mind when making your decision.

First, it is a common misconception that the GRE is an easier test than the GMAT. Although it is true that the Quantitative section of the GRE is, in general, less difficult than that of the GMAT, the difference in difficulty level is virtually unnoticeable unless you are already able to achieve a scaled score of 45+ on the GMAT Quant section. That is to say, only top scorers would notice a significant difference. With regard to the Verbal sections, many people consider the GRE to be harder than the GMAT. Although both tests focus on Reading Comprehension and Critical Reasoning, it's often noted that the GRE's reading passages are more difficult than the GMAT's. Also, instead of testing grammar, the GRE tests vocabulary, which takes most people longer to learn than grammar rules.

Another important factor to consider is whether your target business schools will accept the GRE. Even though there are a lot of schools that do, *most* business schools ***do not*** accept the GRE. Education Testing Service (ETS), the organization that owns the GRE, has a list of the business schools that will accept the GRE on its website. If you are seriously considering taking the GRE over the GMAT, we recommend you take a look at the list to be sure that your schools will accept the score:

http://www.ets.org/gre/general/about/mba/programs/

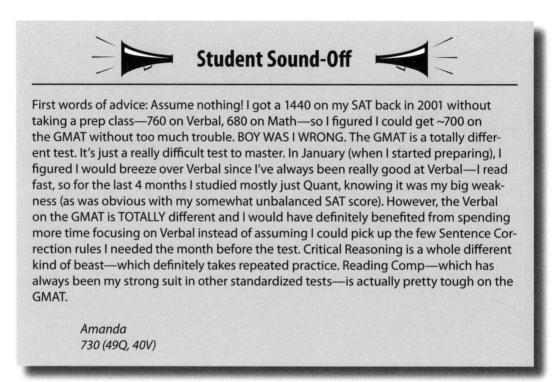

Student Sound-Off

First words of advice: Assume nothing! I got a 1440 on my SAT back in 2001 without taking a prep class—760 on Verbal, 680 on Math—so I figured I could get ~700 on the GMAT without too much trouble. BOY WAS I WRONG. The GMAT is a totally different test. It's just a really difficult test to master. In January (when I started preparing), I figured I would breeze over Verbal since I've always been really good at Verbal—I read fast, so for the last 4 months I studied mostly just Quant, knowing it was my big weakness (as was obvious with my somewhat unbalanced SAT score). However, the Verbal on the GMAT is TOTALLY different and I would have definitely benefited from spending more time focusing on Verbal instead of assuming I could pick up the few Sentence Correction rules I needed the month before the test. Critical Reasoning is a whole different kind of beast—which definitely takes repeated practice. Reading Comp—which has always been my strong suit in other standardized tests—is actually pretty tough on the GMAT.

Amanda
730 (49Q, 40V)

How Is a Computer-Adaptive Test Different?

The GMAT is a *computerized adaptive test* (CAT), meaning it will choose problems according to your performance on preceding questions. The test begins with randomized problems; once it has accumulated a meaningful sample of responses, it will assign subsequent problems adaptively—increasing the overall difficulty if you are answering most problems correctly, and decreasing it if you are answering most problems incorrectly. The questions you receive are also subject to further restrictions—for instance, each test-taker must receive the same balance of topics and question types—resulting in an extremely complicated selection algorithm. Finally, each section of the test will contain 5–10 *experimental questions* (problems being calibrated before they are included in future exam administrations), which are distributed at random and affect neither your score nor your adaptive performance.

TRIVIA

Most test-takers get about 12–14 questions wrong per section.

In general, you shouldn't worry about the exact difficulty level of problems, or about the nuances of the testing algorithm. The test won't show you the difficulty levels of questions, nor will you be able to guess those levels accurately. (Even if you could guess difficulty levels, you still wouldn't be able to identify experimental questions, which could give a completely misleading impression of your performance. For instance, a strangely easy problem *could* mean that you have bombed the last few problems, but is more likely just a random experimental question.) You should therefore focus on how adaptive testing changes *your* strategy and perspective. For instance:

- Because the test chooses questions according to your previous performance, you cannot skip any question, leave any question blank, or return to any previous question. As a result, time management is much more important than on a paper test, because you cannot see any other question until you have answered the current one. Getting hung up on even a single question can have disastrous consequences!

- There is very little correlation between your score and the number of questions you have answered correctly (except at the extremes of the scoring scale). It is possible for a 490 scorer and a 720 scorer to miss exactly the same number of problems!

> **MYTH BUSTER**
>
> "You have to get the first seven to ten questions on each section right to do well on the GMAT." WRONG!! There is nothing magical about those first seven questions. Your score is a function of where you end up and how you got there. The first few problems do not determine your score; they just determine where you will start the next few. It is absolutely possible to recover from a few early errors. We know. We did it ourselves: Instructor Liz Ghini picked C on the first seven questions of an official GMAT and still finished with a 98th percentile score. Of course, we don't recommend that you try this on your own test!

As a helpful analogy, the GMAT can be compared to a resistance-training workout, in which you (1) perform a certain number of sets on each body part, and (2) increase or decrease the amount of resistance until you can perform a set number of repetitions. In the same way, the GMAT (1) gives everyone roughly the same number of each major question type, and (2) adjusts the difficulty until you are getting roughly half of the questions right and the other half wrong.

Finally, the GMAT does not allow the use of calculators. If you've spent the past few years delegating your arithmetic to calculators and Excel, you should practice doing arithmetic by hand—including arithmetic with fractions, decimals, and numbers in scientific notation—until you can reliably perform the calculations quickly and accurately.

Chapter Takeaways

The GMAT is a challenging test, but with the right information, the right strategies, and the right attitude, you can conquer it!

Chapter 2

Getting Organized

In This Chapter...

Determining Your Trajectory up the GMAT Mountain:
Developing a GMAT Study Plan

Getting Back into Academic Mode

Finding Time: The W's to Success

Chapter 2:
Getting Organized

How should you interpret your first practice test?

Your first practice test is a good measure of where you are and what you need to work on—it does not determine your eventual score. Do not be discouraged if the score is lower than you were hoping. If your first practice exam score matches your target score, you just wasted a lot of money buying test prep materials!

So what *should* you take away from the practice score?

If you see...	This could indicate...	You should...
A Quant or Verbal subscore below the 40th percentile*	You need to brush up your basics.	Check out *Foundations of GMAT Math* or *Foundations of GMAT Verbal.*
A content area (such as Geometry or Critical Reasoning) is below 25% correct*	You have a weak link.	Plan extra time to master this area.
A content area above 70% correct*	This area is a real strength.	Plan to cut reading time on this content area.
You finished a section 5 or more minutes early	You are prone to racing through problems without really thinking about them.	Pay special attention to this book's section on timing.
You ran out of time on a section	You have a hard time giving up on problems.	Pay special attention to this book's section on timing.
Percentage correct for easy problems is not higher than that for hard questions*	You have a tendency to make careless errors.	Pay special attention to this book's section on managing your scratch paper.

Data Sufficiency percentage correct is well below that for Problem Solving*	You are struggling with Data Sufficiency logic.	Refer to this book's section on Data Sufficiency.
FDP percentage score below 35%*	Your manual computation skills need improvement.	Plan to do extra hand computation drills.
Reading Comprehension (RC) percentage correct below 35%*	You don't fully comprehend the GMAT passages.	Start RC preparation immediately. Refer to relevant sections of this book.

*See Chapter 9 to learn how to generate an assessment report to see this statistic. Note that if you left more than a couple of problems undone at the end of the section, you will get a low score on that section that may not be due to a lack of content knowledge.

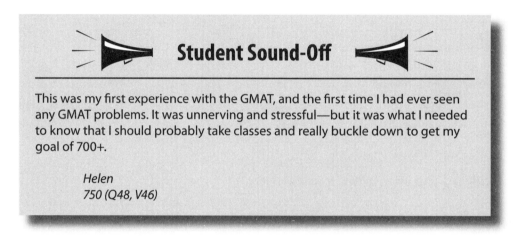

Student Sound-Off

This was my first experience with the GMAT, and the first time I had ever seen any GMAT problems. It was unnerving and stressful—but it was what I needed to know that I should probably take classes and really buckle down to get my goal of 700+.

Helen
750 (Q48, V46)

Determining Your Trajectory up the GMAT Mountain: Developing a GMAT Study Plan
– Abby Pelcyger & Stacey Koprince

Instructor Insights

These days, almost everyone preps for the GMAT—but surprisingly few actually plan how to prep in order to maximize the chance for success. Prepping for the GMAT without a plan is like climbing a mountain without a trail map. You may be just starting out or taking a second crack at the official test, but whatever stage you are at, you need a plan. It's our hope that this article will help guide you on your way to developing your own personalized study plan.

What to Expect During Your Climb

Studying for the GMAT, like mountain climbing, has three phases: reaching base camp, climbing the mountain, and preparing to summit. Each phase has different goals and involves different strategies to help you achieve those goals.

2

Reaching Base Camp

If you are planning on climbing a mountain, you first need to be sure that you have the appropriate tools—you wouldn't want to be halfway up Everest before realizing that you forgot your ice pick. Taking the GMAT is no different. Our GMAT Strategy Guides (and our classes) assume a basic knowledge of math and grammar, as outlined in our *Foundations of Math* and *Foundations of Verbal* books. If your CAT score is below the 40th percentile in a content topic, we recommend that you review the corresponding Foundations book before diving into the Strategy Guides or a 9-week course.

Climbing the Mountain

Climbing the mountain is mastering the material, not including a comprehensive final review. For most people, this will take 8 to 16 weeks, though it may be a bit shorter if you've taken the test before and you're not aiming for a significant score gain. If you take a class, your primary study period will be at least the duration of the class.

Preparing to Summit

Once you have mastered the relevant material, you will need time to review before you take the test. This review period is key to fully developing your timing strategy. Most people spend 2 to 6 weeks on a comprehensive review.

Outside Constraints

You need to factor in external constraints that will affect your study time frame:

- The application deadlines of your preferred schools. You have to work backwards from these set dates. Optimally, get the test out of the way well before you have to start filling out the applications themselves. Your GMAT score is valid for 5 years, so you can get started very early!
- Allow yourself one month of "buffer" time to ensure that you can take the test a second time if you decide to try for a better score.
- You may also want to add in a couple of extra weeks as an additional buffer, just in case. Work gets busy, you get sick, you procrastinate... things happen.

> **TIP**
> You are only allowed to take the GMAT once every 31 days (and five times a year).

Picking the Path That's Right for You

Just as the time you need to climb a mountain depends on the mountain's height, where you start, and your pace, the time you need to prep for the GMAT depends on your target score, current ability level (in terms of content knowledge and standardized test know-how), and your study style.

Target Score: How High Am I Climbing?

2

First, you need to know the score level that will make you competitive at the schools to which you plan to apply. Many business schools post the average GMAT score of incoming students on their websites, often in the admissions or frequently asked questions (FAQ) section. Alternatively, several companies publish "Best Business School" books that list the statistics for incoming classes.

Current Ability Level: Where Am I Now?

Content: How long has it been since you studied grammar, found the prime factors of a number or critically analyzed a reading passage? What's the formula for the area of a trapezoid? When did you last write an impromptu essay?

> **TIP**
>
> If you conduct your research via books, be sure to use those that have been published in the last year or so.

The average MBA applicant works for at least a few years after college before returning to school. Depending on your job, you may or may not have kept up with the content tested by the GMAT. Most of us don't. Knowing how much you don't know is key to establishing your prep plan.

Use the results from your first CAT to help estimate your current ability level. Generally speaking, the larger the desired improvement, the more likely it is that you will need more time and/or more outside help.

Standardized Tests: When you took the SAT, did you do better than, worse than, or about the same as people expected based upon your performance in school? How stressed did you get when you took any kind of exam? Did your exam grades mirror your overall class grade? In a nutshell, do you tend to thrive or falter when you are in high-pressure testing situations? If you underperformed on standardized or other high-pressure tests in the past, you may require more in-depth prep than those who did very well.

Don't forget that the GMAT CAT has an extra complication: you must take it on a computer. If you're not used to taking tests on a computer (and most of us aren't), this could negatively affect your performance. To acclimate to computerized testing, make sure that the practice tests you take are computer-adaptive tests taken under official conditions (75 minutes per section, 8-minute breaks between sections, etc.) Also, when completing practice questions out of a book, prop the book up vertically on your desk. Doing so will force you to look up and down while you use your scrap paper—just like on the real test!

Study Style: What's my pace?

Are you someone who can study for hours on end, or does the book page begin to look like a Jackson Pollock painting after the first hour? How much prime time concentration can you realistically dedicate to studying each day?

Do you struggle to memorize formulas and need to review content often to keep it fresh or do you have a photographic memory? Does it take you a long time to process and truly understand a new math concept, or can you read a concept once and immediately apply it?

Step-by-Step: Working within Your Timeline

Okay, you have your study timeline mapped out. Now, how do you use your time most effectively?

Climbing the Mountain

Look over your study timeline (for many of you, that may be the syllabus for your Manhattan GMAT class). Look at the assignment you have earmarked for the following week. Get a calendar and block off the time periods during which you will study during the upcoming week. Next to each scheduled appointment, list tasks you intend to accomplish during that time slot. Prioritize the areas that address your weaknesses (as indicated by your CAT analysis results) by placing them earliest in the week. Assign only "makeup work" to your last study session of the week—trust us: there'll be plenty of it to do.

If you are planning to study for more than an hour at a time, be sure to mix it up. Either work on a different content area during each hour (e.g., first hour Critical Reasoning, second hour Geometry) or do different types of assignments during each hour (e.g., first hour reading and taking notes on a Strategy Guide chapter, second hour working through and reviewing practice problems). When you do practice GMAT problems, plan to spend two-thirds of your time reviewing the solutions to those problems.

At the end of each study session, jot down what you did that day, what you think went well, and what you think needs more work. If something didn't go as well as you'd hoped, then feel free to adjust your calendar. At the end of the week, review your journal and set up your plan for the next week. Repeat.

Preparing to Summit

By the time you finish working through the Strategy Guides, you will have learned an enormous amount of material; it's only natural that you will need some time to review.

First, make sure to gain an in-depth understanding of your own particular strengths and weaknesses. The easiest way to do this is to use Manhattan GMAT's CAT analysis tools to analyze your practice exams and the online *Official Guide* problem tracker (OG Archer) to analyze your work on *Official Guide* practice problems, although a "gut feel" analysis can also be very helpful. Manhattan GMAT students in the 9-week

2

class can request a post-course assessment (PCA) with their instructor if they have completed three practice tests by the last week of class, including the initial one taken by the second week of class, for help with structuring this review and final exam prep.

Next, set up a schedule. Spread your review evenly over the time you have until your GMAT, leaving the last five to seven days open, just in case you fall behind schedule. During your review, you will need to make decisions about how you are going to handle each type of question on the test based on your strengths and weaknesses, and you will need to plan your time management strategy accordingly.

People often see improvement on a second exam simply because they know what to expect the second time around, but this improvement, by itself, usually isn't enough to justify retaking the test.

Don't Forget to Enjoy the Climb!

Mountain climbers enjoy the climb as well as the summit. Marathoners enjoy the run as well as the finish line. Make sure you find ways to enjoy your GMAT journey. Doing so will help keep you motivated along the trek and keep your mind focused on the learning instead of distracted by thoughts of the other fun things you could be doing. Some ideas of how to increase your study enjoyment include treating problems as puzzles, celebrating mini victories along the way, and creating a study group. If you have a study partner (or two), you can keep each other on track and answer each other's questions. A study buddy also serves as a reminder that you really aren't the only one making sacrifices to achieve your goal.

MANHATTAN
GMAT

2

Dear Jen,

I haven't taken a math class or even thought about math since high school, which was a pretty long time ago. (When you add fractions, you add the tops together and add the bottoms together, and then reduce, right?) I took a practice test and got a 420. I want to get a 700 and I need to take the GMAT in two months.

Dreaming of joining the MGMAT 700 club…

Dear Dreaming,

I hate to be the bearer of bad news, but, while some people have indeed gone from scoring 420 to scoring 700 on practice tests in a couple of months, the initial low score was due to poor time management, massive anxiety, or just never having seen Data Sufficiency or taken a CAT before—not to a lack of basic math knowledge.

If you can't remember the difference between adding and multiplying fractions (adding is the one with a common denominator!), how to factor a quadratic equation such as $x^2 + 2x - 8 = 0$, or how to solve a system of two equations (if $2x + 5y = 27$ and $y - 3x = -15$, what is x?), then it's unrealistic to expect to get a 700—or even to begin your GMAT studies in earnest—until you've done a high school level math refresher.

Our book, *Foundations of GMAT Math*, covers exactly these topics. How long might it take you to relearn everything you knew as a teenager, up through Algebra II? It takes some people a week, and it takes some people a few months. (Just think about how long it took to learn all that material the first time!)

A typical student takes three or four months to study for the GMAT. Some take longer. This three- to four-month time frame does not include time for a high school level math refresher. You need to not only relearn high school level math, but it needs to be second nature to you, and you need to be able to execute it quickly (much more quickly than in high school) without making silly mistakes. Once you can do that, you have the foundation to actually *begin* preparing for the GMAT.

So I think you're going to have to readjust your study plan, and possibly even apply to business schools a year later.

Everything on the GMAT is learnable, and it is definitely possible to climb your way from a total lack of math mechanics to an ultimately high GMAT score, but there's no magic that will take away your need to relearn the basics.

Sincerely,

Jennifer Dziura, MGMAT Instructor, New York

Student Sound-Off

I know it's just a silly test but I'm so excited that I don't even know where to begin or what to do now. I started with a 530 MGMAT CAT score and finished the GMAT with a 740. I am no propeller head, so this can be accomplished with time and good study habits. It may take 1 month for the gifted ones out there, 3 months for others, or maybe even a year if you completely screwed off during high school math classes. But eventually things will click. Below is my debrief:

I first thought about an MBA back in 2001 when every other NYC investment banking turd that I was working with at the time told me that I had to do it. So, being young, dumb, and in over my head with these guys, I followed the crowd. I took a *[competitor's]* class and studied (while working long hours) for a few months before taking the GMAT. (Rule #1 of success on this exam: chill out dude, it's just a test.) 1st try 590 (Q44, V27), 2nd try 630 (Q44, V33). Back then I used to put so much pressure on myself that I'd simply have a meltdown with these things. I was completely crushed, embarrassed, and just gave up on the MBA idea. Although I realize that a 630 isn't bad, I was confident that the net present value of my MBA would certainly be negative. I was not going to get into a top program, and I have a somewhat nonconventional opinion on the MBA degree that just forced me to forget about it.

Fast forward 7 years later… I'm in Boston now, unemployed, and thinking a lot about my future, so I spent a couple of days researching GMAT prep programs. I had never even heard of Manhattan GMAT but most reviews pointed them out as the best of the bunch. So… it was a no-brainer to check out a free class.

The instructor was Eric Caballero and his teaching style actually made the subjects interesting and fun.

About halfway through the syllabus I began to get some sort of sick enjoyment out of this stuff, almost like a puzzle addict. The MGMAT guides were excellent and I followed the heavy syllabus pretty closely.

Relative to other people, I don't think I did nearly as many questions, but I spent an absurd amount of time understanding each one that I did do. The MGMAT explanations to the CATs, Question Banks, and Challenge Questions were thorough and very helpful, but even more discussion on them was available in the forums.

Anyway, I hope that's helpful. Thanks again everyone, especially Eric, Stacey, and Ron from MGMAT. Remember to commit to good study habits, study at your own pace, and most of all remember that it's only a foolish test. Don't beat yourself up if you get knocked down.

Dave
740 (Q49, V41)

Getting Back into Academic Mode

Has it been a while since you last studied for a test? If you graduated from college and have been im-
mersed in a busy professional life for a few (or more than a few…) years, you may have completely
forgotten the academic game. However, if you are preparing to study for the GMAT, you can make
your life a lot easier if you establish good study habits. This does *not* mean that you will be pulling
all-nighters or living in the library. Quite the opposite! That type of cramming is not
particularly efficient or even effective for the GMAT. Here's an overview of what
you need to think about in planning your studying. (For more details and suggestions on how to customize your study time, read instructor Whitney Garner's
article later in this chapter.)

> **TIP**
>
> Establishing good study habits now
> will not only help you prepare for
> the GMAT with minimum anguish,
> but also help you better handle your
> course load in business school.

Carving Out Time

The first thing to think about is carving out time. Here at Manhattan GMAT, we
usually recommend that students devote at least 10–15 hours per week to master-
ing the material. Studying, like exercising, needs to be done regularly, so it's critical to set specific study
times and stick to them. If you have set "appointments" to study, do homework, and take practice tests,
you'll be less likely to procrastinate and fall behind.

Also, studying a little each day is more effective than studying for an extended period of time on only
one or two days a week, so look at your calendar and think about plugging in short blocks of time. If
you don't have a lot of room in your schedule, plan on fitting in 20-minute periods during the workday—one session during the morning (on the subway on the way to work), one during your lunch
break, and one during the evening. You can spend extra time on the weekends for more extended study
sessions and practice exams.

Even then, keep in mind that studying for long hours at a stretch is not the most effective method. In
fact, your study sessions should never exceed two hours at a clip; excessively long study periods overload
your brain and have diminishing margins of return. Sometimes, your brain needs a break! We recommend that you take about a 15-minute break after each hour of studying and a one-hour break after two
hours of studying.

You should also be sure to separate your study time from your down time. You don't want to burn out
and become resentful of your prep time, so it's important to make room to relax. Be sure to schedule in
at least one stress-alleviating activity each week, whether it's a long run, time in the garden, dinner with
friends, movie night, yoga, or an evening at a club. You'll get a chance to unwind, and your brain will
thank you for it.

2

Finding Places to Study

There are many good places to study other than at your desk at home. Most people actually do a better job of learning if they study in different locations, so try mixing it up. Although this may seem surprising, this is in line with what cognitive neuroscientists know about how the brain lays down memories. If you can solve quadratic equations in a café and in the park as well as in the library, you can definitely solve them in a Pearson Vue test center.

Effective Ways to Study

Studying effectively requires intense concentration. There should be no texting or TV distracting you while you study. Turn your phone off. Although some people find soft background music helpful, anything distracting or catchy is counterproductive and will cause you to be less efficient, which will unnecessarily add time to your study session.

It also improves retention if you study the same material using multiple methods. There are many techniques, such as flash cards, reading, timed and untimed practice, writing down notes, and making up mnemonics (do you remember Please Excuse My Dear Aunt Sally?) that can be helpful. For example, if you are trying to learn parallelism, you might read about it, try spotting it in some practice sentences, and then make up your own parallel sentences. It is also a great idea to plan for later review by making a few flash cards out of some of the most interesting problems that you see while you are learning.

TIP

The first letters of the words in Please Excuse My Dear Aunt Sally, or PEMDAS, stand for parentheses, exponents, multiplication, division, addition, and subtraction.

There is no one best way that everyone learns, and the most effective learners typically use multiple techniques. Most people, however, benefit from tracking what they cover in each session. It helps to keep you on task (we all tend to want to study subjects that we are already good at and avoid those we struggle with) and to make future time estimates more accurate. For most people, a simple notebook will serve this purpose perfectly. Log dates and times and a few words about what you did in it. Other people will prefer to use a calendar or a spreadsheet. The key is to pick something that works best for you.

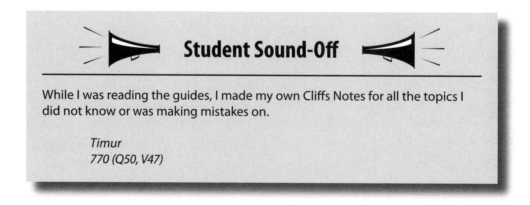

Student Sound-Off

While I was reading the guides, I made my own Cliffs Notes for all the topics I did not know or was making mistakes on.

Timur
770 (Q50, V47)

MANHATTAN
GMAT

We mentioned before that finding a study group or partner can help make studying more fun, but it also offers a unique learning opportunity. Teaching someone else is a very effective method of deeply mastering material—as every Manhattan GMAT instructor will attest—so don't worry if you and your study partner have different strengths or are at different levels. That being said, it is important to pick a study buddy who has some expertise to share with you so that the relationship is a two-way street. Even a friend or significant other who is not studying for the GMAT can help you by quizzing you with flash cards and keeping you accountable to your study schedule.

2

 **Student Sound-Off**

Study groups are one of the most integral parts of successfully studying for the GMAT, but not because you'd necessarily learn more in a group setting, but because it can play a vital role in keeping your sanity and studying interesting through the long-haul marathon known as GMAT prep. Sitting alone in your apartment on a sunny Saturday afternoon, it's hard to focus all your attention on your 20th permutation while you know your friends are finding much more fun in a different combination of things. However, if your friends (the new ones you've made studying for the GMAT) are with you in that study room, it becomes a lot more exciting. You're learning, but you're being social at the same time—missing less of the free time the GMAT has cruelly entrenched upon.

While there are clear benefits to group studying, diversification of your studying habits is key to success. Many times over, I've seen groups spin their wheels for hours on a single math problem trying to solve an extremely tough question. This is valuable, as the process you go through helps deepen your understanding of the core concepts and will benefit you in the long run. However, the GMAT is a numbers game, and it's imperative that, in preparing for the exam, you get through as many types of problems as possible. This is most easily accomplished by doing problems yourself. No matter how efficient your group is, you will inevitably be slowed by making sure every last person of your group understands each explanation.

That's why it's imperative you have a healthy balance of both individual studying and group studying. Spend too much time studying by yourself and you'll end up less happy and ultimately less focused. Spend too much time group studying and you may end up extremely competent in some areas but unable to tackle the diversity of problems the GMAT throws at you. Get the balance right, and you'll not only excel when test-taking time comes, but you may even look back fondly on the time you spent prepping.

My study group—five of us who got to know each other through our MGMAT class—studied together every Saturday afternoon and went out together every Saturday night. Three years later and long after our GMAT, I still hang out with some members of my study group, who have become close friends and even co-founders of organizations with me.

Ajay
740 (Q38, V50)

2

Dear Jen,

Maybe this is a silly question, but are there any special foods I can eat or anything else I can do to get smarter?

Sincerely,

Edge Seeker

Dear Edge Seeker,

I doubt that diet can make you "smarter" on a permanent basis, but it is *absolutely* true that how you treat your body will affect how your brain performs. You've certainly experienced "brain fog," or have been unable to think straight after a long night out or a huge holiday meal. It's not that hard to adjust your lifestyle to produce the opposite effect.

The basics: your brain likes for your body to be fed a steady diet that includes "good fats," antioxidants, and small but regular amounts of quality carbohydrates.

If you are trying to lose weight, consider putting your diet on hold—if not for the entire period of your studies, then at least for the period immediately leading up to your actual exam. Low-carbohydrate diets are especially detrimental to brain function.

A quick internet search will yield suggestions for specific foods that are consistent with these guidelines: salmon, tuna and other fish, oysters, avocado, olive oil, nuts and seeds, eggs (especially the yolks), berries, oatmeal, beans, brown rice, fresh coconut, green leafy vegetables, tomatoes, red cabbage, ginger, rosemary, and even coffee, tea, and chocolate, which are loaded with antioxidants (keep the sugar intake low, though!). Swap out "white" carbohydrates for whole grain versions, eaten in small but regular portions.

Of course, be aware of any food allergies!

There's nothing terribly novel about any of this—the above list is similar to the advice regarding Mediterranean diets, the maintenance phase of the South Beach diet, anti-aging diets, the glycemic index, and many other popular, mainstream programs for health and fitness.

For the record, the most frequently mentioned "brain food" by far is fish; for those who don't eat seafood, the "good fats" in flaxseeds, avocado, olive oil, and nuts are often mentioned as alternatives.

Probably more important than diet, though, is sleep. Various studies list serious consequences of sleep deprivation such as: increased stress hormones, poor digestion, a compromised immune system, inability to put emotional events into the proper perspective, impairment of ability, and serious attention deficits.

According to a study in the *British Medical Journal*, people who have been awake for 17–19 hours are worse drivers than people with a blood alcohol level of 0.05%. You wouldn't take the GMAT drunk, of course. Taking it on too little sleep may be just as bad.

You can plan and schedule sleep just as you can plan and schedule studying. Make a commitment to get eight hours of sleep per night if that's what you need. Figure out a bedtime, and start winding down an hour or two before that. If you have problems falling asleep, take action: a quick internet search offers suggestions including keeping your bedroom very dark and a bit cold, wearing a sleep mask, if necessary, engaging in relaxing rituals before bed, not eating or drinking alcohol too close to bedtime, etc. Do what you have to do to give your brain the sleep it needs.

Finally, exercise is important to brain function. Exercise increases blood circulation, which oxygenates your brain. Various studies have shown that beginning an exercise program can improve learning ability, concentration, and reasoning skills. Exercise is particularly valuable for "executive function," which involves planning, organizing, and managing multiple tasks—in other words, getting things done. There's also plenty of information online regarding the antidepressant properties of exercise.

One study about executive function reported an immediate boost directly after exercise (and a milder effect thereafter), so a study session just after a workout could be a good move. If you're already a regular exerciser, don't skip the workout on the day of the real test. I probably wouldn't go all out on the day of the exam, but a little physical warm-up can also provide a warm-up for your brain.

While many studies about exercise and intellectual functioning have been done on older populations, an interesting study from the University of Illinois at Urbana-Champaign and Vrije Universiteit in Amsterdam (reported in Health Psychology in 2006) compared young people who were physically active to those who were not. After controlling for IQ, they discovered that while the physically active didn't perform more accurately on mental tasks, they did perform more quickly. Did you hear that? Faster performance with no decrease in accuracy? That sounds like the Holy Grail of GMAT performance, if you ask me.

We should insert the usual disclaimers here: we're not doctors, nutritionists, personal trainers, or anything of the like, so consult a doctor or other professional where appropriate. All the information here can be easily found in many, many articles available via a quick internet search, and much of it is just common sense: eat your vegetables, stay active, get a good night's sleep. While it may seem tempting to sacrifice these things for your studies, it's more productive to maintain some balance.

Don't forget that your brain is really just another part of your body. If you want your brain to work well, you have to take care of yourself.

Sincerely,

Jennifer Dziura, MGMAT Instructor, New York

2

Finding Time: The W's to Success
– Whitney Garner

Instructor Insights

Let's face it, many of us have already overpacked our schedule with commitments to job, family, friends, or social associations. How can you find any more time within that busy schedule to carve out quality study time? And if you cannot find *more* time, how do you decide what has to go to make room?

These are tough questions, but ones that you are going to have to answer if you want that top score on the test. Never fear though—you *can* find the time you need if you're willing to get inventive.

When can you find time to study? *Who* can you get to help? *Where* can you find hidden study locations in your life? And *what* types of study fit best into small chunks of time?

Take inspiration from some of the following MGMAT students who found creative ways to incorporate study time into their everyday lives. There is absolutely no reason *why* you cannot find time in the busiest schedule to get the score you want!

WHEN

The most common question I get when students first receive their set of books or see the 9-week course syllabus: "When am I going to have time to cover all of this?"

There are NO Excuses! Most students work long hours during the week, and fill their evenings with friend and family time, chores around the house, and other social commitments such as: church, neighborhood HOA, the gym, the grass, kids' homework/soccer/ballet/music… and the list goes on and on! But here are some examples of the ingenious ways they made time—maybe they can inspire you, too!

WHEN: Before Work

I realized that studying after work during the week was just too hard—I was just too tired and lacked the energy or motivation to pick up a book. It wasn't easy, but I started getting up 30 to 45 minutes early each morning to read chapters. Then I would work on In Action or OG problems during my lunch break at work. Getting up at 5:15 sucked (and eating alone wasn't a thrill either), but my reward was rarely having to do any homework at night.

Marco A. (Private Tutoring Student)

2

WHEN: While the Kids Are Studying

My entire family studies together now—even my husband! I actually find that I'm spending more time with my 5th and 8th grade girls and my husband and I feel like we're setting a great example for them—see how much fun it is to study!

> Erin B. (Online 9-Session Course Student)

WHEN: During the Commute

I used to read my Kindle or the paper on the train, now I take the Verbal Supplement and do RC passages, or take a Strategy Guide and read chapters.

> Sona S. (Online 9-Session Course Student)

I work on idioms every morning with my kids on the drive to school. I pick 1–2 to review/learn and then we go around the car making up sentences using the correct idiom. I feel like I'm helping them and they treat it like a game (who can come up with the best sentence).

> Matt B. (In Person 9-Session Course Student)

WHEN: During Meals

I study or watch Labs during my lunch break. I put the ringer on silent and close my email notifier so that I will not be distracted. Adding this into my schedule 3 times a week allows me to get my weekly homework assignments completed on time. I also like that I don't have to cram all of my study into long blocks at night or on the weekend.

> Anubha K. (In Person 9-Session Course Student)

I watched labs or reviewed class recordings on my laptop while I would make dinner (my boyfriend calls it boiling noodles).

> Olivia D. (In Person 9-Session Course Student)

My roommate and I had a deal at dinner. If I cooked, she read one of the RC passages in depth and reviewed the questions and their answers. Then, while she set the table, I got the 3–4 minutes to read the RC passage and during the meal she tested me with the questions. 6 months later, I'm doing the same thing for her while she studies for the LSAT!

> Lisa M. (Private Tutoring Student)

I got my husband and my son to quiz me on multiplication tables and formulas while I made dinner or did the dishes. Their reward—they didn't have to make dinner or do the dishes!

> Mayura B. (In Person 9-Session Course Student)

2

WHEN: At Sports Practice

My girlfriend plays league softball and I never really went to games, but she told me to come and bring my homework. I was able to be outside, support her when she was at bat, and get over 2 hours of studying in on gorgeous Saturday afternoons (all without feeling like I'd been shut-in all day). I'm just glad she made me do it.

Wayne H. (Private Tutoring Student)

WHEN: Any Time You Can Find 10 Minutes

[My tutor] told me to carry my Foundations of Math *book with me everywhere and do drills whenever I had downtime at work. It was amazing how often I would have 5–10 minutes while waiting for a meeting to start or for a phone call. Rather than check my RSS feed, I was able to get a million times better at exponents! I started downloading middleschool level drill sheets from the internet so that I could have more to work on!*

James W. (Private Tutoring Student)

My friends started to call me a MGMAT rep because I always had a Strategy Guide or the Verbal Supplement Guide with me. On the train, waiting for a friend at lunch, between meetings, and even in the bathroom—I never realized how many opportunities there were in the day to grab 5 or 10 minutes of study or drill time.

Matthew H. (Private Tutoring Student)

WHO

Many of the ideas for *when* should already be sparking some ideas regarding *who* can help you study. The answer: anyone, you just have to ask! Many of my students enlist their friends, spouses/significant others, and even children to help. These people were certainly a part of the decision to pursue b-school in the first place, so get them involved in the preparation as well. Here are some creative ways people have used their support circle to help ace the exam (now see if you can enlist the people in your life).

WHO: The Kids

I had my teenage daughter tutor me in math. At first she thought it was a joke, but once I offered her a 30-minute extension on her weekend-night curfew as payment, she was all in! When I took the test, she was waiting at home like a proud parent— and she actually told me that she was proud of ME. Now she helps me with homework for my MBA classes and says she wants to pursue business (like mom) when she leaves for college in the fall. I feel so blessed!

Martha B. (Online 9-Session Course Student)

My son and I worked on multiplication tables together. Turned out to be great prac-
tice for both the 8 year old and the 34 year old.

Joshua L. (In Person 9-Session Course Student)

WHO: The Carpoolers

My carpool group was great. They would quiz me with formulas and idioms if I
asked, and they instituted a Tuesday/Thursday "Quiet Drive" so that I could use the
30 minutes to study in the back. By the time I was done with the course, 2 other rid-
ers in the car had signed up for a course as well.

Liz M. (Online 9-Session Course Student)

WHO: The Best Friend

A close friend/coworker was a saint while I studied. I really struggled with CR and
RC—I was just too slow. He would read the passages ahead of time (I actually bought
an extra OG for him to have) and then he would quiz me after I read it. It was great
having someone make you accountable to read and study.

Sarah L. (Online 9-Session Course Student)

My roommate came up with a reward system for me. I had 10 weeks to go before the
exam, so he told me to give him $100. I then had to set a schedule each week and give
him a copy. At the end of each week I had a chance to "win" $10 of my money back
by sticking to my study plan. Any week I did not—he got to keep it. Needless to say,
after the test I had $100 to blow at the bar, celebrating!

Greg S. (Private Tutoring Student)

WHO: The Whole Family

I learned quickly that I would NEVER have time to study if my family didn't get on
board—everyone was having a hard time respecting the "study times" I would set and
I was at the point where I thought I would have to rent a study space! My wife sug-
gested that we make it a family plan. They would help me study when they could and
if I put the schedule on the calendar they would promise NOT to bother me during
my study periods. The bribe: a day at a nearby amusement park when the test was
over. It worked—my kids even did extra chores! The excitement got to everyone and
after my test we had a big celebration dinner at home and then packed up the car and
headed to Roller Coaster heaven!

Jared S. (In Person 9-Session Course Student)

2

WHERE

At work, the boss is always swinging by your desk. At home, the phone won't stop ringing or someone is watching the TV too loudly. At the coffee shop, the buzz of local traffic is too distracting. *Where* in our individual worlds can we find a home for our study efforts? Try a few of these suggestions on for size and see if they fit your life!

WHERE: At the Dinner Table

I would make dinner dates with friends and then coerce them into helping me study (bribe is probably more accurate—I offered to buy them a drink or pay for dessert). I would then use them as fake "students" and practice explaining math problems that I struggled with. [My instructor] told me that trying to teach the problem was a good way to solidify understanding and she was right. My friend even considered taking the GMAT herself—she said I was a great tutor.

Christina L. (In Person 9-Session Course Student)

Rather than watch TV with dinner, I would watch online Labs or watch sections of the prerecorded class videos to get even more practice. They might not have liked it very much, and my roommates ended up having to watch quite a few, but I ordered the dinner so they couldn't complain.

Frank Y. (In Person 9-Session Course Student)

WHERE: Anywhere BUT the Dinner Table

My husband helped me convert the corner of our bedroom into a study space when I figured out that this was the only room without a TV, phone or doorbell. We dragged in a chair, table, and small bookcase to house my materials. He even made me a sign for the door to let the kids know that "Mom Is Busy Getting Smart." I put my study schedule on a calendar and posted it to the door so that everyone knew my start and finish times and did not bother me. It also kept me accountable—my kids would check the schedule and be very strict with me if I wasn't studying when I was supposed to (guess it was payback for all the bossing them around I did for their homework)!

Caitlin M. (Private Tutoring Student)

WHERE: Library Study Rooms

My local library has rooms that you can reserve, and many even have computers, so I would go there to take my CAT exams. It was nice to have a place that was meant for study. I could also go there directly from work so that I wouldn't get home and get tempted by all of the other nice relaxing things I'd rather do, like nap.

Greg C. (Private Tutoring Student)

WHERE: Trains, Planes & Automobiles

I travel a TON for work, mostly long boring flights, so I would take books along for the ride. Coast-to-coast flights gave me a chance to finish half of a Strategy Guide and still have time for the in-flight snack.

Olivia D. (In Person 9-Session Course Student).

The commute on the train into the city every morning became a great way to catch up on drill sets and RC passages. I started to get much better at reading complicated stuff without losing focus. I figure if you can read with the noise of the NYC trains, you could kill it in the quiet testing center!

Tanvi D. (In Person 9-Session Course Student)

[My tutor] gave me a link to "Speed" Math audio quizzes online for free download. Although these were for long multiplication or division practice, they gave me a good idea. I used the "Voice Memo" function on my phone to pre-record my own flash cards. I would ask the question, wait 20 seconds, and then answer the question (like, What is the formula for the area of a trapezoid or What is 15% of 300). Then, in the car, I would practice answering them.

Matt B. (Private Tutoring Student)

WHAT

By now you've read a *ton* of examples from real students finding time in *really* busy schedules, and you can find the time, too. Here are some ideas to fill any space of time you have available.

WHAT Can Fill 5–10 Minutes?

I am not a native English speaker so [my instructor] told me to practice an idiom-a-day. I would pick an idiom from the list [in the SC book], and if I knew it, I would write 2 simple sentences using it. If I didn't know it, I would write 5 simple sentences with it. And if I knew that I used it incorrectly (or might), I would write 10 simple sentences with it. The whole thing never took me more than 10 minutes.

Biresh P. (Online 9-Session Course Student)

The Foundations of Math *book drills went everywhere with me and I would do short 5 question sets whenever I had downtime at work. Once those had been done several times over, [my instructor] suggested I google "middle school math worksheets" for whatever topic I wanted to cover. I found a TON of drill sets and by the time I was taking my test I had stopped making so many careless errors.*

Robert B. (In Person 9-Session Course Student)

2

I would read Strategy Guide chapters in the morning before work and then during the workday I would do (and review) one OG problem or In Action problem any time I had a free 5 minutes.

Matt B. (Private Tutoring Student)

WHAT Can I Accomplish in Just 30 Minutes?

I started the course thinking that I could sit and do 3 hours of study at a time and that I could easily finish a book in one evening. It didn't take more than a week to see that this wasn't working (and I would dread the study time so I'd avoid it like the plague). [My instructor] recommended short study bursts—work as hard as you can for 30–45 minutes and then take a break; repeat. I started throwing these 30 minute "bursts" into a typical day. It was enough time to review 1 chapter, or to do a 15 minute timed OG set and review. Then, I would schedule them like I would an appointment. If I completed all of my study bursts for the week (usually 2 a day during the week and 4 a day on the weekends), I was allowed a nice dinner or a pedicure or the chance to sleep in on Sunday morning.

Olivia D. (In Person 9-Session Course Student)

I found out pretty quickly that much more than 30 minutes and I was zoning out. It was then that I figured out that almost all of the studying I had to do would fit into 30-minute chunks: 1 chapter in the Strategy Guide, 1 set of In Action problems, a set of 7–10 OG problems with time to review, etc.

Greg C. (Online 9-Session Course Student)

WHAT Can I Do to Set an EFFICIENT Schedule for Myself?

During the first week of study, I timed myself like crazy. I tried to figure out how long it actually took for me to accomplish different tasks. Then, for the next weeks, each Sunday night I would set a schedule that I knew I could keep and broke up long study times into smaller periods throughout the week. It made everything more manageable, and I was actually able to get more studying in.

Adam W. (In Person 9-Session Course Student)

When I started to be realistic about the amount of work I could do in a given time, studying got really easy. I would look at my week and set a schedule: I would put in 10–15-minute blocks, 30-minute blocks, 45-minute blocks, and even hour blocks of time. I would schedule meals during/around these times, and just got really regimented. Because I was actually accomplishing the amount of work I planned (thanks to being realistic), I had more motivation to stick to the schedule.

Greg S. (Private Tutoring Student)

For 3 weeks I tried to tell myself to study 2 hours a night during the week and 4 hours a day on the weekends. The plan was to force 13–15 hours a week. Not only was I miserable but I was behind and by the end of week one I was giving up. [My instructor] helped me break up study time throughout my day and set a schedule I could stick to. During the week: 45 minutes in the morning before work, 20–30 minutes at lunch, and then 30–45 minute review in the evening (I would sometimes do 20 before dinner and 20 after). Weekends: up early and do 1 hour, have breakfast and do 30 minutes. Then come back and do something similar later in the day. I was getting 6 hours on most weekends, and 2.5 hours a day during the week (I took Friday nights off). Add to that the tons of 5–10 minute drills and problems I would work on whenever I had a free moment and I was probably studying 20+ hours a week without even noticing!

James W. (Private Tutoring Student)

The takeaway—with a bit of planning and resourcefulness, you *can* find ways to build an efficient and effective study plan into your already busy life. Of course, some things will have to go—gone are the days of going out every night and sleeping in every weekend. But remember that this is a *temporary situation*, and that when you are honest with yourself, you can deal with just about anything on a short-term basis. Committing to a realistic study plan will make you more productive when you are studying and allow you to reach your goal that much faster.

We've given you the ideas for *when, who, where,* and *what.* All you have to do is start asking yourself *why* you're still sitting here reading this article when you could be getting a study calendar together!

 Student Sound-Off

You know yourself best—listen to what your body and mind say. And when it's time to study, FOCUS. Don't waste your time half-assing it. Either you are focused, or you walk away from the work and come back in 15 minutes when you are ready. You should have only two types of modes: high-focus or decompressing. If you don't feel yourself 100% there, go smoke a cigarette, take a nap, take a shower, eat a snack, watch an episode of your favorite show—just stay away from GMAT stuff until you've fully recharged. Then go for it.

Helen
750 (Q48/V46)

2

Dear Jen,

I'm not working right now, so I study for the GMAT eight hours a day. But I don't think it's working very well. What am I doing wrong? Should I study more?

Hard Working Harry

Dear Harry,

Some incredibly accomplished and ambitious people come through our doors here at Manhattan GMAT, so it's not uncommon that I hear from people who are really giving their GMAT studies top priority.

Just keep a few basic principles in mind:

- There's no prize for sitting in a chair for eight or more hours.
- There's no prize for suffering.
- There's no special virtue in the number of hours you put in. There's just a score at the end.
- This is another way of saying *work smarter, not harder.*

Your brain probably can't do heavy intellectual lifting for 10 hours straight. I have tutored students who told me they were putting in 12 hours of studying per day every Saturday and Sunday. One student who was doing this was so burned out and miserable that I refused to tutor him any further until he made plans to live like a human being: eat lunch with a friend, throw around a Frisbee in the park, etc. He made much more progress afterwards, studying in two 4-hour sessions and deliberately planning something fun in between.

Students who are not working often tell me they're studying "full-time." Upon further examination, it's rarely a focused, productive, 40-hours-a-week effort. It's usually a wandering, unfocused mess: because you have all the time in the world, you don't bother to plan.

Make a plan. Start with your GMAT date and work backwards. Perhaps you decide that you are going to work through one Manhattan GMAT Strategy Guide per week, do an hour a day of timed drills, and take a practice test every week. Okay, now break that up into even smaller tasks, and set goals for each day. Maybe on a particular day, you do four chapters of *Word Translations*, do two timed 10-question drills (one math, one Verbal), do two chapters of *Sentence Correction*, and go over problems from a practice test taken the day before. That's four big things. Make a schedule for your day (e.g., two big things before lunch, two big things after lunch), and don't forget to take breaks, exercise, eat real meals, and do the other things you need to do to stay positive (and even happy)!

MANHATTAN
GMAT

2

If you're studying on your own, consider sharing your plan with someone to help stay focused. This could be a GMAT study buddy, but could also just be a friend, parent, or spouse—someone who can check in and ask how it's going, even without any special knowledge of the GMAT.

Overall, focus on *goals*, not time put in. Studying for eight hours straight is not going to impress anyone, especially if you can't say what you've accomplished during those eight hours. I'd much rather hear "Today I finally got a handle on rates problems where you can add and subtract rates" than "I'm so tired because I've been glued to my chair all day long." Focusing on goals instead of time also gives you license to stop and celebrate when you achieve a goal, and might even subconsciously motivate your brain to learn more efficiently.

Sincerely,

Jennifer Dziura, MGMAT Instructor, New York

Chapter Takeaways

1. Your first CAT is not particularly predictive of your final score. The most predictive indicator is the quantity and quality of your studying—you need both to significantly impact your score.

2. Do not underestimate the challenge of getting back into studying mode! Get started now. Make an actual plan; don't expect to wing it.

3. A realistic approach is important. You will be busy. Schedule in breaks and rewards —maintaining your motivation is essential.

4. If you signed up for an MGMAT class, take advantage of the time before your class starts to brush up on some foundational skills.

5. Do not sacrifice sleep and a healthy lifestyle to studying. It is counterproductive and will backfire.

Chapter 3
of
GMAT Roadmap

How to Learn Content

In This Chapter...

Chapter 3:
How to Learn Content

At Manhattan GMAT, we know that test-taking tricks will only take you so far; in order to do well on the GMAT, you *have to* learn the content. This chapter focuses on how to master the core concepts and skills tested by the GMAT.

Many students find it very helpful to understand the big picture of learning content. The GMAT is not a straightforward test that requires you to regurgitate memorized facts. Rather, it is very much a test of analyzing clues in problems to determine the correct concepts to apply to solve those problems. Remembering the definition of something, such as a prime number or the predicate of a sentence, is simply not sufficient for solving a GMAT problem. For a more thorough explanation of what you need to know and the skills you need to master, read on.

How to Learn: An Education Theory Perspective
– Abby Pelcyger

Instructor Insights

When not spending my evenings teaching GMAT, I spend my days learning education theory. So now you get to benefit from what I've been learning as I work towards my doctorate in education at UPenn: how to study in a way that will result in maximal learning based on some serious education theory.

Bloom's Taxonomy is a widely applied theory that breaks down cognitive learning into six intellectual skills. They are shown in the chart from simplest to most complex. It is believed that, when learning something new, lower level categories must be mastered before higher ones can be achieved.

Increasing Critical Thinking

Skills	GMAT Examples	GMAT Learning Tools
Remembering	You can recall that the inside angles of a triangle add up to 180 degrees. You identify that the correct idiom is "whether," not "whether or not."	Memorize key rules and formulas from the Strategy Guides, using cheat sheets or flash cards.
Understanding	You followed the process your instructor, classmate, or study buddy used to solve a GMAT problem. You can restate an OG problem solution in your own words.	Read the Strategy Guide. Pay attention in class. Read given solutions to GMAT-like problems (such as on practice tests and *Official Guide* problems).
Applying	When faced with a GMAT problem and told what that problem is testing (e.g., subject–verb agreement or prime numbers), you correctly apply a pre-learned strategy or algorithm.	Complete In Action problems at the back of each Strategy Guide chapter. Complete the Benchmark GMAT problems listed in each Strategy Guide.
Analyzing	You can use clues in a GMAT problem wording to categorize the problem and its features (e.g., Yes/No DS divisibility problem).	Complete practice GMAT problems. Create a flash card deck of problems that you learn from.
Evaluating	Data Sufficiency, anyone? You can correctly identify the assumption on which a Critical Reasoning argument depends. You can identify and skip problems that will take you too long to solve.	Practice timed sets of GMAT problems.
Creating	You can construct creative solutions to solve GMAT problems that have nuances requiring adaptation from the basic strategy for that problem type.	Group problems that have similar techniques or traps and be able to visualize 3–5 common "variations" of each. Take practice CATs.

So what do these charts have to do with how I should study?

Well, everything, actually. When learning new GMAT content, the first thing to do is to make sure that you understand the content and remember any pertinent rules, formulas, facts, and strategies. Reading the Strategy Guides and making cheat sheets on them will help you to do this. Taking a class (and attending regularly) will help you

3

to learn more about how to apply those rules, formulas, facts, and strategies on GMAT problems.

But here is the vital point that many students miss: just reading the Strategy Guides and/or attending class is NOT enough! While those actions can help you to remember and understand the content, you will not be able to successfully solve GMAT problems—especially during a time-constrained test—if you do not practice applying your new-found knowledge on the types of problems that will be on the test! To learn how to apply your knowledge and to strengthen your analyzing, evaluating, and creating abilities (all skills tested on the GMAT), you need to be able to independently work through problems that require that skill set—problems that will test your knowledge and thinking in the same way that the GMAT will. Luckily, you have the *Official Guide* (OG), a whole book full of genuine, retired GMAT problems.

Too many students come to us confused about why their practice test score is not going up since they have read all of the Strategy Guides, only to admit that they never did any OG problems. Don't let this happen to you! I recommend that my students complete at least three OG problems for each Strategy Guide chapter that we covered in class before beginning to read the next Strategy Guide. If a choice needs to be made, I would rather that they get through less of a Strategy Guide and master fewer content areas, than—by avoiding GMAT-like practice problems—they expose themselves to a wide range of content, but master none of it.

Basics of Quant and Verbal

What does the GMAT test?

The GMAT is a sophisticated, high-level test of your reasoning skills, but it is built on top of concepts that you learned in high school. That's right—the "facts" that you need to reason about in order solve GMAT problems are things that you learned in high school, if not earlier. However, knowing the content is not enough for a high score; you also have to know the reasoning tricks and be able to think through problems quickly and effectively. However, even if you are an excellent thinker and can do analytical reasoning very quickly, do not assume that you will ace the GMAT without preparation. If you aren't rock solid on the basic high school math and English content, the GMAT will trip you up. The Manhattan GMAT curriculum (for both our Strategy Guides and our courses) is designed to review the content while at the same time teaching the reasoning strategies.

You may wonder exactly what this high school content is. In math, it is arithmetic, algebra (primarily Algebra I), geometry (but no trigonometry), and a smattering of probability, statistics, counting, and set theory at the level typically covered in an Algebra II class. Although this material isn't particularly difficult, you need to know this basic stuff really, really well. It's not breadth, it's depth. For example, since the test covers arithmetic, you may realize that you have to know about fractions, roots, exponents, and prime numbers, and be perfectly fine with these concepts as long as you have a calculator and the problem is straightforward computation. However, on the GMAT you will not have a calcula-tor, and computation problems often look impossible unless you know how to use prime factors to simplify horrendous-looking exponents and roots. You will also encounter questions that cannot be solved correctly unless you really understand your basic arithmetic definitions, such as the fact that 0 is an even number, although it is neither positive nor negative.

On the Verbal side, the content is American English grammar and sentence structure, reading comprehension (and indirectly, vocabu-lary), and the logic of argument construction. In order to do well, you have to be able to comprehend what you read precisely and analyti-cally while under pressure. At the micro level, you have to be able to read sentences for grammar, meaning, and concision. This means that you need to know the basic parts of speech, understand the logic of sentence construction, and be able to recognize the gram-mar patterns of the English language. At the macro level, you have to be able to read academic essays and arguments and be able to parse each sentence accurately for meaning as well as determine the overall logical structure of each passage and reason about the logic flow of the writing. This requires that you recognize passage-level, structural, patterns in academic writing. Some of the most common passage-level patterns are detailed below:

> **TIP**
>
> Taking our classes? Sprinkled throughout the Manhattan GMAT course, along with the review of basic content and introduc-tion of reasoning techniques for solving different types of problems, are a bunch of "magical" shortcuts developed by our in-structors that can really boost your score. For example, whenever the GMAT asks you to add or subtract two exponents with the same bases (or bases that can be made the same), try factoring out the smaller power. Look for these tricks in class and put the ones that are new to you on flash cards.

- Introduce a theory and then present evidence that supports that theory.
- State the common view and then explain a different view and provide supporting evidence.
- Compare and contrast two theories and then support one of them.
- Present an ordered timeline of events.
- Introduce two seemingly very different phenomena and show how they are con-nected.

So what do I really need to learn to get a high score?

If you want to get a very high score, even having both deep content knowledge and excellent reason-ing and logical inference skills is not sufficient. You also need to be able to manage your time and your stress level on the test. Exemplifying the truth of the hierarchical nature of learning, it is exceedingly difficult to master the higher level skills and be able to use them with facility if you do not deeply un-derstand the foundational content. Our Strategy Guides and 9-week GMAT prep courses assume that you have mastered the foundational skills already. The classes, in particular, focus on the higher level skills such as: applying, analyzing, and evaluating.

There are two foundational skills in particular that are essential to GMAT success: reading for compre-hension and computing without a calculator. If your practice test indicates that you need to do some pre-work in these areas, read on.

Reading Comprehension
– Tommy Wallach

What's in a name?

Reading Comprehension is, for many people, the most difficult section of the GMAT. Where most Quantitative and Sentence Correction questions only take up a line or two on the page, and even Critical Reasoning prompts top out at a paragraph, RC passages can be four long paragraphs of dry and confusing text. And while the questions may look simple at first glance, the answer choices tend to be convoluted, obscure, and seemingly different from anything mentioned in the passage. In order to improve at RC, it's necessary to fundamentally change the way one reads and takes notes, at least relative to how we might have gotten used to performing these tasks in school.

The name "Reading Comprehension" is comprised of two words. In my experience, the biggest mistake students make is thinking that the focus should be on the *first* word. "Reading!" the student thinks, "I'm great at that! I've been doing that for years! I'm going to own this test." And the student proceeds to miss question after question.

As it turns out, the GMAT takes advantage of people who think that RC is a test of reading ability. Those people will depend on their memory, playing what I like to call "the matching game," as opposed to attempting a more thorough understanding of the underlying concepts and structure of the passage. The focus must always be on the second word: *comprehension*. Unsurprisingly (though ignored by many students), the GMAT will naturally assume you know how to read. But do you know how to understand? That is the question.

The Matching Game

Over the years, I've tutored everyone from ESL (English as a Second Language) students who barely speak English to English majors with national publications to their names. Yet no matter what the student's background is, he or she is likely to make the same fundamental mistake on RC. I'll go through a question with a student, and they'll pick an answer. When I ask why they think that particular answer choice is the right one, they respond, "Because that was talked about in the passage." When asked to explain why the wrong answers are wrong, they explain simply, "The passage didn't mention those."

Notice that neither of these answers has anything to do with comprehension. Imagine I say to you, "The car is on fire," and then ask you what you can infer from that statement. If an answer choice read, "The car is very hot," that would be correct. But did we ever *talk about* heat directly in the original statement? No. However, comprehension of the statement would lead one to the understanding that anything on fire is very hot, so the car must be very hot.

A student playing the matching game would not choose the answer, "The car is very hot." They would look for whichever answer choice mentioned both "the car" and "fire," and choose that, even if it were logically incorrect. For example, "The car will remain on fire until the fire naturally dies out." This answer doesn't mention anything *new*, but it's also incorrect; the car fire could conceivably be put out by an *unnatural* cause, like a fireman, or a pack of very wet dogs coincidentally shaking out their coats at exactly the same time in the vicinity of the flaming car.

The matching game centers around *reading*, rather than *comprehending*. The student thinks that they can *Where's Waldo* their way to the answer by using the words in the passage. On the contrary, the GMAT usually seeks to punish those students who try to play the matching game. The correct answers to RC questions, more often than not, include numerous words not used in the original text. As it turns out, in English, we can say the same thing in an infinite number of ways.

For example, "I have a lot of money" means the same thing as "I'm rich as Croesus" or "My investments have matured handsomely in the past decade" or "My bank balance has more zeroes than the National Debt." Understanding is a function not of the specific words used, but of their underlying meaning.

I Still Don't Understand

All of this may make RC sound pretty darn easy; all you have to do is understand! But comprehension can be quite difficult. RC passages are deliberately written with obscure words and confusing constructions. Even people who read all the time can struggle to make sense of a tough passage. To someone who reads only rarely, the words on the page might look more or less like gibberish.

However, you can improve your odds by taking a number of steps, the most important of which is to begin taking notes. Though it's well-known that one must take notes to improve, I've heard every excuse in the book for why my students refuse to do it: "I don't have enough time as it is."; "I can remember what I read just fine."; "It doesn't help me to take notes." But if you want to get better at RC, you have to write something down. Until you're willing to give it a try, you're unlikely to see your score improve.

The note-taking process for RC is different from what you might expect, and it again revolves around the distinction between *reading* and *comprehension*. When we took notes back in middle or high school, or even in college, it was usually with an expectation of eventually being tested on the facts. If we read something like "Napoleon was

3

born in 1804," we'd immediately write down "N born 1804," because that would likely be on the test.

But this kind of note-taking would be useless on the GMAT. Why? Because the passage doesn't go anywhere. The fact about Napoleon is worth writing down only because you don't get to have the book in front of you on the test. But on the GMAT, the passage stays visible while you answer the questions. This means you simply won't be asked any easy factual questions like "What year was Napoleon born?" So why write it down?

In fact, it's not particularly useful to write down any fact-based information. This isn't because you won't be asked any fact-based questions (you will), but because the questions will be so tricky that you'll have no choice but to read back over the relevant portion of the passage to find the answer.

Let's consider an example. Imagine the passage is about chlorofluorocarbons, the organic compounds that were once responsible for ozone depletion. Imagine you read this paragraph, culled from Wikipedia:

> "The physical properties of the CFCs and HCFCs are tunable by changes in the number and identity of the halogen atoms. In general they are volatile, but less so than parent alkane. The decreased volatility is attributed to the molecular polarity induced by the halides and the polarizability of halides, which induces intermolecular interactions."

I dare you to write notes for that paragraph that capture all of the relevant details you might be asked on the test, without more or less writing it down word for word. It isn't possible, so why bother?

Instead, your notes should be *adding value* to the passage. You should be writing down things that are *never* explicitly stated in the actual passage. I have my students write down two things and two things only.

Main Idea

The first thing you must write down is the main idea of the passage. RC passages generally have either an opinionated point to make (a thesis) or else a simple topic. Whatever it is, you have to find it and write it down *in your own words*. Sometimes it's explicitly stated in the passage, and sometimes it isn't, but either way, you must find it. Recognizing the main idea is critical on RC for two reasons. First, you'll be asked about the main idea on a good 50% of passages. Second, writing down the main idea allows you to prove to yourself you understand what the passage is really about.

Use as few words as possible. Don't include random facts that look important. If the passage is about the history of chlorofluorocarbons, just write "History of chlorofluoro-

3

carbons." Don't add, "Also some stuff about halogen and alkane, and something about volatility and polarity that I don't really get." The main idea should apply equally well to *any* paragraph in the passage, so if you find what you've written doesn't apply somewhere, you've probably been a bit too specific.

Each Paragraph's Structural Purpose

Remember that even though the passages are written using obscure words and difficult constructions, the structure will always be logical. Every paragraph is there for a reason. It's up to you to work out what those reasons are and to write them down (again, in your own words). I tell my students to try and keep this part of their outline entirely content-neutral. In other words, try to leave out *all* the details. Your outline should be so general that it doesn't even make clear the *topic* of the passage. Here are some examples:

Example 1:

> P1: Intro to theory
> P2: Examples of theory
> P3: Recent problems with theory
> P4: Possible solutions to problems

Example 2:

> P1: Background on subject
> P2: New discovery about subject

Example 3:

> P1: Old way of doing things
> P2: New way
> P3: Possible improvements in future

Notice that in each example, content has been left out. These passages could be about business, history, biology, literature, psychology, or anything else. The point is to focus on the structure.

At first glance, this might seem silly. Why not include a bit of content, just in case? The problem is that I've seen too many students use note-taking as a crutch. They figure that if they can only write down enough of the passage, it won't matter if they didn't totally get it, because they can refer to their notes. Unfortunately, their notes will not save them if they didn't comprehend what they read. In fact, their notes will just get in the way, adding no value but sucking up valuable seconds.

The Main Idea/Paragraph Structure outline *forces* you to comprehend. Also, because you *don't* have any specific details written down, you have no choice but to look back at the passage to answer specific detail questions, which is universally acknowledged to be the only way to get these questions right. If you depend on your memory (or a flawed set of notes), you're far more likely to make a mistake.

Practice, Practice, Practice

Improving at RC is difficult. These methods will not be easy to put into practice, and it might take 30 or 40 passages before you see the fruits of your labor. But trust in the method. Would you go to one week of soccer practice and then quit, because you still kinda sucked at soccer? Of course not! Everyone knows that improvement takes weeks or even months. The key is to start right now.

Never let yourself read an RC passage or answer a question without employing the method. Don't let yourself off the hook because you're low on time or energy, or because you think the passage is simple enough that you can answer the questions without notes. Even if it works on that passage, as the passages and questions get harder, you'll find yourself missing more and more. With a good process, you'll be safe no matter the difficulty of the passage or the questions at hand.

GMAT-like Articles to Practice Your Reading Comprehension On

(We recommend you read these for 20 minutes a day for at least three weeks straight in the subject area(s) in which you struggle.)

Humanities:
Smithsonian: http://www.smithsonianmag.com/
Harvard Alumni Magazine: http://harvardmagazine.com/

Science:
Scientific American: http://www.scientificamerican.com/sciammag/
MIT Technology Review: http://www.technologyreview.com/

Business:
The Economist: http://www.economist.com/

Ready, Set, Compute!
– Liz Ghini Moliski

Instructor Insights

Many students are surprised to discover that, unlike many other standardized tests, the GMAT does not allow you to use any type of calculator. This can be an issue even for people who are good at math because most of us simply haven't done calculations without a calculator or spreadsheet since junior high, and so we have forgotten all of the techniques that make hand calculations easier.

Compute This

Even if you are comfortable with math in general, if your initial CAT indicates that Fractions, Decimals, and Percents (FDPs) are a weakness, or if you struggled with exponent problems, you should brush up on hand computation skills before your GMAT prep class gets under way. Can you quickly compute the following (without a calculator)?

$$\frac{\frac{3}{4} - 0.60}{(3/10)^2} = ?$$

The answer is:

$$\frac{\frac{3}{4} - 0.60}{(3/10)^2} = \frac{0.75 - 0.60}{(0.3)^2} = \frac{0.15}{0.09} = \frac{15}{9} = \frac{5}{3}$$

If that wasn't so easy, take a look at Manhattan GMAT's *Foundations of GMAT Math* book. The drill sets for FDPs and exponents are very helpful if you just need to brush the rust off of your computation skills. The chapter reading explains basic techniques such as cancelling, factoring, and finding common denominators in case you have forgotten how (or even never really knew how) to do these things.

You can also help yourself get better at computation by putting down your calculator when you shop. Sum the cost of your groceries on a little notepad while you are waiting in the checkout line. Figure out things like: What is 20% off of merchandise that has already been reduced by 30%? Which is a better deal: buy 2, get 1 free or 35% off?

Building Speed and Accuracy

One of the keys to building speed and accuracy is doing your computations on paper instead of in your head. It really helps to write down your math steps—otherwise you are much more likely to make silly mistakes.

MANHATTAN
GMAT

Another thing that helps is to develop your ability to approximate, which is tested directly on the GMAT, and your number sense (an understanding of whether an answer is within a reasonable range), so that you can quickly ballpark what an answer has to be and catch any silly mistakes. For example, if you are given that 77% of a room's area is 273, you could solve exactly by setting up the equation and then doing long division:

$$0.77x = 273 \rightarrow x = \frac{273}{0.77}$$

However, on the GMAT, an approximation is usually good enough for a computation problem like this because the answers tend to be spread apart. So it would be much easier to do the following approximate math instead of long division:

$$\frac{273}{0.77} \approx \frac{270}{0.75} = \frac{270}{3/4} = 270 \times \frac{4}{3} = 270 + \frac{270}{3} = 270 + 90 = 360$$

The actual answer is closer to 345.5, but it is unlikely that you would need to be that precise on an actual GMAT computation problem. With regular approximation practice, you will be able to look at the equation and say that x has to be larger than 300 because 75% of 300 is 225, but also less than 400, because 75% of 400 is 300. This kind of number sense is very helpful because it lets you quickly check your work without redoing calculations.

In order to develop your number sense, spend time playing with numbers. Try approximating the total of your groceries and seeing how accurate you can be. Try ballparking multiplication and division as well. For instance, if 21 servings of crackers come in a box, and each serving is 11 crackers, about how many crackers come in a box?

Memorizing some of the most commonly needed arithmetic for the GMAT can also help. Here are some student favorites:

Things to Memorize

- Times tables through 12×12
- Perfect squares through 15^2, as well as 20^2 and 25^2
- The first ten powers of 2
- The first 15 prime numbers (helpful for factoring and divisibility)
- Fraction to decimal equivalents for 1/2, 1/3, 1/4, 1/5, 1/6, 1/8, and 1/12
- $\sqrt{2} \approx 1.4$ (remembering that 2/14 is Valentine's Day might help)
- $\sqrt{3} \approx 1.7$ (remembering that 3/17 is St. Patrick's Day might help)
- The divisibility rules for 2, 3, and 5 (in *Foundations of GMAT Math*)
- The exponent rules (in *Foundations of GMAT Math*)

3

If you know that $15^2 = 225$ and $20^2 = 400$, you are likely to realize that 16×18 has to be between 225 and 400, and so catch yourself if you made a mechanical error and computed it as 488 instead of 288.

Seemingly Magical Computation

Although the GMAT doesn't actually test your ability to do enormous calculations, it does test your ability to figure out how to *avoid* doing enormous calculations when performing computations. For example, if you see the following:

$$\frac{14^7 - 14^6}{13} = ?$$

You should know that you do *not* have to compute 14^7 or 14^6 to solve the problem. There is a computation shortcut! In this case, the trick is to factor out from the numerator:

$$\frac{14^7 - 14^6}{13} = \frac{14^6(14 - 1)}{13} = \frac{14^6(13)}{13} = 14^6$$

The clever tricks for avoiding computation that you need to solve the most challenging GMAT computation problems are based on the arithmetic rules that you learned long ago (PEMDAS, factoring, properties of addition and multiplication, and exponent rules) and use without thinking. The first step in mastering the clever tricks is to make sure that you deeply understand the logic behind arithmetic rules. This is the key to doing seemingly impossible math. All the great computation tricks are just clever applications of the arithmetic rules you learned in grade school. By building your intuitive understanding of computation, seemingly impossible math will become as easy as one plus one.

Takeaways

Computation matters on the GMAT. Even if you excel at thinking through the toughest math problems, if you can't do computation without a calculator, you won't get the problem right or achieve your target GMAT score. To remedy this:

- Read *Foundations of GMAT Math* (FoM).
- Memorize common math facts.
- Do drills in FoM. (Use the online FoM Question Banks.)
- Practice computation, estimation, and testing your math sense whenever you can (even in the grocery store).
- Look for the basic rules that are hidden in seemingly impossible computation problems: if you master the basics, the "seemingly impossible" aspects of many problems disappear.

3

How to Build Drills
– Jon Schneider

Instructor Insights

There are a lot of mechanics that we need to be able to perform in order to do well on GMAT Quant. Arithmetic and algebra, in particular, often involve a lot of steps. As you study, make it your goal to first understand the meaning of the rules surrounding the manipulation of arithmetic and algebra. You'll find that you are able to repeat the steps more easily if you understand why you can perform certain operations but not others. (Really try to talk out the meaning of it to yourself.)

But after you've come to understand the meaning of the manipulation, you'll want to practice these mechanics over and over to solidify your new skill. Sometimes, you'll be able to find lots of OG or other questions on which to practice. But oftentimes, you won't. Let's say, for instance, that you find that you need more practice with FOIL-ing and factoring quadratic forms. Well, if you can't find a bunch of problems to practice on, don't worry! You can make such forms yourself. In fact, the process of making them will often help solidify your understanding. Moreover, making drills is often easier, and faster, than finding drills.

I've listed here several methods for creating a drill for yourself to practice. Start by trying any of the suggested drills that strike you as relevant to your current needs. Later, use the general idea of these drills to make your own drills. Often, it is not a whole GMAT problem but rather one part of the problem that gives us trouble. If this is the case, practice that one aspect of the problem repeatedly, until you feel comfortable with it.

Finally, note that scrap paper processes are very important for all aspects of math mechanics! So, commit to the following principles:

- Write down given information as given.
- Only perform one operation of math per line of math.
- Double-check each step as you perform the step.
- Work neatly, and give yourself enough clean space on the page to properly solve.

To practice long division:
Needs: Notebook, pen, calculator

How to: Write out various numbers and divide them by each other. Try dividing primes by each other, as these numbers will often yield interesting decimal results. Check your answers on a calculator.

Purpose: To get faster at long division; to recognize when a decimal will begin to repeat; to work neatly; to be able to rely on long division on the test when you need it; to memorize some common decimal equivalents.

To practice prime factorization of numbers:
Needs: Notebook, pen, calculator

How to: Multiply numbers together on the calculator. Start by multiplying various small primes together. For example, multiply $2 \times 2 \times 3 \times 5 \times 5 \times 7 \times 11 \times 13$. Write down the resulting product in the notebook. Do this again 5–10 times. Next, take each number and create a factor tree.

Purpose: To get faster at prime factorization; to build clean work habits; to learn divisibility tricks (how to tell if a number is divisible by 9, for example).

To practice manipulation of fractions:
Needs: Notebook, pen

How to: Write out a random series of fractions with various mathematical operations connecting the numbers. For example, write:

$$\frac{1}{3} + \frac{2}{4} + \frac{5}{3} - \left(\frac{2}{7} \left(\frac{1}{\frac{3}{2}} + \frac{\frac{3}{7}}{\frac{2}{9}} \right) - \frac{2}{6} \right) + \frac{3}{7} - \frac{1}{9}$$

Now simplify and solve. Carefully check your work to make sure you are solving correctly. Solve the same formation multiple times to make sure that you arrive at the same solution.

Purpose: To get faster at fraction manipulation; to practice clean work; to better understand the rules of arithmetic.

To practice manipulation of exponents:
Needs: Notebook, pen

How to: Write out random exponent patterns above integers and fractions connected by various mathematical operations. For example, write:

$$\left(\frac{1}{3} + \frac{4}{5} \right)^2 + (2 \cdot 3 \cdot 7)^2 - \left(\frac{\left(2 + \frac{1}{4} - 3 \right)^{-3}}{\left(\frac{3}{1} + \frac{2}{5} \right)^5} \right)$$

Now simplify and solve. Carefully check your work to make sure you are solving correctly. Solve the same formation multiple times to make sure that you arrive at the same solution.

Purpose: To get faster at fraction manipulation; to practice clean work; to better understand exponent rules.

To practice algebraic manipulation (part one):
Needs: Notebook, pen

How to: Write out random algebraic forms using one or more variables. Use exponents, and connect the forms with various mathematical operations. For example, write:

$$(x+y)^2 + 3(x+x^2 - 2y + y + 5y - 3x + z) - 5(z+z^3 - y^2)^2 + xy(y+z)^2$$

Now simplify the form. Carefully check your work as you proceed. Note that the form is not part of an equation, so you will not solve to an actual value for any variable; rather, you are just looking to boost your speed at combining like terms. Remember to try each form more than once to make sure that you arrive at the same answer each time.

Purpose: To get faster at simplification of algebra and grouping of variables; to practice exponent manipulation, factoring, and distribution.

To practice algebraic manipulation (part two):
Needs: Notebook, pen

How to: Write out various equations each involving three variables. For example, write:

$$5x + 7(y + x - z) = 3z$$

Now solve for each variable. What is x equal to, in terms of y and z? What is y equal to, in terms of x and z? etc. Solve the same formation multiple times to make sure that you arrive at the same solution.

Purpose: To get faster at algebraic manipulation; to gain comfort solving for one variable in terms of other variables.

To practice factoring and distributing Quadratic Equations:
Needs: Notebook, pen

How to: First, create several sets of parentheses on your paper:

(   )(   )   (   )(   )   (   )(   )

3

Next, write in *x* at the beginning of each parenthetical:

$(x \quad)(x \quad)$ $\qquad$ $(x \quad)(x \quad)$ $\qquad$ $(x \quad)(x \quad)$

Next, write in various numbers at the end of each parenthetical:

$(x \quad 16)(x \quad 3)$ $\qquad$ $(x \quad 1)(x \quad 5)$ $\qquad$ $(x \quad 3)(x \quad 7)$

Finally, write in either "+" or "−" in the middle of each parenthetical:

$(x + 16)(x + 3)$ $\qquad$ $(x - 1)(x + 5)$ $\qquad$ $(x - 3)(x - 7)$

Now, FOIL each form, and combine like terms for the simplest expression in each case. On a separate sheet of paper, rewrite the simplified, distributed forms in a different order. Now factor these forms back into parentheticals. Check that you have arrived at the original forms.

Repeat this exercise until you can factor or distribute basic Quadratic Equations in under 30 seconds.

Purpose: To get faster at factoring and distributing Quadratic Equations.

Learning to Think Like a 99th Percentile Scorer

Now that you know the content you will have to review (or relearn) and have an understanding of the level of skill that you will need, you may find yourself getting a little wary. You're probably wondering how you are going to manage to think quickly enough through all of this material in order to complete the GMAT in the allotted time.

The solution lies in learning to think the way a GMAT expert does. Our instructors actually do *less* thinking to solve GMAT problems than most students do. When tackling a tough problem, they zero in very quickly on what's important and draw on their past experiences with similar problems to help themselves solve efficiently. It's a valuable skill set to have, and one that you will be working towards as you prepare for the GMAT.

The Dual Process Model
– Liz Ghini Moliski

Instructor Insights

There is a lot of great research on how experts reason, solve problems, and make decisions that is very applicable to the GMAT. When I was a student in the PhD program at the University of Chicago's Booth School of Business, I became fascinated by this sort of research and even ran studies on doctors making hypothetical medical decisions to test my theories.

3

That's nice, you may think, but how is this relevant to getting a better GMAT score?

Well, getting a high GMAT score is all about becoming a GMAT expert. Understanding the way experts think through and solve complex problems, both in general and on the GMAT, can help you more efficiently master the thinking skills that you need in order to become a GMAT expert.

There is general agreement among psychologists that there are two fundamentally different ways to think. The psychologist Daniel Kahneman (who you will run into again in business school when you study prospect theory and behavioral economics) laid this out in his Dual Process Model of thinking. He called the two basic methods that people use system 1 and system 2, or intuition and logical reasoning. Intuition is associative thinking, which is fast and relies on shortcuts like pattern matching, whereas logical reasoning is slow and effortful because it relies on step-by-step, rule-based thinking.

For thousands of years, people have argued about which method was the overall best one. The ancient Greek philosophers typically favored step-by-step, rule-based thinking, whereas artists and other creative types throughout history generally favored intuition. Modern psychologists have concluded something rather commonsensical and practical, though: the best problem solvers use both of these styles of thinking and move back and forth between them fluently.

Intuition is fast because pattern recognition is fast. It relies on the brain's ability to distinguish patterns and associate them with something previously experienced. With practice, people learn to almost instantly recognize groups of squiggly lines as letters, groups of letters as words, and then groups of words as algebra word problems. Categorization is a natural response to recognition and it makes possible the next step in this process—associating a response with a certain stimulus (such as recognizing an algebra word problem and then knowing to create a variable table and set up equations). Your brain needs to make sense of the input stimulus at whatever level you perceive it (be it letters, words, or an algebra word problem) in order to know how to respond.

In contrast to pattern recognition and associative reasoning, rule-based reasoning is slow and effortful because it relies on methodical step-by-step thinking. Although babies recognize patterns, most people do not develop the ability to engage in rule-based, step-by-step reasoning until they are somewhere between 7 and 11 years old. This kind of reasoning requires thinking explicitly about each step taken and checking to see that it follows correctly from the previous step. When teachers teach students something new, such as how to manipulate a quadratic expression, they generally start with step-by-step, rule-based reasoning that details exactly how students should proceed with the task.

3

As students become more expert at doing something, they shift some of their thinking from effortful, step-by-step thinking to faster pattern recognition and association, thereby tying the two distinct types of reasoning together.

For example, a student might see the following quadratic and think about how to solve it using the rule-based, step-by-step process that most people learned in Algebra I as FOIL (First, Outer, Inner, Last):

$$(x+y)(x-y) = x^2 - xy + yx - y^2$$
$$= x^2 - y^2$$

A more experienced student might recognize this as a factored difference of squares and rewrite it immediately as without the intervening steps. A true expert will recognize even disguised versions of the "difference of squares" pattern and make the connections necessary to solve problems that do not, on the surface at least, even look like the algebra problems where he or she first learned the pattern:

$$(7+3\sqrt{5})(7-3\sqrt{5}) = 7^2 - (3\sqrt{5})^2$$
$$= 49 - (9 \times 5)$$
$$= 49 - 45$$
$$= 4$$

When an expert seems to "magically" instantly know how to start solving a problem, he or she has usually recognized a chunk of the problem as falling into a particular category that he or she has an associated "shortcut" for dealing with. However, the expert can also explain the rules governing each step and why the shortcut works. He or she typically knows and uses explicit rules and follows an organized solving process (such as the UPS process in math or the 4-step process in Critical Reasoning), especially when facing problems that are harder to categorize or that don't have shortcuts.

Having the ability to think in a step-by-step way on the GMAT is crucial because you need to be able to plan the solution technique, figure out how to deal with weird little problem quirks, and execute solving processes accurately. However, having the ability to see patterns, spot clues, and make quick associative connections is what allows you to finish the test in the allotted amount of time because you don't need to try every rule and technique on every problem.

The difference between a solid novice problem solver and an expert problem solver is often just that the expert recognizes bigger problem pieces and more subtle instances of patterns than the novice does. For example, although two chess players might both know all of the rules of chess, the more expert one will usually recognize more patterns of pieces on the board as favorable or unfavorable, and so will have to do less explicit step-by-step thinking in order to figure out what to do next.

If you work to develop both types of thinking skills and make an effort to use them synergistically as you solve GMAT problems, you will have a huge advantage when it comes to test day.

Logical Inference—The Secret Nexus – Dmitry Farber

Drawing Conclusions

The ability to make inferences, or draw conclusions, is one of the most important elements of a successful GMAT performance. This may not seem very intimidating—after all, we come to conclusions all day long. The problem is, we are not usually held to very exacting standards in that department.

What's an Inference?

You may be wondering what an inference is, and how it is different from a conclusion. Here are the GMAT-ese definitions:

- **Conclusion:** An opinion that we draw based on an interpretation of the facts.
- **Inference:** The recognition of an additional fact that must be true given the previous information.

Oh, and by the way, the GMAT never wants you to draw a conclusion in Critical Reasoning questions. When they specifically ask you to "draw a conclusion," they actually want you to make an inference. Logical, right?

Let's look at an example. Suppose you're at work and your friend Lothar tells you, "The boss is not my biggest fan right now." There are many inferences you might come to:

(A) The boss is angry at Lothar.

(B) The boss's opinion of Lothar has declined.

(C) Lothar is the boss's least favorite employee.

(D) Lothar has said or done something recently that the boss found upsetting.

(E) If someone is going to propose a risky new idea to the boss, Lothar should not be the one to do it.

In real life, most or even all of these inferences would probably be correct. So which of these can we conclude on the GMAT? None of the above! All we know is that the boss

3

is not Lothar's biggest fan at the moment. We don't know why this is the case, how long it has been going on, or what effects, if any, it has had on their working relationship. So what would a good GMAT conclusion look like? These should work:

Lothar has a boss.

Lothar has some ability to discern his boss's opinions.

At least one person is a bigger fan of Lothar's than the boss is.

Even that last one is a stretch, because we are assuming that Lothar has a biggest fan. If we wanted to be technical, we might say, "If Lothar has one or more fans, at least one of those fans thinks more highly of Lothar than the boss does." Not exactly inspiring stuff here, but that's what makes these inferences correct. The more interesting conclusions tend to be extreme, to grasp at weak connections, or to make reasonable but unsupported assumptions. The correct inference usually states something rather mild and boring.

Getting Clear on the Mission

You may have noticed that in the last example, we were quite wary about making even small assumptions, but at the same time, we never bothered to question a very fundamental one—that what Lothar is saying is true. That's one step we don't have to worry about. Whenever the GMAT gives us information—whether it's a set of statements, a Reading Comprehension passage, or an equation—we can treat it as true, at least for the duration of the problem. Let's try another problem. To be fair, we'll throw in a correct answer this time:

> The novelist Charles Dickens was an enthusiastic follower of the *Star Wars* films, and liked to entertain dinner guests by doing uncannily accurate impressions of the characters. In fact, an early draft of *A Tale of Two Cities* uses Yoda as a narrator, beginning with "The best of times, the worst of times it was…. "
>
> The statements above, if true, most strongly support which of the following conclusions?
>
> (A) Dickens had access to a time machine.
> (B) Dickens removed the Yoda character to avoid copyright infringement.
> (C) Dickens regularly had guests over for dinner.
> (D) The Star Wars films were popular in the 19th century.
> (E) More than one draft of *A Tale of Two Cities* was written.

Okay, so we won't see this on the GMAT, but let's not worry about that. The point is that we have been asked to identify what else we know **if the statements are true**. Let's see what we can do with the answer choices:

(A) Watch out for answers that try to explain the premises. We don't know why or how Dickens became a *Star Wars* fan. We just know it happened.

(B) Again, we don't know why Yoda was cut from the story. We might reasonably infer that he was cut, since the text above makes a point of saying that he was featured in an "early draft," but that's as far as we can go.

(C) We know that Dickens liked to entertain dinner guests, so (C) seems pretty safe. But do we know how often this happened? Nope. We have to cross this one out. If (C) had said "Dickens sometimes had guests over to dinner," it would have worked. Notice that incorrect conclusions will often add a degree word (regularly, most, all, etc.) that is not supported by the text.

(D) This might explain the weirdness of the above statements, but we don't know when the films were popular, or if they were popular at all.

(E) This is our only safe bet. If we are told about an early draft of the book, we can infer that there was at least one later draft.

The key to cutting through the wrong answers quickly is to know how far we can go with the information we've been given—not far at all. Often, students who struggle with this question type find that they are giving the right answer to the wrong question. So make sure you're clear on the mission—we don't want to explain the information, amplify the points that have been made, or "back the author up." We just want to find something, however trivial, that seems to be true based on the information.

The Secret Nexus

Taken alone, Critical Reasoning inference problems don't constitute a big part of your GMAT experience—you should only see a few of them on your exam. But the ability to see what makes an inference shaky will help you on just about every Critical Reasoning question, and making inferences is also a core skill in Reading Comprehension. And then there's the Quant section. Oh yes. This test isn't really about calculation; it's about problem solving. You need to know what you can conclude from the data at hand. That's the secret to success in Data Sufficiency, in Geometry, and in quite a few other situations throughout the test. This is why I refer to logical inference as The Secret Nexus—this one concept connects many seemingly dissimilar portions of the test, and mastery of this skill will have a tremendous impact on your GMAT performance. If you know how to make logical inferences, you will frequently avoid getting tricked, or getting stuck between answer choices. If you jump to wild conclusions, you are toast.

3

Mathematical Inference

Data Sufficiency is all about making inferences. The point is to find out what information, if any, will give us a definitive answer to the question, so we need to determine exactly what we know from each statement. Let's try a problem:

> While on summer vacation in Hawaii, Carla goes for an ocean ride on a mystic porpoise named Noelani. If Noelani maintains a constant speed for the entire trip, does the ride take less than 3 hours?
>
> (1) Noelani swims faster than 6 miles per hour.

One possible interpretation of this is "Noelani swims at least 7 miles per hour." However, this interpretation requires an assumption that the porpoise's speed is an integer. What about 6.5 or 6.0002? What we can really conclude is this: In 3 hours, the porpoise swims more than 18 miles. So if the trip is 18 miles or less, the answer to the question is yes. If the trip is more than 18 miles, the answer is maybe. It depends on how fast the porpoise really swims.

> (2) The ride is 20 miles in the winter, but is then reduced by a mile per month until the fall.

We might think "So what?" or say "Okay, the ride is less than 20 miles—but this statement doesn't tell us how fast they're going." Still, let's see exactly what we know. Carla is on summer vacation, so the earliest it could be is June. Winter must be at least 3 months away, so the ride has been reduced to 17 miles (if this month's reduction has already happened) or 18 miles (if it hasn't). Very nitpicky work for an insufficient statement, but now we know exactly what we have.

(1) & (2). If the trip is 18 miles or less, it will take less than 3 hours. The trip is 18 miles at the absolute max, so it takes less than 3 hours. Both statements together are sufficient to answer the question. For those familiar with Data Sufficiency, that would be an answer of (C).

Okay, you might say, but that problem was like a little story. Sure I have to use my reading comprehension skills there, but what about the pure math problems? Well, try this:

> If $xy \neq 0$ and $x^2y = y^2$, which of the following must be true?
>
> (A) $x > y$
> (B) $y > x$
> (C) $x^2 < y^2$
> (D) $y > 0$
> (E) $x < 0$

If you've looked at much GMAT material, this question type should look familiar. We are often asked which of the choices *must* be true, *could* be true, or *cannot* be true, and to tackle these questions, we need to be ready to make careful inferences. In this case, the correct choice will be something that *must* be true, so what do we know about the rest? They may be true under some circumstances, or they may not be true at all. In short, they *could* be false.

In a sense, each step we take in manipulating an equation is an inference, and as we go, we need to keep checking to make sure that our inference is a logical one. For instance, your first instinct might be to divide both sides of the equation by y. This makes sense, as long as y is not 0. Since we have been told that $xy \neq 0$, we can infer that $y \neq 0$, so this step is okay to take:

$$x^2 y = y^2$$

$$x^2 = y$$

Now we know that x^2 equals y. What can we infer from this? It would be tempting to infer that y must be greater than x, since we have to square x to make it equal to y. That is a dangerous inference, though, because we are assuming some things about our numbers. We might slow down and ask ourselves, "Could x be equal to or greater than y and still fit this equation?" Sure—x could be 1, in which case $x^2 = y = 1$, or x could be a fraction, in which case x^2 (and therefore y) would equal a smaller fraction. These possibilities allow us to eliminate answer choices (A), (B), and (C).

So what is a safe inference? Answer choices (D) and (E) are dealing with positive and negative. What do we know there? If $x^2 = y$, we don't know much about the sign of x. Whether x is negative or positive, we'll get the same result when we square it—a positive number. From this, we know that y must be positive. The answer is **(D)**.

At this point, you might be noticing a difference between mathematical inferences and verbal inferences. To make mathematical inferences, you have to apply mathematical rules! If you feel confident in your ability to apply those rules, you might find mathematical inferences easier and more comfortable than verbal inferences. On the other hand, if you feel shaky about math, each new problem may feel like a fraternity hazing. In either case, the important thing is that you focus not just on memorizing an endless list of rules, but on carefully applying what you know in order to make inferences. In fact, we might sum up the formula to getting a top GMAT score this way: "Learn the relevant content, and use it to make inferences while keeping an eye on the clock." It sounds easy now, right?

How to Use Your Strategy Guides

If you wanted to meet every neighbor on your block, you wouldn't reintroduce yourself to your best friends who live a few doors down, or to the guy who has you over for a barbeque every fourth Sunday. Rather, you would identify which neighbors you don't know, and go knock on their doors. The same is true for learning GMAT content. If you are already solid on a bunch of content, reading a whole book on stuff you already know and doing practice problems you could do blindfolded with your hands tied behind your back won't improve your score. You need to identify the content that you do not yet know, or are still shaky on, and concentrate your efforts there.

The Strategy Guides are written to provide comprehensive coverage of GMAT-level content. It is your job to ascertain how to most effectively use the guides. Here's what we recommend:

- ***If you know that you don't know*** the content covered in a Strategy Guide chapter, are shaky and/or rusty on the material, or feel that there must be a faster way than how you currently approach the subject, read the chapter. Create a cheat sheet for the chapter by taking notes on key points that you want to remember, but don't yet have memorized. Then, test your learning by completing all of the In Action problems at the end of the chapter. Make sure to check your answer and review the solution after completing each problem—not after completing the whole set. There is no better way to internalize how *not* to do something correctly than to repeat an incorrect method 15 times in a row!

- ***If you know that you know*** the content covered in a Strategy Guide chapter, quiz yourself to prove it! Turn to the In Action problems at the end of the chapter. They are listed from easiest to hardest, so try numbers 3 and 8. If you do not get those problems right, read the chapter. If you do get those problems right, complete numbers 11–15. Make sure to check the answers after completing each problem. If you get them all right, move on to the next chapter. If you get them mostly right, skim the chapter and focus in on the pieces of information that you need to fill the holes in your knowledge.

- ***If the Strategy Guide leaves you confused,*** it is likely that you have holes in the foundational knowledge on which the GMAT content is built. While reading the Strategy Guide, refer back to the appropriate chapters of the Foundations books, as needed, to fill in these gaps.

Student Sound-Off

The Manhattan GMAT guides were excellent but I had to read them once, absorb the information by taking the practice tests, and then come back to review in order to truly understand the subtleties of the GMAT.

Timur
770 (Q50, V47)

3

Chapter Takeaways

1. In order to do well on the GMAT, you have to know how to apply the content you learn to new types of problems. Memorizing facts can help, but the key is really to learn how to analyze and evaluate GMAT problems.

2. The "facts" that you need to remember to do well on the GMAT are drawn from typical high school Algebra and English Composition classes.

3. If your pre-test showed a low Quant or Verbal score, you should start the recommended pre-work *before* you start working through the Manhattan GMAT Strategy Guides or begin the class.

4. Exploit everyday opportunities (e.g., shopping, splitting checks, and calculating tips) to practice hand computation. There is no calculator on the GMAT and most students, including those who are good at math, are relatively slow at hand computation.

5. Whether your natural thinking style tends to be more intuitive and pattern based or more rule and formal logic based, it is important to develop both styles of thinking as you learn to analyze GMAT content.

6. Learn or review the language of logical inference because it will make understanding many GMAT questions much easier.

7. You do not necessarily need to do all of the homework, but you do need to figure out what you don't know so that you can focus on homework that will correct your weaknesses.

Chapter *of* 4

The Big Picture of GMAT Quant

In This Chapter...

Chapter 4:

The Big Picture of GMAT Quant

The GMAT Quant section—unlike those math tests in high school—is designed so that you cannot get every problem right. On a typical high school math test, the hardest part of what you will need to do is the mechanics of the math; however, on the GMAT, it is the higher-level reasoning and time allocation. In order to be fast enough, you will have to reason intuitively as well as in the step-by-step, show your work style so popular with high school math teachers.

The best GMAT Quantitative problem solvers are able to move back-and-forth between intuitive pattern recognition style thinking (speed) and step-by-step logical reasoning (error prevention) as they work through problems. They are also good guessers, and spend time reasoning and eliminating whatever answer choices they can, rather than struggling futilely when they don't see how to fully solve a problem mathematically.

TIP

Test-takers at the 700 level and below are only getting an average of 60% of the questions correct! That's only 3 out of 5. Even 99th percentile test-takers miss 20% of the questions—that's one out of five!

The following articles will guide you through learning the types of reasoning that you will need to succeed on the GMAT.

Understand, Plan, and Problem Solved!
– Abby Pelcyger

Instructor Insights

Too often I see confident students pick up their pencils as soon as they are given a new math problem and start rapidly scribbling down equation after equation. Their math is often correct, but the problem they're solving is not. Solving the wrong problem on the GMAT is like running a race in the wrong direction. While you can run the required number of miles, you will not end up at the finish line.

Likewise, students who are insecure about their math competence often stare blindly at a math problem, pencils poised but frozen in air. These students believe that they are *supposed* to be rapidly scribbling down equations, but don't know where to start.

Whether you are confident in your math prowess or shudder at the thought of algebra, the odds are that the same issue is holding back your math score: if you do not understand the problem, you cannot solve it. It is crucial to invest time making sure that you understand the problem *before* you try to solve it. *Time?* You may ask. *I don't have time to sit back and worry about understanding!* The truth is, though, that you don't have time not to.

Six years ago, when I first moved to Philadelphia, I was teaching elementary school full-time and working on my Masters in Education as a first-year Teach For America Corps Member. I was pretty busy. During that first year, there was a contest going on between the number of parking tickets that I got and the number of times that I locked my keys in my car. Imagine how much time I would have saved not waiting for AAA to break into my car had I taken 30 seconds each time I left my car to go through a short mental check list. The same is true for GMAT problems: spending time up front to make sure that you understand the problem will save you time in the long run.

The problem solving process that we recommend you use for every math problem is: Understand, Plan, Solve[1] (UPS). UPS is a step-by-step methodical process that will maximize your chance of recognizing patterns, give you concrete steps to take until pattern recognition sets in, and provide you with an overarching framework within which to go back-and-forth between these two types of thinking.

> **TIP**
>
> For more information about the two types of thinking, see Instructor Liz Ghini Moliski's article on the Dual Process Model in Chapter 3.

Let's look at this sample GMAT-like problem as an example:

> Reggie was hiking on a 6-mile loop trail at a rate of 2 miles per hour. One hour into Reggie's hike, Cassie started hiking from the same starting point on the loop trail at 3 miles per hour. What is the shortest time that Cassie could hike on the trail in order to meet up with Reggie?
>
> (A) 0.8 hours
> (B) 1.2 hours
> (C) 2 hours
> (D) 3 hours
> (E) 5 hours

---

1   This approach was popularized by the mathematician Georges Polya in his seminal book *How to Solve It: A New Aspect of Mathematical Method*. Fascinating read… you know, for all of your spare time.

MANHATTAN
GMAT

Understand

The GMAT simply doesn't use cookie-cutter problems: the writers are constantly crafting new twists and turns to throw at you. For this reason, it is essential that you understand the nuances of the problem in front of you and consciously decide how to approach it before you begin to wildly throw equations down on the page.

In order to understand a Quant problem, begin by asking yourself these two methodical questions:

(1) What am I given?

(2) What do I need?

Because Quant problems are often chock full of information, it is important to work your way through the problem sentence by sentence, phrase by phrase, to ensure that you pull out all of the information. *Write down all of the information that you gather on your scrap paper;* attempting to store information in your head reduces the available brain power that you have to apply towards actually solving the problem. Also, putting all of the information down in one place will help you see the relationships between the pieces of information, recognize patterns, and minimize the probability that you will forget a pivotal caveat at a crucial time during the solving process.

Looking at this problem, the first thing that jumps out is that it's practically a *paragraph* written in the *Quant* section. This is the pattern of word problems—that should alert you to the fact that you need to translate the English into Math. Also, you should identify questions that take up more than two lines as ones that can often be translated into equations with the help of a picture and/or a chart.

A key word in this problem is *rate*. Whenever a problem involves a rate, the equation Rate × Time = Distance should pop into your head. Problems involving rates almost always require this equation. It's a good thing to write down at the top of your page. Also, you should recognize that rate problems can often be drawn, so try sketching a diagram!

Once you've noticed a couple of big-picture elements in the problem, it's time to dissect the question methodically, starting at the beginning. The first sentence begins *Reggie was hiking on a 6-mile loop....* Aha! There's a path. It's 6 miles long. And it's circular. Draw it! Make sure to write down that it is 6 miles long. Also, draw an arrow to show Reggie walking along it. Choose the variable "R" for Reggie because it will be the easiest to remember.

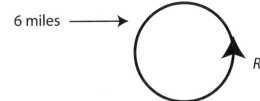

The sentence continues *at a rate of 2 miles per hour.* Add Reggie's rate to your picture. Continue drawing until you have worked through the entire question. Write "G:" for *given* to the left of all the information that the problem provides. Your picture will likely look something like this:

$$G: R \times T = D$$

Note that Cassie is drawn two miles away from Reggie. This is to take into account the two miles that Reggie hiked during his one-hour head start.

The picture helps you realize that there are two directions that Cassie can walk in if she wants to meet up with Reggie:

(1)　She can walk in the same direction as Reggie.

(2)　Since the trail is a loop, she can walk in the opposite direction of Reggie.

Very interesting, you think to yourself: you now understand that, in order to find the shortest time that it will take Cassie to meet up with Reggie, you will have to compare the time that it will take her to walk in each direction!

If you want to, you can also put all of the information that we know into a chart under our equation:

	R	×	T	=	D
R	2		$t+1$		
C	3		t		

However, note that if you *only* had the chart, it would be very easy to miss the subtlety that Cassie can choose to walk in either of two different directions.

Once you have consolidated all of the information that you have been given, it is time to ask the second question: *What do I need?* Rate problems fall into one of two patterns. Some require investigating an overall average rate when two different rates are given for specified distances. Alternately, others require calculating the rate or time needed to accomplish a certain distance or amount of work. In this question, you are asked for the smallest amount of time that it would take Cassie to meet up with Reggie. Thinking about this, you realize that this question falls into the latter category. You need to solve for Cassie's time hiking, or "*t*" in our *RT = D* chart.

I advise writing "N:" for *need* to the left of what you are looking for. I also strongly suggest boxing in what you are looking for so that, if you forget what you're asked to solve for when you're mired down in the details of the problem, you can quickly look above and get yourself back on track. For this problem, I would write something like this:

N: Cassie's minimum time—compare walking in each direction

Plan

Once you understand everything that the problem has to offer, it's time to decide *how* to get from what you were given to what you need. Math is cool. There is only one right answer, but there are many ways to get there. The better you become at math, the more options you will have.

Maybe you recognize what to do from solving other problems with similar patterns. Maybe you can quickly and methodically solve the problem algebraically. Even if you are not sure how to solve the problem algebraically, because you took time to understand the question, you can still use logic to reason through it. You know how fast Reggie and Cassie are each hiking, the length of the trail, and how far away from each other they start. You can use this information to figure out approximately when they meet by moving time forward in one hour segments to find out where they are at each hour. You can then choose the answer closest to your approximation. You just need to remember to compare the times of the two different directions that Cassie can hike in. We will walk through this approach below.

Solve

First, label the miles on your path so that you know where Reggie and Cassie are on the path at any given amount of time:

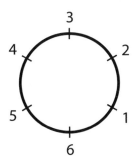

4

Cassie Walks in the Same Direction as Reggie		
Time (hours)	R	C
0	2	0
1	4	3
2	6	6

Cassie Walks in the Opposite Direction as Reggie		
Time (hours)	R	C
0	2	6
1	4	3

Aha! If Cassie tries to catch up to Reggie, it will take her *two hours*. Although that is one of your answer choices, we must remember that the GMAT writers often throw in trap answer choices to make questions trickier! Don't forget to compare Cassie's time walking from the other direction.

Whoa! Glad you checked this second way—it's faster! If Cassie walks in the opposite direction as Reggie, they pass each other in *less than one hour!* You do not know exactly how much less than one hour, but there is only one answer choice that is less than an hour, so choose it: **(A) 0.8 hours**.

Takeaway

Using the Understand-Plan-Solve framework can help you think through tough Quant problems. To use the framework as you work through the problem, ask yourself the following questions—and write down the answers: *What am I given? What do I need? How will I get there?* Spending time up front can save you a lot of time in the long run!

Translating Words into Math
– Stacey Koprince

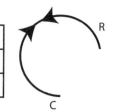

Instructor Insights

I've spoken with several students recently who are struggling with translating wordy Quant problems into the actual math necessary to set up and solve the problem. Some people make too many mistakes when doing this, and others find that, though generally accurate, they take more time than they can afford. In this article we're going to talk about how to translate efficiently and effectively.

We're going to do this by example. I'll provide short excerpts from GMAT-like problems, and then we'll discuss how to *know* what to do, how to *do* the actual translation, and how to do so *efficiently*. Note that I'm not going to provide the full text of problems—and, therefore, you're not going to solve fully. That's not your goal today.

The Basics

Before we dive into more advanced issues, there are some basics we all need to know. We're not going to spend a lot of time on the basics because all GMAT books out there already explain this; I'll give a quick introduction, and if you need more instruction on

MANHATTAN
GMAT

this topic, take a look at the Algebraic Translations chapter of the *Word Translations* Strategy Guide.

First, when the problem introduces certain people, objects, or other things, you will likely need to assign variables. Cindy can become C and Bob can become B.

Next, the words will give you some kind of relationship between variables.

For instance, a sentence might tell you that Cindy is five years older than Bob. You've already decided to use C for Cindy and B for Bob, and the "is" represents an equals sign. Five, of course, represents the number 5. Finally "older than" indicates addition; you need a plus sign. Your translated equation becomes $C = 5 + B$. (Another very common word is "of," which typically means to multiply. For example, 1/2 of 6 would be written: $1/2 \times 6$.)

Notice a couple of things about this equation. You have two unknowns in the sentence, so you should expect to have two variables in the equation. Also, how can you quickly check the equation to see that it makes sense? There are two common ways. You can plug in some simple numbers to test the equation—this might take a little bit longer, but it's the more certain method. Or you can think about the concepts that have been presented. Who's older and who's younger? To which person do we need to add years in order to make their ages equal? You want to add to the younger in order to equal the older. Bob's the younger one, so you want to add to his age. Does the equation do that?

Here's an excerpt from another question:

> "Daniel has d snow globes, which is 1/3 as many as Pete and twice as many as Jennifer."

They've already defined one variable for you: d for the number of snow globes Daniel has. Let's use j for Jennifer's snow globes and p for Pete's snow globes.

Next, take each piece of information separately:

Daniel has d snow globes, and d is (=) 2 times as many as (multiply) j, so $d = 2j$.

Daniel has d snow globes, and d is (=) $\dfrac{1}{3}$ as many as (multiply) p, so $d = \dfrac{1}{3}p$.

Task 1: Translate *everything* and make it real.

Another problem first tells you that a bakery sells all of its doughnuts at one specific price and all of its cupcakes at another specific price. It also tells you:

"On Saturday, the store sold 14 doughnuts and 8 cupcakes for a total of $40.00, and on Sunday the store sold 16 doughnuts and 12 cupcakes for a total of $52.00."

What should you do? First, set variables. Let d = the price for one doughnut and let c = the price for one cupcake. Then, pretend you own the store and a customer walks up with 14 doughnuts and 8 cupcakes. What do you do? Make it real—actually visualize (or draw out) what needs to happen.

First, I'd figure out how much I need to charge for the doughnuts: $d each for 14 = $14d$. Similarly, the cupcakes would cost $8c$. You want to buy all of them? Excellent! You owe me $14d + 8c = 40$. If you do the same thing with the second half of the sentence quoted above, you get $16d + 12c = 52$.

So, you're done with that—now, you just need to solve for d and c, right? Not so fast! Read the actual question first:

"How much less does a doughnut sell for than a cupcake?"

Hmm. They're not just asking for the price of a doughnut or the price of a cupcake. They're asking for the difference ("less than") between the two. Which one costs more and which one costs less?

The sentence is telling you that the doughnut is cheaper. Okay, so if you want the difference in cost between a cupcake and a doughnut, and the doughnut is the cheaper item, how do you do that subtraction? Write $c - d$. You actually want to solve for that overall combination ($c - d$); if you can find a way to do that without solving for c and d individually first, you can save time. (That topic, however, we'll save for another time.)

Task 2: Where appropriate, use a chart or table to organize.

Let's try another:

"A painter painting a building at a constant rate takes 7 hours to paint 2/5 of the building."

Again, visualize—you're standing there (for 7 hours!) with a paintbrush, painting the building. How does it work? *RTW*: Rate × Time = Work. Make a chart:

	Rate	Time	Work
First Sentence	R	7	2/5

Okay, so you have one formula: $R \times 7 = 2/5$. The next sentence says:

"How much more time will it take to finish painting the building?"

To finish painting… hmm, how much more do you have to paint? An entire job = 1. You've painted 2/5, so we have 3/5 to go, right? Add another row to your chart:

	Rate	Time	Work
First Sentence	R	7	2/5
Question	R	T	3/5

Hey, you've got another formula: $RT = 3/5$. You can use the first one to solve for R, and, since the rate stays the same, you can then plug into the second to solve for T.

One more! Let's try this one:

"Jose is now 9 years younger than Beth. If in 6 years Jose will be half as old as Beth, how old will Beth be in 3 years?"

First, set a chart up. You need a row for each person in the problem, and you also need to represent all of the time frames that are discussed. Careful—there are three time frames, not two!

	Now	+3 y	+6 y
Jose	J		
Beth	B		

Assign variables—decide whether to use one variable or two and decide when to set each base variable (most of the time, you'll set the base variable to the "Now" time frame). In the above chart, I've set two variables in the Now time frame.

Next, if you want to use one variable, try to use the simplest piece of information given in the problem to simplify to one variable. In this case, the first sentence is the simplest information because it is set in the "Now" time frame for both Jose and Beth.

"Jose is now 9 years younger than Beth."

$J = B - 9$

Remember, "is" means "equals" and "younger than" means "subtract." Do you remember how to check your equation quickly to make sure it makes sense?

Who's older, Jose or Beth? According to the sentence, Beth. The equation subtracts the 9 from the older person, Beth. That makes sense.

Okay, so you can either remove the J from our table and insert $B - 9$ instead, or you can flip the equation around (to $B = J + 9$), then remove B from the table and insert $J + 9$ instead. Does it matter? Mathematically, no, but practically speaking, yes—make your life easier by keeping the variable for which you want to solve! You want to solve for Beth, so your new table should look like this:

	Now	+3 y	+6 y
Jose	$B - 9$		
Beth	B		

Now fill in the remaining timef rames (you have the info to do this already—just add 3 for the middle column and 6 for the final column!):

	Now	+3 y	+6 y
Jose	$B - 9$	$B - 6$	$B - 3$
Beth	B	$B + 3$	$B + 6$

What now? Oh, right—now you have that harder second statement to translate:

"If in 6 years Jose will be half as old as Beth...."

Okay, what time frame do you need to use? "In 6 years"—okay, go to that column. In 6 years, Beth is $B + 6$ and Jose is $B - 3$. Make sure to use these as you translate.

Next, "will be" is a variation of "is" and means "equals." "Half" means 1/2, and "as old as" means multiply. Here's the translated equation:

$$B - 3 = (1/2)(B + 6)$$

Hey, you have an equation with one variable! Now you can solve.

Key Takeaways for Translating

1. Know the basics. Certain words consistently mean the same thing (e.g., forms of the verb "to be" generally mean "equals"). There are lots of great resources out there already that will give you the basics.

2. Those annoying wordy problems have a lot going on. Make sure you are translating every last thing, and also try to make it real! Insert yourself into the situation; imagine that you are the one doing whatever's happening and ask yourself what you'd have to do at each step along the way.

3. When there are multiple variables, multiple time frames, or other kinds of moving parts, use a chart or table to organize your info. Label everything clearly and only then start filling in.

Disguising — and Decoding — Quant Problems

How can the GMAT disguise a prime number (or any other) problem? We're going to use the concept of prime to describe this, but the general process of disguising—and studying how to decode—problems is applicable to a great number of problems on the test. You can use these concepts when studying a number of different GMAT content areas.

What Is the Exact Mathematical Definition of a Prime Number?

Most people, when asked to define or describe the concept of prime, will say that a prime number is a positive number that is divisible by itself and 1. (A number is said to be divisible by another when the result of that division is an integer.)

However, in order to recognize a disguise, you have to precisely understand the fundamental concept at play, and, in this case, that means recognizing that *any* positive integer is divisible by itself and 1. The number 1 is divisible by itself and 1. The number 2 is divisible by itself and 1. The number 9 is divisible by itself and 1. Yet only one of those numbers is actually a prime number. If ALL positive integers are divisible by themselves and 1, then what is *different* about prime numbers? This is the key to understanding the difference between an everyday language definition and a precise mathematical definition.

When considering positive integers, there are three categories: prime, non-prime (or composite), and the number 1. Although the number 1 is divisible by itself and 1, "itself" equals one. The number 1, then, has only one factor. A prime number is divisible by itself and 1, where "itself" is a *different* number than the number 1. In other words, a prime number has exactly two factors. A composite number is divisible by itself, 1, and at least one other number; a composite number, then, has *more* than two factors (itself, 1, and at least one number in between).

(In case you have forgotten the exact definition, a factor is a positive integer that divides evenly into an integer. For example, 6 is a factor of 12 because 12/6 = 2, and 2 is an integer. In fact, 1, 2, 3, 4, 6, and 12 are all factors of 12 because when 12 is divided by each of those factors, the result is an integer.)

How Will the GMAT Disguise a Prime Number Problem?

There are a number of ways that the GMAT can test our knowledge of some concept in general. One common theme on more difficult problems is an attempt to disguise the fact that the problem is about prime numbers. Often, the word prime will not even appear in the problem. Essentially, the test writers are testing whether you can decode the language in order to realize what the problem is really asking.

For example, a Data Sufficiency problem might tell you about the positive integer *x*, which does not equal 1. Are there two integers, both of which are greater than 1, that can multiply to give you *x*?

What am I really asking you there? Can you think of a specific value for *x* that would allow you to answer "yes" to that question? And a specific value that would give a "no" answer instead?

4

Let's see. $2 \times 2 = 4$. Those are two integers (they're not different, but notice that my question didn't specify two *distinct* integers) and both are greater than 1. They multiply to equal 4. So, if positive integer x is 4 then, yes, there are two numbers, both greater than 1, that multiply to give us 4.

On the other hand, $1 \times 5 = 5$. That doesn't work because both numbers are not greater than 1, so the answer to the question (for this specific example) is "no." For the integer 5, the answer will always be no. Why? Because there's no way to express 5 as the product of two integers without using 1; there are no factors of 5 that are *between* 1 and 5.

What's the difference between those two numbers? The first is composite and the second is prime. A composite number will always result in a "yes" answer for this question, because a composite number, by definition, has at least one factor between 1 and itself. A prime number, by contrast, will always result in a "no" answer for this question, because a prime number has exactly two factors, 1 and itself.

Back to the question: Are there two integers, both of which are greater than 1, that can multiply to give you x? I'm really asking you whether x is prime or composite (or, because this is Data Sufficiency, whether you can't tell at all). In formulating my question, I incorporated the distinction between prime and composite numbers: I used the definition so that I could avoid giving you the term "prime" in the question.

Why Is This Broadly Applicable to the GMAT?

This is one of the fundamental ways in which the test writers can make any question harder: ask you about a concept without using the actual name. It's not enough just to know the concept; you have to figure out that they're referring to it in the first place.

Your task as a student is to figure out how the test writers can ask about various properties or principles without using the names of those properties or principles. The only way to do this is to give the definition instead, so study *how* that will look on a GMAT problem. What is the definition, as precisely as possible? What are the different ways in which that could be worded in a question? Can you find two or three OG (*Official Guide*) questions that ask about the same fundamental principle using somewhat different wording?

Check out the following two DS problems:

Does the integer x have 3 or more distinct positive factors?

(1) x is odd
(2) $23 < x < 29$

Does there exist an integer d such that $x > d > 1$ and x/d is an integer?

(1) $11! + 2 \leq x \leq 11! + 12$
(2) $x \geq 2^5$

Do they look familiar in some way? The structure of the two problems is almost identical, although the harder one also incorporates additional concepts. In addition, you could solve the easier one by testing real numbers, so you don't absolutely have to figure out the "prime" aspect in order to answer that one. For the harder one, though, you do actually have to recognize that the problem is testing the concept of prime. Here's the kicker: it's easier to *figure out* the "prime disguise" on the easier problem; then, all you have to do is *recognize* it on the harder problem. That ability to recognize the fundamental issue will then give you time to deal with all of the additional complexity in the harder problem.

Takeaways

1. Know the definition of prime, but also know the difference between prime and non-prime (or composite) numbers.

2. Know how the test writers can ask about prime without using that specific word. Don't stop with prime! What other concepts can they ask about without using the specific words? What are the very precise definitions, and what are the different ways in which they might word a problem to reflect each definition?

3. How will you recognize similar wording on future problems?

Data Sufficiency Reasoning (without the Math!) – Jennifer Dziura

Instructor Insights

For students just beginning a GMAT course of study, Data Sufficiency problems can be very challenging because they combine a new and unusual problem type with math knowledge many of us haven't seen in years.

Data Sufficiency may also prove difficult for those who are more advanced in their studies: many students feel as though they've "got the math," but somehow are still picking the wrong answers to Data Sufficiency questions.

This article is designed to help you learn and practice the mechanics of Data Sufficiency questions—without the math. (Well, we might sneak a tiny bit of math in at the end, but it's for your own good!)

Let's try a totally math-free example:

Is the rock in my pocket blue?

(1) The rock in my pocket is either blue or red.

(2) The rock in my pocket is either red or purple.

(A) Statement (1) ALONE is sufficient, but statement (2) is NOT sufficient

(B) Statement (2) ALONE is sufficient, but statement (1) is NOT sufficient

(C) BOTH statements TOGETHER are sufficient, but NEITHER statement ALONE is sufficient

(D) EACH statement ALONE is sufficient

(E) Statements (1) and (2) TOGETHER are NOT sufficient

What a strange way to ask a question! The main idea behind Data Sufficiency questions is that you're not *actually* being asked the question, "Is the rock in my pocket blue?" Instead, you're being asked *how much information you would need* to answer the question.

Let's attack. First, note that "Is the rock in my pocket blue?" is a yes or no question. You wouldn't necessarily need to know the color of the rock in order to answer that question. (For instance, "It's not blue" would tell you exactly what you need to know, even though you still wouldn't know the rock's color.)

Examine Statement (1) alone: "The rock in my pocket is either blue or red." Is this statement enough to answer the question, "Is the rock in my pocket blue?" Many people get confused here, because, according to Statement (1), the rock *could* be blue. You could say that Statement (1) is consistent with the possibility that the rock is blue. But it definitely is NOT enough information to allow you to answer the question with a definite yes or no. If the rock is blue, the answer is yes; if the rock is red, the answer is no. Since Statement (1) allows for the possibility of either a yes or no answer to the question, Statement (1) is NOT sufficient.

If Statement (1) is NOT sufficient, answer choices (A) and (D) are now impossible and can be eliminated (look back up at the answer choices to determine why).

Now move on to Statement (2). It is very important here to consider Statement (2) *independently*—that is, you must momentarily forget that you ever saw Statement (1). Statement (2) tells you that the rock is either red or purple. Is this enough to give a definite yes or no to the question, "Is the rock in my pocket blue?" Indeed, it is! Statement (2) does NOT tell you what color the rock is—it gives you two possibilities, red or purple. But either way, you can be sure that the rock is NOT blue. That is, each of the possibilities presented by Statement (2) yields the same answer to the question— no, the rock is not blue.

Statement (2) IS sufficient. The answer is **(B)**.

Note that you ended up finding out from Statement (2) that the answer to the original question was "no." This throws some people off, because they end up confusing "no" with "insufficient." Keep in mind that what you're being tested on is *whether you have enough information to get a definite answer to the question.* You shouldn't particularly care what that answer happens to be. For your purposes, *No is just as good an answer as Yes.*

Also note the *order* in which you proceeded above. You considered Statement (1) independently, then considered Statement (2) independently. *This is always how you are going to begin.* (One exception—if the second statement were obviously much easier than the first, you could consider them in reverse order, but the principle still holds that your first step is to consider each statement independently, ruling out (A), (B), and (D) before combining). If Statement (2) had also been insufficient, only then would you have gone on to combine the statements.

Let's try another example. Pick a letter answer for yourself before reading the explanation below. (On the GMAT, you will be required to answer every question in order, without going back to previous questions, so in many cases you will be forced to make a guess. So get used to giving it your best shot!)

> Am I 32 years old?
>
> (1) I am either 29 or 37 years old.
> (2) I am over 35 years old.

(A)   Statement (1) ALONE is sufficient, but statement (2) is not sufficient

(B)   Statement (2) ALONE is sufficient, but statement (1) is not sufficient

(C)   BOTH statements TOGETHER are sufficient, but NEITHER statement ALONE is sufficient

(D)   EACH statement ALONE is sufficient

(E)   Statements (1) and (2) TOGETHER are NOT sufficient

Note that this is another yes or no question. You don't necessarily need to know the speaker's age to know that he or she is or is not 32.

Statement (1) tells you that the speaker is either 29 or 37. You don't know which age he or she actually is, but you DO know enough to know that he or she is not 32! Statement (1) IS sufficient! (That is, both possible ages yield a "no" answer to the question.) You can now eliminate answer choices (B), (C), and (E) (look up at the answer choices to figure out why).

Next, move on to Statement (2). If the speaker is over 35, he or she is definitely not 32. The answer to the question is definitely "no." Statement (2) IS sufficient. Your final answer is (D) (look up at the answer choices to figure out why).

Note that, by combining the two statements, you could determine that the speaker is actually 37. However, you do not ever have to get to the point of combining the statements, since you don't really care about the speaker's real age—you already had answer choice (D) before even getting to the point of combining.

An important idea in Data Sufficiency is *Never combine the statements until you've ruled out the possibility that either is sufficient independently.* If you had skipped the steps above—considering each statement in isolation—and just lumped the statements together and figured out that the speaker was 37, we probably would have picked (C) (look up at the answer choices to figure out why), which would be incorrect. You must ALWAYS consider each statement independently before you even think about combining.

Let's try a third example:

What is my brother's name?

(1) My brother's name is Sandeep, Vijay, or Tom.
(2) My brother's name is not Tom.

(A)   Statement (1) ALONE is sufficient, but statement (2) is not sufficient
(B)   Statement (2) ALONE is sufficient, but statement (1) is not sufficient
(C)   BOTH statements TOGETHER are sufficient, but NEITHER statement ALONE is sufficient
(D)   EACH statement ALONE is sufficient
(E)   Statements (1) and (2) TOGETHER are NOT sufficient

This question is a little different. It is not a yes or no question—to answer this question, you need an actual name.

Statement (1) gives you three possibilities. This is definitely NOT enough to answer the question, "What is my brother's name?" Eliminate (A) and (D).

Remember, *when considering Statement (2), forget you ever saw Statement (1).* Statement (2) tells you that the brother's name is not Tom. That is definitely NOT sufficient to tell you what his name actually is! Eliminate (B) (look up at the answer choices to figure out why).

Only once you have eliminated (A), (B) and (D) do you combine the statements. That means *you will never consider both statements in combination until you are down to only two possibilities for your final answer—(C) and (E).*

Statements (1) and (2) together tell you that the brother's name is Sandeep, Vijay, or Tom, and then that it is NOT Tom. Therefore, his name is Sandeep or Vijay. That's STILL not enough to answer the question, "What is my brother's name?"

The answer is **(E)**—even with both statements together, you cannot give a definitive answer to the question.

Now, consider how you would have given different letter answers to this problem if the question were changed. For instance, what if the question read:

> Is my brother's name Joe?
>
> (1) My brother's name is Sandeep, Vijay, or Tom.
> (2) My brother's name is not Tom.

Now, the answer would be (A). Statement (1) gives you three possibilities, but each of them yields a "no" answer to the question. However, according to Statement (2), the brother's name could be Joe—or it could be any of a million other things.

Here's another version:

> Is my brother's name Tom?
>
> (1) My brother's name is Sandeep, Vijay, or Tom.
> (2) My brother's name is not Tom.

Now, the answer is (B). Note that the answer to the question is "no" (his name is not Tom), but that you are answering (B) because Statement (2) is *sufficient* to answer the question. *No is just as good an answer as yes.*

One more version:

> Does my brother's name have more than three letters in it?
>
> (1) My brother's name is Sandeep, Vijay, or Tom.
> (2) My brother's name is not Tom.

Statement (1) is now NOT sufficient. If his name is Sandeep or Vijay, the answer to the question is yes, but if his name is Tom, the answer is no. Statement (2) alone is also not sufficient. If his name is not Tom, it could be Al, or Joe, or Balthazar, or anything, so you have no way to answer the question.

Only now that you have ruled out the possibility that either statement alone is sufficient do you combine the statements.

Statements (1) and (2) together tell you that the brother's name is Sandeep, Vijay, or Tom, and then that it is NOT Tom. Therefore, his name is Sandeep or Vijay. You still don't know his name, but since Sandeep and Vijay each have more than three letters, you have a definite answer to the question—yes, the brother's name has more than three letters in it. The answer is **(C)**.

A few ground rules, by the way: the statements in Data Sufficiency do not lie, and do not contradict each other. So if one statement says, for instance, that x is 2 or 3, and the other says that x is 3 or 4, then x is definitely 3! The statements can be thought of as different windows towards a single truth—some of those windows allow you to see more of that truth than do others, but the windows are pointing at the same value of x, or the same brother Vijay.

Above, you considered four different versions of the "brother" problem. Note how adjusting the question drastically changed the correct letter answer to the problem. This is why some people feel that they understand all the math being tested, but are still missing Data Sufficiency questions—often, such students are not reading and understanding the question carefully. As you have done above, always note whether you have a yes or no question or a question requiring a specific answer, such as a numerical value.

Let's match up the questions we've looked at so far with more realistic GMAT question stems.

YES OR NO QUESTIONS	SPECIFIC ANSWER QUESTIONS
Is the rock in my pocket blue?	What is my brother's name?
Am I 32 years old?	What is the value of x?
Is my brother's name Joe?	If two bagels and one drink cost $3.25, what is the cost of one bagel?
Is x even?	
If n is an integer, is $3 < n < 13$?	What is $4p^2 + 2q^2$?
Does $3x + y = 12$?	
Is $xy > 0$?	

Before you take the real GMAT, or even begin your studies in earnest, you want to memorize/internalize what each of the choices means.

A short version might be:

    (A) (1) only
    (B) (2) only
    (C) Together
    (D) Either
    (E) Not Enough

In Manhattan GMAT classes, we instruct students to write the following on their papers for each Data Sufficiency question:

AD
BCE

Here are the steps for using this grid:

If statement 1 is SUFFICIENT, cross off BCE.

>Then, if statement 2 is SUFFICIENT, pick D. You're done!

>Or, if statement 2 is NOT sufficient, pick A. You're done!

However, if statement 1 is NOT sufficient, cross off AD.

>Then, if statement 2 is SUFFICIENT pick B. You're done!

>Or, if statement 2 is also NOT sufficient, combine the statements.

>>If both statements together are SUFFICIENT, pick C. You're done!

>>Or, if both statements together are NOT sufficient, pick E.

>>You're done!

Here is an example using the grid.

>How many 40-cent stamps did Alejandro purchase?

>(1) Alejandro bought more than three of these 40-cent stamps.
>(2) Alejandro spent less than $2.00 on 40-cent stamps.

Write the grid on your paper:

AD
BCE

Note that you have a specific answer question. You need a number of stamps to achieve sufficiency.

Consider statement 1. Alejandro bought more than three stamps, but he could've bought four stamps or a million stamps. This is NOT sufficient. Cross off AD.

~~AD~~
BCE

Consider statement 2. Alejandro spent less than $2. Since stamps cost 40 cents each, you know he bought fewer than 5 of them. But he could've bought anywhere from 1 to 4 stamps. NOT sufficient. Cross off B.

~~AD~~

~~BCE~~

ONLY NOW do you combine the statements. If Alejandro bought more than three stamps and spent less than $2, do you know how many stamps he bought? Well, "more than three stamps" means the same as "at least four stamps." If he bought four stamps, he spent $1.60. If he bought five stamps, he would've spent exactly $2.00. But you know he spent less than $2.00. So he must have bought exactly four stamps. SUFFICIENT.

The answer is **(C)**. There's no need to check (E); you're done!

Backup Approaches for Quant Problems – Jon Schneider

Knowing the textbook solution for a GMAT problem feels great. But on an adaptive test, you're unlikely to know the textbook solution for every problem that you see. Many test-takers panic when they can't find the "best" solution to a problem. They fear making a random guess, so they spend too long searching for the textbook solution, even though they're not sure how to set it up or execute it. But for many problems there is a lot of room between the textbook solution and a random guess. Having a practiced and consistent set of backup approaches will allow you to switch from the hunt for the right answer to the hunt for a good guess before resorting to a random guess. This will not only improve your GMAT score, it will also boost your confidence. After all, having a practiced arsenal of backup approaches gives you a safety net, a line of defense between the "right" approach and a total guess.

Of course, this requires that you (1) know the backup approaches applicable to the common problem types, and (2) have a practiced method of using these backup approaches, so that they can be used quickly and properly.

This worksheet is designed to help you learn the basic backup approaches, and gives you suggestions for how to practice those approaches. Remember that not all backup approaches fully "solve" GMAT problems; more often, a backup approach will just help you to make some process of elimination, so that you have a better chance when guessing. Finally, not all GMAT problems have a decent backup approach, so don't get stuck searching for one. In general, follow the "1–2–3 Approach": try the textbook solution first, but when you are stuck (or staring for 10+ seconds), switch to a backup approach; if you find yourself staring for 10+ seconds while trying the backup approach, make a random guess. Successful implementation of this strategy will allow you fewer random guesses, but it will also make those random guesses happen faster. After all, if we're really stumped on a problem, the best thing to do is move on.

MANHATTAN
GMAT

Backup Approaches for Problem Solving

I Back-solving

    a. Back-solving is the most applicable, and the most underused, backup approach. When you're stuck on a tricky Number Properties or Algebra problem, look at the answer choices. Can you use them to work backwards?

        i. To back-solve quickly, it is generally best to start with the middle number (answer choice (C)), so that you will know if you need to pick a larger or smaller number.

            1. If (C) is incorrect and you know the answer must be smaller, try (B); if it does not work, then (A) is your answer. Likewise, if you know the answer must be larger, try (D); if it does not work, then (E) is your answer.

        ii. Sometimes it is easier to start with the numbers that will be simplest to use. For example, if two of the answer choices are complex fractions, and three are integers, it may be easiest to start with the integers.

    b. Remember, back-solving is a Process of Elimination. You should write out ABCDE and cross off the incorrect choices as you go.

    c. Practice back-solving even when you know the full "textbook" solution to a problem. It is a valuable skill, and one that you will probably need on test day.

II Smart Numbers

    a. Sometimes the answer choices do not offer numbers that you can plug in, but you can still plug in numbers. You just need to invent your own.

    b. The "Smart Numbers" technique works well for questions when there are variables in the answer choices. It also works well when the entire problem consists of fractions, percents, or ratios, but when no real numbers are given.

    c. For these types of questions, create a chart, marking the numbers that you select for each variable. Create a "Target Value." Plug the Smart Numbers into the answer choices until you match the Target Value. If you can, plug in small, distinct prime numbers, as these will give you the least chance of multiple matches. If you are plugging in the integers 1 or 2, or any integer that you feel will likely give multiple matches, don't stop when you get the first match, but continue to plug your Smart Numbers into every answer choice. If more than one choice matches, pick new numbers, create a new Target Value, and test out just those answer choices that remain.

    d. For fraction word problems, pick numbers in the following way:

        i. If two fractions are given for the same type of item, pick a Smart Number equal to the common denominator of the fractions involved. For example, if told that a small bag of apples is 1/2 full, and a second bag, which is twice as big, is 3/5 full, pretend that the small bag has a total capacity of ten apples.

  ii. If multiple fractions are given for different types of items, choose Smart Numbers for each item set (again using the common denominators). For example, if told "Tommy owns 3/4 as many baseball cards as Jack, but he has 7/3 as many toy cars as Jack," call Jack's number of baseball cards 4 and his number of toy cars 3.

e. For percent questions, start with the Smart Number 100.

f. You should write out ABCDE and cross off incorrect choices as you go.

III Estimation

a. Estimation works well for Geometry, Arithmetic, Probability, Rate, and Weighted Average questions.

b. If the answer choices are far apart, estimation is especially useful.

c. When working with a tricky Geometry problem (for Problem Solving only), estimation should be your primary backup approach. If you are solving for the length of a certain line, how long does the line appear to be?

  i. Some drawings are said to be "not to scale." In this case, consider whether you could redraw the diagram to scale. Occasionally, it is possible to redraw the diagram to scale and then estimate the correct answer.

d. For tough Arithmetic questions, consider the relative size of the numbers involved. If working with a tricky fraction, remember that the smaller the denominator, the larger the overall number.

e. For Probability questions, ask whether it is reasonable to presume that the probability is more or less than 1/2.

f. For Rate questions, estimate in the following way:

  i. When working with two bodies in motion, determine which is faster; this may help to determine where the two objects end up relative to each other.

  ii. For Combined Work questions, consider the individual rates: does it make sense that the combined rate would be faster than each individual rate? If so, by about how much?

IV Number Properties

a. This is the rarest type of back-solving, but it can be very effective. There are times when you know something about the answer, even if you don't know the full solution. For example, perhaps you know that the answer must be odd, or that it must be divisible by three.

b. Elimination via Number Properties works well when the word "must" or the word "could" appears in the question stem.

c. Elimination via Number Properties works well when working with Digits problems. It also works well for some exponents problems.

i. Unsure of the value of $79^5 - 36^5$? Well, 79 is odd, so 79^5 must be odd; and 36 is even, so 36^5 must be even. We have an odd minus an even: the result must be odd.

V Brute Force
  a. This works well for Rates questions. Imagine that you are asked to find when two cars will meet, after traveling at their respective rates from opposite ends of a straight road. Construct a picture and map out where the cars will be after each hour, until you've found where they meet.

Backup Approaches for Data Sufficiency

Note: All backup approaches for Data Sufficiency require that you use a Process of Elimination grid. Remember to start with the easy statement, and write out either $\frac{AD}{BCE}$ or $\frac{BD}{ACE}$ on your paper.

I One Statement is clearly insufficient.
  a. Remember to start with the easy statement!
      i. Here, eliminate either AD or BD.
  b. This pattern often occurs when the question asks about more than one variable, but the statement does not mention one of the variables.
      i. Note that occasionally this occurs for both statements! Sometimes you can move quickly to considering (C) vs. (E).

II The Statements together are too clearly sufficient.
  a. This often occurs when one statement is clearly insufficient, but it gives you the value of one variable and the other statement gives you a simple equation that you could plug that variable value into.
      i. For example, consider the question, What is $x - y$?
          1. $x = 4$
          2. $x = y + 6$
      You could obviously plug in the value of statement 1 into statement 2 to get the value of y and then solve for $x - y$, but you should ask yourself, "Is this too obvious?"
  b. If the Statements together are too clearly sufficient, the answer cannot be (E). However, the correct choice is unlikely to be (C), either. Instead, give that more complex statement a second look. It might be capable of solving the problem alone.

III The Statements do not cooperate.
  a. There are times when, although they provide different information, the two statements do not cooperate. In this case, the answer cannot be (C).
      i. For example, imagine that you have two statements:

1. $x > 4$
2. $x > 6$

What do you know if you combine both statements? Just that $x > 6$. But this is what Statement 2 tells you. If this is sufficient information, Statement 2 is already sufficient. The answer cannot be C because Statement 1 does not add anything useful to Statement 2.

IV The Statements provide equivalent information.

    a. If the statements, when reduced are exactly the same, then the answer cannot be (A), (B), or (C).

        i. For example, imagine that you have two statements:

            1. $x + y = 5$
            2. $3x + 3y = 15$

        These are essentially equal statements (just divide the second equation by 3). As a result, the answer must be either (D) or (E).

V The Statements do cooperate, but not in a way that makes the solution obvious.

    a. In this case, (C) is a good guess.

        i. For example, imagine that you have two statements:

            1. $x + y = z + w$
            2. $z - p = w - y$

        Depending on the question, (C) might be a very good choice here. You could manipulate the statements in interesting ways, but they do not obviously give you the value of each variable.

        ii. Of course, don't pick (C) without first considering the merit of each statement alone. It's still possible that one of the above statements is sufficient, depending on the question.

        iii. When you are working with four or more variables, (E) is unlikely to be the correct choice. The harder the algebraic manipulation, the more likely that sufficiency will occur somewhere. This is not a guarantee, of course. You should try to solve the question first, and if you can prove that it's (E), pick (E). But if you're stuck, this can be a good pattern to fall back to.

Practice

It is essential to practice each of the backup approaches listed above. Look at each of the first 20 PS and 20 DS questions in the OG, and try to find the relevant backup approach. In the future, always consider the backup approaches when reviewing a problem, and switch to backup approaches when you are stuck on the textbook solution.

Make sure that you know what two minutes feels like while solving math questions. Work with a stopwatch until you can feel the timing without looking at the watch. Develop the discipline to know when your primary solution isn't working, so that you can switch to a backup approach before it's too late. Knowing backup approaches is a huge help on the GMAT, but it won't serve you well if you only think of these strategies after two minutes have gone by; you'll need to use these tools proactively when stuck in order to preserve your overall pace.

Finally, remember that not all questions can be tackled using a backup approach. If you find such a question, don't worry! It's probably just a very hard question. Guess and move to the next question; your score will thank you!

 Student Sound-Off

Content knowledge is very important, but it is equally important to know the "back up methods" to help you when the textbook methods fail. The GMAT is intentionally designed to be solved with these backup methods. Using the backup methods, you can actually solve about 80% of PS and 50% of DS.

Please see Ron Purewal's "Thursday with Ron" recording and find the study hall on backup methods. Practice those and you will see your score go up substantially. It also helps you with the timing because you won't be tempted to spend too much time trying to solve a problem via textbook. The backup methods are very mechanical—if one doesn't work, you quickly abandon and move on.

Of course, still know your content… review every OG you do and try multiple ways to solve a problem. Practice makes perfect.

James
750 (Q49, V44)

Chapter Takeaways

1.   Understand–Plan–Solve is a step-by-step methodical process that provides you with a scaffolding to guide you through solving math problems. This technique helps you figure out the tricky problems you don't know how to solve when you first see them.

2.   Learn the standard ways of translating information from words to math so that you will be faster at solving word problems.

3.   Learn the GMAT's Quant "code." Quant questions are often asked in very tricky ways and being able to quickly determine what the actual content is will make some impossible looking problems quite doable.

4.   It is very easy to become confused about the goal when working through Data Sufficiency problems; make sure that you deeply grasp the meanings of the different answer choices and that you are reasoning in the correct direction.

5.   Learn and use back up methods; they are often partial solutions that will lead you to greater insight about a given problem type. An educated guess made within two minutes is better than a perfect solution in four.

Chapter 5 of GMAT Roadmap

The Big Picture of GMAT Verbal

In This Chapter...

Chapter 5:
The Big Picture of GMAT Verbal

Efficiently solving Verbal problems on the GMAT requires that you be able to identify the functions of different components of language. In order to master GMAT Verbal, you have to understand parts of speech, basic sentence structure, and the organization of written passages. Although it is helpful to know particular little "zinger" rules (such as when to use "rather than" versus "instead of" or that answer choices with extreme language are less likely to be correct), the core of GMAT Verbal is really being able to reason and understand about language structure.

Like expert GMAT Quant problem solvers, the best GMAT Verbal problem solvers use both pattern recognition (i.e., reading an argument and predicting the nature of the correct answer) and rule-based, step-by-step solving processes (i.e., reading and carefully parsing exactly what the test writer wrote and eliminating answer choices for specific reasons).

How to Correct Sentences

Sentence Correction (SC) questions make up slightly more than a third of the Verbal questions on the GMAT. Each SC question has two basic parts:

- A sentence with an underlined portion.
- Five different options for replacing the underlined portion. The first option is always identical to the original underlined portion.

When beginning their GMAT preparation, students often tell us that they chose an SC answer choice because it "just sounds right." However, Sentence Correction is not about writing style or what sounds right: it is about correct usage, otherwise known as grammar—American English grammar, to be specific. It does not matter whether you know the technical name of each grammar rule. Rather, you have to know how to apply these rules in context and under exam pressure.

The good news is that, if you've read this far, you already know a lot of grammar. So how do you transform your current knowledge into a high SC score on the GMAT? There are two skills you need to develop:

1. Learning to recognize the patterns of the language (this is how native speakers usually learn a language).

2. Learning the explicit grammar rules that govern the language (as someone learning English as a second—or third—language generally would).

While most people prefer to rely on one of these skills or the other, an expert at Sentence Correction recognizes the patterns of the language but also knows the explicit rules and can reap the benefits of both knowledge bases. Even an English major will profit from learning the actual rules, just as English language learners must rely somewhat on their ability to recognize the patterns of the language.

5 The Importance of Splits in Sentence Correction

Whether you prefer to be more grammar rule based or more language pattern based when you work through Sentence Correction problems, you will benefit from being methodical in your use of splits. A split is a systematic difference between answer choices in Sentence Correction. Splits make us more efficient; by grouping answers, we can quickly eliminate in groups, and avoid rereading the large chunks in each answer that are the same. However, some students tell us that they struggle to spot splits in the first place. If this describes you, try the following approach:

1. **Read the entire sentence—note anything that seems suspicious.**

   If you found something that stood out, vertically scan the region of the answer choices where it should appear to see if you can find a split based on what stood out.

2. **Check the beginning and the end of the underlined section for splits.**

   The test writers chose to start and end their underlining there for a reason!

3. **Scan the middle of the underlined section or go word by word between two choices.**

   Sometimes, when you are deciding between two answer choices, you will have to go word by word through them to find a split. This is OK to do when you have just two choices, but far too time consuming when you are looking at five answer choices. Vertically scanning is much faster.

As soon as you have found a split that tests a grammar rule that you know (splits on rules that you don't know will not help you, and there are also red-herring splits where both options are correct), either explicitly or implicitly, you can use it for wrong answer elimination.

Your *Sentence Correction* Strategy Guide (and your instructor, if you are taking a class) will provide you with comprehensive coverage of the rules tested on the GMAT so that you can identify useful splits when you see them. Meanwhile, in the following three articles, veteran instructor Ron Purewal (of the ever-famous "Thursdays with Ron") will guide you through how to use your innate knowledge of the patterns of language to help yourself decide splits more effectively.

Sentence Correction for Native Speakers of English – Ron Purewal

Instructor Insights

Our courses and books are designed to fulfill the needs of both native and non-native speakers of English. We've done a remarkable job of addressing the needs of both groups—but, as would be true of anything intended for a diverse audience, some specialized bits and pieces had to be left out.

At first glance, this warning may seem to pertain mostly to non-native speakers; the course, you may figure, is primarily aimed at people who grew up speaking English. However, that's not really true; the course and books assume *competence* in the English language, but are not necessarily aimed at native speakers.

In fact, if you're a native speaker of English—and especially if your parents are too—then you should modify our base approach in a couple of ways.

1. For verb tenses, turn on your ear.

Verb tense is one of the few aspects of English used almost flawlessly in the spoken English of educated individuals. In fact, if you are a native speaker, *you should not study verb tenses*, unless you are actually getting them wrong on actual GMAT SC problems.

Native speakers' understanding of verb tenses (in any language, not just English) is extremely subtle and nuanced. It's also completely subconscious, so systematic study is more likely to diminish your skill than to improve it.

Consider the following two examples:

> *Jake has never been to Disneyland.*

> *Jake never went to Disneyland.*

Which one is sad, implying that Jake will never get the chance? Which one is just a statement about what Jake hasn't done yet?

When you answer these questions, you don't need to identify or analyze the tenses—in fact, you might not even be *able* to identify them. Still, you just *know* how they work: you can feel the implications of each sentence deep in your subconscious, with an understanding that's as much emotional as analytical.

TIP

Intuition and instinct as discussed in this article stem from subconscious language pattern recognition.

If you're a native speaker of English, you should test this intuition before diving into the formal study of verb tenses. Go through some of the *Official Guide* problems classified as "Verb Tenses" in our SC Strategy Guide, use your ear to identify the tenses, and see whether you actually get any of them wrong. If you don't, *do not* study them!

2. For the rest of Sentence Correction, test your instincts.

Consider the following sentence:

A puck is to hockey similar to a ball is to soccer.

That's ugly, right? Horrible.

If you're a native speaker and regular reader of English, you can without a doubt reject the above sentence immediately. *You may have no idea why*—but that's not the point! The point is that you know it's wrong.

Think a choice that ugly couldn't possibly appear on the test? Think again! That sentence is written in exactly the same way as an official answer choice.

Remember—at the end of the day, if you can consistently tell right from wrong, *you don't have to know why*. You can probably reject the sentence above in a matter of seconds, but you would most likely have difficulty coming up with a formal justification. So, don't!

If you've read enough well-written English, your "reader's instinct"—the intuition you've developed throughout all that reading—will be able to tell correct from incorrect sentences in most cases. If you can reject a flawed sentence by using that instinct, *you don't need to analyze the sentence!*

The keys, then, are to determine the extent of your "reader's instinct" and to identify any error types that consistently sneak past it. Before studying the full SC curriculum, test yourself: go through a fairly large number of *Official Guide* problems *using only your intuition* to determine what's right and what's wrong. If there are any error types that you never miss, even after solving many problems, then avoid formal study of those types.

Most good readers and writers have mastered the language primarily through intuition, not analysis. If you already have that intuition—at least to some extent—then don't try to replace it with analysis. Approach SC as you would a complex machine: don't take apart the pieces that are already working! The only parts you should disassemble and examine are those that actually need to be fixed.

Parallelism Is a Beauty Contest
– Ron Purewal

Consider the following SC problem:

> Virginia is one of very few U.S. states <u>where lacrosse is played by a sizable proportion of high school athletes, and in which</u> the sport attracts as many spectators as does football or basketball.

    (A) where lacrosse is played by a sizable proportion of high school athletes, and in which

    (B) where a sizable proportion of high school athletes play lacrosse, in which

    (C) that has a sizable proportion of high school athletes who play lacrosse and where

    (D) in which lacrosse is played by a sizable proportion of high school athletes, and

    (E) where a sizable proportion of high school athletes play lacrosse and where

If you try to approach this problem with memorized rules and formal grammatical analysis, it will be extremely difficult—perhaps even impossible—for you to solve. If you approach the problem with an understanding of what parallelism actually means, though, you may find it quite easy.

Here's the secret:

Parallelism is a beauty contest!

In an actual beauty contest—whether that contest involves people, livestock, architectural designs, or whatever else—the judges don't need a theoretical understanding of beauty, nor do they need objective criteria for the beauty of an individual person (or animal, or design, etc.). Their task is much simpler: they only need to make *relative* judgments.

The same is true of parallelism. In general, you don't need to perform detailed formal analysis on parallel structures; instead, *you only have to decide which structure is **most** parallel*—a much easier task.

If one structure is clearly more parallel than the others, then that structure is right, and the other structures are wrong. *Do not overanalyze!*

In the problem quoted above, there are two parallel facts about Virginia: first, many of its high school students play lacrosse, and, second, it is a place where lacrosse is as popular as football or basketball. Because both of these facts about Virginia are presented with equal priority—and because neither is subordinate to the other—they should be expressed in parallel.

If you attempt a formal analysis of the answer choices, you may not be able to eliminate (A), (C), or (E) at all—because those choices are, from a strictly grammatical standpoint, *not wrong*. However, it should be clear that the parallel structure in choice (E)—*where X and where Y*—is vastly superior to that in any of the other choices, so (E) is the correct answer.

This kind of dichotomy—in which formal analysis is difficult or even impossible, but conceptual judgments are quick and easy—is not accidental. **The GMAT writers emphasize parallelism because it is grammatically complex, but conceptually straightforward.** If you can see the "big picture" of these relationships, you can resolve them quickly and accurately; if you get mired in grammatical details, on the other hand, then the problems can become impossibly difficult.

The Meaning Behind Sentence Correction – Ron Purewal

If you have a technical background, your first inclination may be to view SC problems as though they were systematically designed gadgets or even giant algebraic equations. In other words, you may want to approach them by disregarding their meaning, memorizing a huge number of mechanical rules, and trying to apply those rules to a mass of lifeless words.

Unfortunately—as many students before you have discovered through a painful, lengthy process of trial and error (and error and error and error)—this kind of approach just won't work. Almost *everything* in SC depends on the *intended meaning* of the sentence—a meaning that must be deduced through a combination of context and common sense.

Every **major SC error type is easier to identify if you understand the intended meaning of the sentence; many of them** *require* **you to understand that context.**

Consider:

- Verb tense is impossible to determine without context.
- Verb voice is impossible to determine without context.
- Modifiers are assigned according to grammar rules, but it's impossible to determine whether those assignments are *correct* without meaning.
- Pronouns are subject to grammar rules, but it's impossible to determine whether they are *correctly assigned* without meaning.

- Parallelism involves grammatical forms, but it's impossible to determine whether structures *should* be parallel without meaning.
- Idioms have specific meanings; an idiom can be correct in one context but wrong in another.
- Subject-verb agreement is mechanical, but you need context to tell whether the subject makes sense.

Also notice that the GMAT largely *does not* test things that are purely mechanical, such as punctuation, spelling, and the use of articles.

Concentrating on meaning is even *more* important for second-language speakers of English! If this statement surprises you, consider that it's usually pretty easy to figure out the meaning of a sentence, even if it is riddled with grammatical errors:

Freeway accident on, me behind, late hours will be two at the least.

The grammar of this sentence is essentially 100% incorrect, but its meaning is still obvious: I'm stuck behind an accident on the freeway and so will be at least two hours late. If you aren't a native speaker of English, you may not be able to fix the sentence perfectly—but you can still *understand* it perfectly.

That's the secret—grammar varies considerably from language to language, but objective meanings are essentially universal. Therefore, if English isn't your native language, it's even *more* important for you to focus on meaning before considering any finer points of grammar.

How to Reason Through Critical Reasoning

Of all of the problem types on the Verbal section, Critical Reasoning (CR) is the most time-consuming for a majority of students. Although there is no way to get around the time constraints for CR problems (there is just a lot to read per question), an efficient approach will make a huge difference in both your accuracy and your speed.

Critical Reasoning: Processes and Patterns
– Ian Jorgeson

Instructor Insights

CR questions make up roughly one-third of the Verbal questions on the GMAT. Superficially, these problems resemble short Reading Comprehension questions. But while reading skills are important for both, there are significant differences. The most important distinction lies in the goal of each question. Reading Comprehension is mostly concerned with identifying relevant pieces of text buried within the larger passage, while Critical Reasoning asks you to actually do something to, or with, the important information. For instance, an RC problem might ask what the author said about a certain topic; a CR problem takes the next step and asks you to weaken or strengthen the author's position, identify an underlying assumption of the argument, or identify a logical flaw in the argument. CR questions might even ask the test-taker to evaluate an argument or explain a contradictory situation.

Each CR problem is composed of three basic parts: a short passage, which we will call the argument; a question; and five answer choices. The passage is known as the argument because, in the classic sense of the word, that is what it is. In most CR passages, the author presents a point of view (conclusion) and supports it with evidence (premises). The passage may also contain background statements, or even counterpoints, but the core of most arguments is a conclusion supported by one or more premises.

An expert CR solver follows a specific series of steps—steps that ensure that they are able to understand the question, identify the relevant information in the argument, understand the structure of the argument, and efficiently eliminate incorrect answer choices. While working through these steps, a CR expert is also on the lookout for patterns they are familiar with that, when recognized, will help them to more quickly answer the question. These patterns appear in the way the test phrases the question, in the structure and logic of the argument, and in the answer choices. It should come as no surprise at this point that the knowledge and recognition of common patterns in GMAT CR questions can speed up your solving process and increase your accuracy. But having a solid process that can be applied to each CR problem is even more fundamental, because the process helps you to recognize the patterns, and because many questions do not conform to standard patterns.

What follows is a process that can be used to solve any CR problem in a step-by-step, logical manner. We will also discuss the points in the process when pattern recognition can help tremendously to increase understanding and efficiency.

> **Step 1: Read and identify the question.**
> **Step 2: Read and deconstruct the argument.**
> **Step 3: Pause and state the goal.**
> **Step 4: Work from wrong to right.**

Step 1: Read and identify the question.

The simplest, and perhaps most important, advice to someone new to CR is to always read the question first. Understanding the question is, of course, key to recognizing which answer is correct, and which four are wrong, but it also can affect how we read the argument. A CR expert doesn't look at every argument in the same way. They want to focus on the most important information in each argument and recognize that different question types require different pieces of important information. Additionally, some CR questions hide important information by placing it in the question instead of in the passage. Spotting this information early can be very helpful.

The question presents our first pattern recognition opportunity. Although it may seem that there are a number of different question types, there are actually only a few, asked in a variety of different ways. Regardless of the phrasing, every weaken question, for example, is asking the test-taker to do the exact same thing—attack an underlying assumption in the argument.

The questions on the GMAT fall into three broad families, based on what information in the passage is important. By identifying the family a question belongs to, we can focus on the most important part of each passage and avoid wasting time trying to understand information that is not important. For example, all of the questions in the assumption family revolve around an unstated assumption that the argument relies on. To determine the underlying assumption, you need to identify the argument's conclusion and the premise or premises that support it. Any additional information may provide context, but is not core to the argument.

Within these broader categories, the questions can be further divided into 10 types, based on the goal that the correct answer must accomplish. A precise understanding of the goal for each question drives your ability to recognize patterns in the answers—both in the correct answers and in the incorrect answers.

5

Q Family	Q Type	Common Question Phrasing	Goal
Structure Based Family	Describe the Role	In the argument given, the two boldface portions play which of the following roles?	Identify the role of the bold portions.
	Describe the Argument	In the passage, the author develops the argument by….	Describe the structure of the argument.
Assumption Based Family	**Assumption***	The argument depends on which of the following assumptions?	Identify an unstated assumption.
	Weaken*	Which of the following, if true, most seriously weakens the argument?	Weaken the author's conclusion by attacking the assumption
	Strengthen*	Which of the following, if true, provides the most support for the argument above?	Strengthen the author's conclusion by supporting the assumption.
	Evaluate	Which of the following must be studied in order to evaluate the argument presented above?	Identify information that would help to determine the validity of the argument.
	Flaw	Which of the following indicates a flaw in the reasoning above?	Identify a logical fallacy in the argument.
Evidence Based Family	**Draw a Conclusion***	Which of the following can be logically concluded from the passage above?	Identify an additional fact that must be true.
	Explain	Which of the following, if true, most helps to explain the surprising finding?	Reconcile two contradictory statements.
	Complete the Argument	Which of the following most logically completes the argument given below?	Identify the statement that most logically fills in the blank.

*These four questions are more common than the other six.

Learn to spot the language used by each question type, and work on your ability to categorize new question phrasings into one of the types you've learned. A helpful exercise is to go through the *Official Guide* reading only the questions, and practice identifying each type. You can check yourself online using the Manhattan GMAT OG Archer, which identifies the category for each question.

Step 2: Read and deconstruct the argument.

Once you've identified the question type, and the family it belongs to, you're ready to look at the argument with a clear idea of the important information you need to detect. This allows you to avoid the trap of passive reading. Since you know, based on the question type, what sort of information is likely to be most important, you can actively search for that information. What you are doing here is deconstructing the argument; identifying the purpose of every part of the argument, and extracting the key parts from the rest. This can be done fairly mechanically. With a bit of practice, you can begin to consistently identify the author's conclusion and the premises that support it, counterpoints that the author is arguing against, and background information, all by recognizing the words and phrases the GMAT uses in these parts.

While deconstructing the argument can be mechanical, it is also an opportunity to use pattern recognition. The GMAT test writers tend to reuse the same handful of arguments over and over. While not every passage falls neatly into a category, a number of them do, and recognizing these common arguments can provide a tremendous shortcut. For example, a number of arguments present two topics in the premise, and repeat one of them in the conclusion, while adding a new topic. For instance, a simple argument might state that *"All dogs make great pets. Thus, Fido must be a great pet."* In this case, both the premise and the conclusion discuss great pets. But the premise refers to *all dogs*, and the conclusion refers to *Fido*. In order for the conclusion to be drawn, you must assume that Fido is actually a dog. Spotting this pattern in an argument (A related to B, therefore B related to C—assumes A is related to C), even when the argument is much longer and more complex, allows you to easily recognize the underlying assumption.

There are several argument patterns that you can learn to spot. The one discussed above, in which there is a well-defined gap between the premise and the conclusion, is quite common. Other patterns include arguments about causality, arguments that put forth a plan to solve a problem, arguments based on an analogy, conditional (if/then) arguments, statistical arguments, and arguments comparing percentages or other numerical data. In each of these cases, there are specific assumptions underlying the arguments, or precise inferences that can be drawn from the evidence.

These patterns are useful because they allow you to quickly recognize what kind of answer will be correct, given a specific question type. For example, once you spot that the argument about Fido above has a logic gap, you know what the assumption is. If this argument were associated with a weaken question, you would know that the right answer would provide information demonstrating that Fido is not, in fact, a dog. If it were a strengthen question instead, you would know that the answer would demonstrate that Fido is a dog. And if it were an evaluate question, the correct answer would present a method to determine whether Fido is a dog. Spotting the underlying argument pattern puts you in a position to be able to answer any possible question associated with the argument.

Look for these common argument patterns. Keep a list of them and identify OG problems by number within your list. Your *Critical Reasoning* Strategy Guide will point out these patterns, as will your instructor (if you are taking a class), but you need to actively look for them in problems to truly learn how to recognize them. At the same time, you should also practice mechanically deconstructing the argument into its component parts; this will ensure that you're able to solve even the most unusual argument problems, and unlock the patterns hidden in complex arguments.

Step 3: Pause and state the goal.

The GMAT is a very time-limited test. You never want to waste valuable time. However, taking a moment to crystallize your understanding of the argument, and of what the question is asking, will save time when evaluating the answers. Pause for a moment and summarize in your head the important parts of the argument. Remind yourself what type of question you're working on. Anticipate the general form of the answer; while it's often impossible to predict the correct answer, in most cases you should be able to predict what type of answer will satisfy the question. Taking this time will help you to recognize the correct answer, but, more importantly, it will help you to efficiently eliminate the wrong answers.

Step 4: Work from wrong to right.

If you've done a good job with the previous steps, you should be in an excellent position to correctly answer the question. It would be tempting to immediately choose the best sounding answer. However, the GMAT is especially good at crafting trap answers that look good at first glance and correct answers that are convoluted and difficult to spot.

To avoid the traps that the GMAT sets, you should find reasons to eliminate each of the four wrong answers. You will never have to decide which of two correct answers is best. Every wrong answer will be wrong for an identifiable, though sometimes hidden, reason. Finding a reason to eliminate each wrong answer will ensure that you are not fooled, and will make you more confident that you've picked the correct answer. No matter how sure you are that an answer is correct, you should still identify reasons to eliminate the other four.

> **TIP**
>
> Looking for advice on Reading Comprehension? Instructor Tommy Wallach's article in Chapter 3 will tell you everything you need to know, but if you are still looking to improve, our best advice for you is to read. We've found that students who make an effort to read every day for an extended period of time ultimately see a marked improvement in their Reading Comprehension scores. The catch is that you need to be reading GMAT-like articles, and it is even better if they are online because reading from a computer screen is a little different from reading from paper. There is a box at the end of Tommy's article with a list of recommended sources.

Many of the wrong answers follow patterns that are repeated over and over again. Recognizing these patterns in the wrong answers is a skill that can be learned and practiced. We will discuss wrong answer analysis in great detail later, both as its own topic and as part of our discussion of each question type. For now, force yourself to identify an explicit reason before eliminating each wrong answer.

How to Make Educated Guesses on Verbal – Stacey Koprince

Everyone will have to guess at some point on the GMAT; there's no way around that. The test *will* give you things that you can't do. (Most people have to guess on between four and seven questions in each section.) The trick is learning how to guess in a manner that will give you the greatest probability of success.

What is educated guessing?

Generally speaking, there are two kinds of guessing: random and educated. A random guess is one in which you really don't have any good idea how to choose among all five answer choices. An educated guess is simply one in which you have used good reasoning to eliminate a wrong answer or answers before you make a random guess from among the remaining choices.

It is often the case that you can figure out that some answers are wrong even when you have no idea of how to find the right answer. When you narrow your options in this way, you give yourself a better chance of guessing correctly when you finally do guess. In order to narrow your options effectively, though, you have to have studied this in advance; it is not something that you just "know" how to do.

When should I make an educated guess?

On Verbal, you use a different process to choose an answer than you do on Quant. You are actually making an educated guess right from the beginning of each Verbal problem.

Your first pass through the five answers is used to determine which answers are definitely wrong and can be crossed out immediately (and ignored from then on). You should not attempt to determine which answers are correct on this first pass; you should only cross off the ones you know are definitely wrong (and this is already educated guessing, because you are eliminating answers!). It is rare not to be able to eliminate any answers on the first pass, though this can happen occasionally. (If ever it does, you will need to consider making a random guess on this question and moving on.)

On your second pass, you should take a more careful look at any remaining answer choices. If you get stuck, you may need to use more sophisticated means to continue to narrow down your answers through the use of educated guessing.

Techniques

There are many different techniques that you can use to make educated guesses. For the most part, the techniques will be specific to a problem type (e.g., Sentence Correction, Critical Reasoning, or Reading Comprehension) or even to a sub-type (e.g., Draw a Conclusion on CR). We'll discuss some of the most common techniques below, but you should consider this just a starting point. As you study from now on, ask yourself: *How can I eliminate wrong answers on this question? How do the test writers make wrong answers tempting on certain types of Verbal problems?*

Note: What we discuss in this section still involves making guesses based on certain common traps during your second pass through the answers; it is not the case that these guesses will always result in correctly eliminating wrong answers. These tactics should be used only when needed—they should not be your first line of attack. One caveat is to leave an answer choice "in" if you aren't sure it's wrong and you don't have a clear reason for crossing it off—it is better to recognize that you are guessing than to delude yourself into believing that you know more than you do.

Sentence Correction: Play the Odds on Certain Splits

There are certain pairs of differences, or splits, in the answer choices that more often resolve one way than the other (more often, but not always!). If you know what these are and you have to make a guess, then you can "play the odds" by guessing the variation that is more often correct. For instance, in a split between "like" and "such as," the phrase "such as" is more likely to appear in the correct answer. (This is because people often make the mistake of using "like" when they actually should use "such as," so the trap is to think that "like" is okay to use in place of "such as.") In a split between "rather than" and "instead of," "rather than" is more likely to appear in the correct answer.

When you're studying and see a split that you've seen before, ask yourself: Does this tend to go one way more than the other? If so, why? There should always be a good reason.

Critical Reasoning: Know the Common Traps

In Critical Reasoning questions that include a conclusion in the written argument, the right answer needs to be connected to the conclusion in some way. Wrong answers are

sometimes not tied to the conclusion at all. If you're debating between two choices and one is tougher to connect to the conclusion, don't guess that one.

When you are asked to draw a conclusion or make an inference, wrong answers will often go too far—they will go beyond the scope of what you can reasonably infer from the given information. If you are debating between two choices and have to guess, choose the one that doesn't go as far from the premises given in the argument. (Note, however, that strengthen and weaken the conclusion questions do include new information in the correct answer; on those types, you can't use this same technique.)

Reading Comprehension: Know the Common Traps

In Reading Comprehension, again, the common traps tend to be specific to the problem subtypes. On General (main idea) type questions, the wrong answers will often be either too specific or too broad; if you have to guess, pick a "middle of the road" type answer. Extreme words are often included in wrong answers.

On Inference questions, wrong answers will often go too far (much like wrong answers on CR Draw a Conclusion or Inference questions). Choose an answer that doesn't stray as far from the text of the passage. Wrong answers may be what we call "plausible in the real world" but not addressed by the passage. If you read something and think, "Hey, that's probably true!" but realize you think that because of your own knowledge of the world, not something you read in the passage… don't guess that one.

On Specific questions (both inference and look-up) beware of the "mix-up" trap. If the answer choice includes language directly from the passage, but that language is found in two or more separate paragraphs in the passage, then the answer is more likely to be a trap.

Your Turn!

It's up to you now to keep studying and find more of these. Talk to your friends. Ask your instructors. As you study, ask yourself: How do the test writers get someone to choose this wrong answer? How do the test writers get someone to eliminate this right answer? And, of course, if you did fall into a trap yourself, figure out precisely why so that you don't make the same mistake in future.

Chapter Takeaways

1.　In SC, use splits to figure out what is being tested and to eliminate more than one wrong answer at a time.

2.　Intuitive recognition of language patterns, combined with an understanding of the meaning of phrases, can be used to effectively solve SC questions, particularly those with parallelism and/or modifier errors.

3.　CR problems can be solved with a straightforward four-step process. To implement it, you must be able to identify the role of each sentence in the argument (conclusion, premise, counter premise, or filler) and determine the question type.

4.　Wrong answers on Verbal are always wrong for a specific reason. As you become a Verbal expert, you should be able to articulate what makes each wrong answer choice wrong.

5.　There are common wrong answer patterns in Verbal. Learn to recognize them so that you will be more likely to eliminate wrong answers rather than right answers when you have to guess.

Chapter 6 *of*
GMAT Roadmap

From Content Knowledge to GMAT Problems

In This Chapter...

Chapter 6:

From Content Knowledge to GMAT Problems

Dear Jen,

I feel like I understand everything in class (or I feel like I understand everything I read when studying for the GMAT), but then when I actually take the test, I get almost everything wrong and I'm scoring really low. What's going on?

Confused in Conshohocken

Dear Confused,

There are two things that occur to me here. One is that you mention "understanding" everything when you study or attend class—and not that you are *doing* the related problems successfully, in two minutes each, during class or anytime. When I watch Serena Williams play tennis, I *understand* exactly what's happening—but that certainly doesn't mean I could execute it on the court.

Of course, understanding the material is important, but *doing* the material—regularly, the way you would physically practice for a sport—is the other half of that.

Make sure that when you review your class notes, you actually pull out a timer and *do* the problems in your notes, even though you already know what the answer will be. If you are doing an *Official Guide* problem (just a reminder: you should always be doing those with a timer) and you get it wrong, you take more than two minutes, or it just feels weird, then put it on a list of problems to review, or make a flash card.

I like making flash cards because when you pick up a flash card, it is really obvious that you are supposed to *do something*. (Specifically, you're supposed to re-do the problem in two minutes or less.) Conversely, when people look over their notes, they just tend to nod and turn the pages.

Before taking the real GMAT, you should have done (*done*, not *looked at*) every problem in the *Official Guide*. A good goal is being able to execute each one within the time limit, and then being able to explain it to someone else. After mastering a problem, ask yourself how it could've been different (because you won't see those exact problems on the GMAT; you'll see "similar but different" problems). For instance: What if the rate, rather than the distance, had been unknown? What if the Data Sufficiency problem had specified that *x* was positive? What if the 400 were a 100 instead? If someone reached in and changed the problem around in ways like those I'm describing, could you still do it?

What I'm getting at here is a level of *deep interaction* with a problem. You could say that understanding is the first level, followed by being able to execute it, then being able to execute it within the time limit, being able to teach it to someone else, and finally being able to apply what you've learned to a body of "similar but different" problems.

That should give you some ideas for studying (actually, "practicing") more actively.

Jennifer Dziura, MGMAT Instructor, New York

Introduction to the OG

6

You've learned the content by reading the Strategy Guides and completing the In Action problems. You may have even taken a class and gotten a taste of what GMAT problems testing that content might look like. Now it's time to master GMAT problems by practicing them independently…. **Welcome to the Official Guide (OG).**

The OG is a book produced by the Graduate Management Admission Council (GMAC), the people who write the GMAT. It is largely composed of hundreds of retired GMAT problems, organized by problem type and roughly increasing in difficulty as the problem numbers increase. Completing and thoroughly reviewing practice problems from the OG is the secret sauce that will take you from understanding content to being able to apply that understanding to solving problems on the GMAT. This chapter will walk you through the intricacies of OG problems, how to solve them, and how to review them so that you can master them!

First, though, here's how to pick which problems to do! Just like the MGMAT Strategy Guides, the OG is written to provide comprehensive coverage of GMAT-level content. Your current ability level on various problem types will determine how to most effectively incorporate OG problems into your studying. We recommend that everyone begin by trying to tackle a few **benchmark problems** (and make sure to review them thoroughly).

The OG is roughly organized from questions that test-takers are more likely to get correct to questions that test-takers are less likely to get correct. Benchmark problems come from the middle of the book; they are

TIP

For now, only work through problems in the OG, not the Verbal or Quantitative supplement OGs. Part of the challenge of taking the GMAT is that you have to recognize what the question is about (e.g., Is this asking about primes? Is this a percent problem?) before you can solve it. That takes practice. Right now you are consciously building proficiency on specific topics. It's like doing skills drills when you are learning a sport: working only on your forehand in tennis or learning how to dribble a basketball. Later, you will be doing sets of random problems. That's like playing mini-practice games—something you can't do well until many of the component skills are in semi-decent shape. It is important to save the supplement OGs for this time, so that you have fresh problems to practice on.

of mid-range difficulty. As such, they serve as an important diagnostic tool. (If you are taking our course, you can find a comprehensive list of benchmark problems near the end of your class syllabus.) As a general rule, problems numbered lower than those of the benchmark problems in the same topic are easier, and problems numbered higher than the benchmark problems are more difficult.

> **TIP**
>
> Problems preceded by a D refer to problems in the Diagnostic test at the beginning of the 13th edition. These problems tend to be difficult.

Use those initial benchmark problems to help determine the appropriate next steps to improve your GMAT score. Here's what we recommend:

- If you struggle with the benchmark problems: Stop completing them! Instead, try lower-numbered OG problems on the topic (find these on the OG Archer in your online student center or in the Strategy Guides). Use the relevant Strategy Guide as a reference tool and the *Foundations of GMAT Math* guide as needed to learn how to approach and tackle these problems. Also, refer to the OG Archer to see MGMAT solutions to the OG Quant problems.

  Once you are able to consistently solve these easier problems, go back to the benchmark problems and try them again.

- If you are acing the benchmark problems: Make sure that you can consistently complete the lower numbered OG problems on the topic quickly and accurately (find these on the OG Archer or in the Strategy Guides). If you have extra time, read Part II in your Strategy Guides and try the higher numbered OG problems on the topic.

  Until you are consistently getting 600–700-level questions correct within the two-minute time limit, you cannot hope to increase your GMAT score by mastering 700+ level questions. This is because you will not be given significant numbers of 700+ level questions to solve on the GMAT if you do not solve the lower level questions correctly. If there are significant gaps in the knowledge that the GMAT considers lower-level, it will not test you on the higher-level concepts.

6

6

 Student Sound-Off

I treated OG questions as very precious. They are straight from the horse's mouth.

Also, every OG question has a lesson to be learned. On average, if I took two minutes to solve a problem, I took 5 minutes to review the question, even when I got that question right. That is correct. Rather than trying to solve too many problems left, right, and center, concentrate on a few problems and study the problems you solved.

Remember quality over quantity. And, review is more important than getting the problem right.

If you get a problem correct, you remember very little, but if you get a problem wrong, you'll never forget the problem. Or you *should* never forget that problem. I started tracking all my mistakes in an excel sheet and added comments to it after searching in the forums. The best thing about forums is that you get to see many different angles on how to attack a problem. Different people have different amazing ideas.

Gova
740 (Q49/V41)

Do You Know Where I Can Get Some Advanced Quant Problems to Work On?
– Horacio Quiroga

Instructor Insights

If only I had $1 for each time I have been asked this question…. Needless to say, the students who ask it think that working on harder stuff almost exclusively will greatly help them to improve their GMAT Quantitative score; nothing could be further from the truth.

Obviously, students whose math is less than super solid will not benefit from working with advanced stuff; not only do they not understand most of the reasoning behind the problem, but also they miss a great opportunity to hone their basic skills by working with easy and mid-level problems.

Still, I believe that even students with solid math skills, aiming at a 700-plus score, benefit very little from working almost exclusively on tough stuff. Why? Hard problems, more often than not, tend to focus on some not-so-frequently tested piece of trivia. More importantly, when all is said and done, a hard problem is simply several easy problems put together. And so even for the advanced student, shaving seconds from solving that quadratic equation or adding those two fractions will give her more time to focus on the big picture.

I have taken the real GMAT more than a dozen times and scored almost always in the 700s (that 690 will forever blemish my GMAT record), yet I have not seen many hard problems; what I do see is usually a lot of easy and mid-level problems. That means that those who go deep into that complicated rates problem are most likely practicing for less than 10% of the test.

> **TIP**
>
> San Diego instructor Stephanie Moyerman is a judo champion. She practices twice as long off the mat as she does on the mat. The same is true when studying to become a GMAT champ: plan to spend twice as long reviewing a problem as you do solving it.

As a 99th percentile scorer, I am often asked what the secret of my success is. I tell them that it has nothing to do with my being particularly smart but with the fact that I am simply able to fly through the easy problems, and thereby through the mechanical, easy parts of hard problems as well. So, if what you want to do is ace the Quant part of the GMAT, I say dump that advanced set of problems and work on easy and mid-level problems until you are blue in the face!

6

Know Your Per-Question Time Constraints and Track Your Work

When practicing GMAT-format problems, ALWAYS keep track of the time for each question, whether you are doing one problem at a time or a set of problems.

> **TIP**
>
> Remember: The OG Archer will track your time for you on OG problems.

If you want to finish the test on time, GMAT Quant and Critical Reasoning questions need to take about two minutes each. Reading Comprehension questions also needs to take no more than two minutes each on average. We suggest you accomplish this by spending no more than three minutes on your initial read of passages (less than 50 lines long) and no more than four minutes on your initial read of longer passages. Doing so will leave you with about a minute for each question. Sentence Corrections (SC) questions need to take, at most, a minute-and-a-half. If you can get SC questions down to a minute and 15 seconds each, or even a minute each, that's more time you will have to devote to the other Verbal question types.

Question Type	Average timing
Quant	2 minutes
Critical Reasoning	2 minutes
Reading Comprehension	2 minutes, including reading (We suggest you spend up to half of your per-question allotted time on your initial passage read through.)
Sentence Correction	1–1.5 minutes

Breaking Down Two Minutes: Time Management Within a GMAT Problem

You *won't* correctly answer every Quant problem on the GMAT in the allotted time. Even 99th percentile performers typically don't do this. Through a 700, GMAT-takers are getting about 60% of the problems correct: that's only three out of five! Even individuals who score a 750 are only getting about four out of five questions correct. That's why time management is *essential* on the GMAT. Why spend time on a problem that you won't get correct anyway, when you could invest that time on a problem where the time will make a difference?

As you are working through a GMAT problem, you also need to evaluate whether you are using your time efficiently. For instance, if you are attempting to solve a problem that you know you wouldn't get right in 10 minutes, let alone two, you are not using your time effectively. Likewise, if you are working on a problem and you know that you *can* get right, but that it will take five minutes, you are also not using your time effectively. *Any time that you spend on a problem over two minutes is time that you are taking away from a problem that you have not even seen yet.*

So how *should* you use your time? While no two problems will take you exactly the same amount of time to work through each step, using this timeline to structure your time working on GMAT practice problems will help you to make wise (but difficult) decisions on test day:

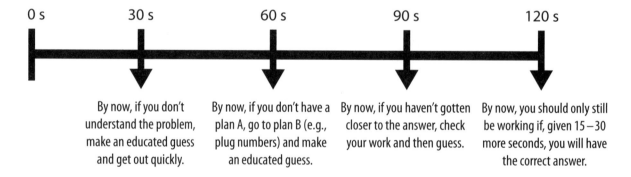

Note: While having a plan for a problem may mean an algebraic method to solve, it doesn't have to. Backup strategies such as plugging in numbers and picking smart numbers are just as valid approaches—and sometimes quicker!

Once you have used this strategy to work through a practice GMAT question, write down (or better yet, input into the OG Archer) your best guess. Then, draw a line under your scrap paper notes and continue to work on the problem until you have exhausted every potential line of your thinking. Providing your brain with the opportunity to think through new material most often takes more than two minutes. The trick is to do the heavy thinking now, during practice, so that on test day there's very little new: all you will have to do is recognize, remember, adapt, and solve!

After you have given a problem your all, make sure to review the solutions both in the OG and on the OG Archer (our MGMAT take on how to solve the questions). For *how* to review, read on!

Develop Your "1-Minute" Sense – Stacey Koprince

You can't check the clock after every problem on the real test—you'd drive yourself crazy before the test was even over! Instead, develop a "time sense" so that you can make appropriate, timely decisions as you move through the test.

WHY are you developing a 1-minute sense?

One of the key time frames on this test is the 1-minute mark on a question. For Quant, CR, and some RC questions, this represents the halfway point, and there are particular things that you need to have accomplished by that time in order to have a reasonable shot at finishing the question correctly in two minutes. For SC and some RC questions, the 1-minute mark represents the "wrapping up" point—you should be close to done with the problem.

Be honest with yourself: by one minute into a problem, you should know whether you'll be able to solve it. However, don't let intimidation get the best of you. If you find yourself skipping problems within less than 20 seconds, it is likely that you are not spending the time to carefully read the problem and thus have not given yourself a true opportunity to evaluate your know-how.

For 2-minute questions (Quant and CR), by the 1-minute mark, you need to have a very good idea of what else needs to happen in the second minute as well as confidence that you're capable of doing that work. If you don't, you need to move from trying to find the right answer to trying to find wrong answers. Spend up to one more minute eliminating wrong answers, then guess and move on.

For most other questions (SC and RC questions), your expected time frame is 1.5 minutes or less. When you get that 1-minute feeling and aren't on track, start to eliminate aggressively. You cannot spend up to another minute on these.

HOW do you develop a 1-minute sense?

Get a stop watch (physical or electronic) that has "lap" timing capability. (Most electronic stopwatches will do this; only some physical stopwatches will.) When using "lap" timing, pushing the "lap" button will not stop the stopwatch; rather, it will mark the time at which you

> **TIP**
>
> If you're done with the question before you think it has been a minute, check your work. If you were really that fast, you have the time to check, right? Make sure you didn't make a careless mistake simply due to speed. While checking your work, still push that button when you think it has been a minute since you started in the first place, and again when you're done with the problem.

pushed the button, but the timer itself will keep running. You can push the "lap" button multiple times, and the timer will record all of the times at which you pushed the button while continuing to run.

> **TIP**
>
> You can also train yourself when you're doing anything that requires extended mental concentration, even if it's not GMAT-related. Have to write up a report or memo for work or do some research? Set up your timer and push the button every minute until you've pushed it ten times. Then check your data.

Set yourself up with a set of 5 or 10 Quant or CR practice problems. (It's best to practice this with 2-minute questions to start.) Start your timer and cover it up so that you can't see what it says (but still give yourself access to the "lap" button). Dive into the first problem; when you think it's been about a minute since you began, push that lap button. When you're done with the problem, push the lap button again. Start your second problem; when you think it's been about a minute since you began, push that lap button. When you're done, push the button again. Keep repeating this process until you're done with your set.

Then review the data. For the 1-minute part, anything between 45 seconds and 1 minute 15 seconds is good. Anything outside of that range is too fast or too slow. Note your tendencies and, tomorrow, adjust accordingly when you do your next set of problems. Most people find it takes three to four weeks of regular practice with this in order to develop a time sense that is reasonably accurate most of the time.

Once your time sense is relatively reliable, you can start to implement your "am I on track?" and "if not, I'm moving on, or I'm moving to guessing" strategy.

Takeaways

1. Do timed sets! They will develop your mental flexibility and your time management skills in ways that other homework can't.
2. Take practice CATs under official timed conditions, with essays; skipping the essays can result in an artificially inflated multiple-choice score.

Chapter Takeaways

1. Do OG problems in sets customized to your current ability level. If the assigned benchmark problems are too difficult, try easier problems on that topic. If the benchmark problems are too easy, prove it by doing easy problems on that topic in half the time.

2. Don't worry about problem difficulty ratings—focus on content and solving techniques.

3. Start using a rigorous problem-solving timeline and develop your one-minute sense. Assess where you are at the one-minute mark. If you still don't have a clear picture of what to do, bail out before you waste three minutes on a problem that you can't solve.

MANHATTAN
GMAT

Chapter 7
of GMAT Roadmap

From Mastering Problems to GMAT Mastery

In This Chapter...

Chapter 7:
From Mastering Problems to GMAT Mastery

When you study practice problems, your overall goal is to *master* the problem you're solving. What does mastery mean? When you have mastered a problem, you have the ability to do the following:

1. Rapidly recognize a problem's features and associate them with solution techniques that you have successfully applied to problems with similar features.
2. Adapt the solution techniques to the current problem.
3. Execute those techniques efficiently and flawlessly.

These skills enable you to recognize what to do on a future problem—a problem you've never actually seen before. It's necessary to get to this level of mastery because the problems you study will never be the actual problems you're expected to do on the test. But you will see similar problems—problems that test the same concepts and so have similar features to the problems that you've already studied.

This mastery comes from the analysis you do *after* you've already finished trying a new problem for the first time. So, how do you analyze practice problems after you've tried them?

Well, the first thing everybody does is check the answer, right? Interestingly, the analysis doesn't depend much on whether you got it right or wrong! But we all want to know, so go ahead and check the answer. Just be aware that this doesn't change your review process much.

When reviewing a Quant problem, work through the question analysis chart detailed below.

Quant Question Analysis by Problem Solving Stage

Step	Issue	Situation	Fix
Understand U1	Did not understand	I guessed or got the problem wrong. After reading the solution, I am still confused.	Reread the relevant Strategy Guide chapter and redo the In Action questions at the end of the chapter. Plan to guess on this type of problem *until* you learn how to solve it.
Understand U2	Misunderstood	I got the problem wrong—or right accidentally. I know how to do it, I just read the problem incorrectly!	Read questions at a speed that allows you to absorb all of the relevant information. Always write down everything given on your scrap paper, even if you are not sure how to write it in "math."
Understand U3	Could not categorize	I did not recognize what type of problem this was. (I may have solved this problem, but not efficiently.)	Look up the problem's classification in OG Archer. Identify question language that would help you recognize this type of problem. For help, look at examples in the relevant Strategy Guide chapter and in the list of OG problems for that chapter.
Plan P	Could not strategize	I categorized this problem correctly, but could not adapt an appropriate strategy to solve it.	Put this question on a flash card. Look up problems in the same category and review their solutions. Try the MGMAT online flash cards for this problem type.
Solve S1	Missed something critical to solving	My method would have worked! I did not remember a rule, formula, math fact, or simplification technique that I needed.	Put the forgotten rule, formula, math fact, or technique on your cheat sheet. Complete extra drill sets (check *Foundations of GMAT Math* and other Strategy Guides) on the forgotten topic.
Solve S2	Made a careless error	I made a mechanical error while solving that led to an incorrect answer.	Drill! Work on scrap paper organization. Write out each math step. Learn backup strategies so you can rule out silly answers quickly.
Master M	Mastered	I know how to optimally approach a problem like this.	Congratulations! Later, when you review, try the advanced questions on this topic.

Student Sound-Offs

The OGs have some gems hidden in them. I noticed that even after going through these several times, I still could find something new each time I reviewed these books.

I went through these questions several times and copied all the questions that I thought were out of the ordinary or the concepts were tricky. Also, for the ones that I repeatedly made mistakes, I wrote my own questions testing that concept to thoroughly understand the tricks and traps.

I CANNOT EMPHASIZE THIS ENOUGH: Reviewing and dissecting the question is the most important thing you need to do to get the fundamentals right. After all, there are only so many concepts that GMAC can test, but they can do so in a billion ways. That is why it is so important to understand the fundamentals.

>   *Soomodh*
>   *700 (Q46, V41)*

Problem Solving/Reviewing: I've learned that it is not so much about the answers, but more about the process by which you get the answer. When reviewing problems, there are three things I want to make sure I can do before moving on:

1. Do I know why every wrong answer is wrong?

2. Double check for tricks and short cuts.

3. If something in the stem was changed, would I still know how to solve the problem? (This is something they did a lot in the MGMAT classes. They take an OG problem and change it slightly (by changing a positive integer to a negative integer or a fraction or zero), and then it becomes not about the answer but about the makeup of the question.

If you can do those three for an OG problem, you're done with it—and you should be able to solve anything even similar to it on the real test.

Also, eat right and exercise. Sleep. If you stay in shape, your mind can work faster and better.

>   *Helen*
>   *750 (Q48,V46)*

7

How to Learn from Your Errors
– Stacey Koprince

Instructor Insights

When I make an error, I get excited. Seriously—you should be excited when you make errors, too. I know that I'm about to learn something and get better, and that's definitely worth getting excited about!

Errors can come in several different forms: careless errors, content errors, and technique errors. We're going to discuss something critical today: how to *learn* from your errors so that you don't continue to make the same mistakes over and over again. First, let's define these different error types.

Careless Errors

Remember those times when you were sure you got the answer right, only to find out that you got it wrong? For a moment, you even think that there must be a mistake in the answer key. Then, you take a look at the problem again, you check your work, and you want to slap yourself on the side of the head. You knew exactly how to do this problem and you should have gotten it right, but you made a careless mistake!

By definition, a careless mistake occurs when you did actually know all of the necessary info and you did actually possess all of the necessary skills, but you made a mistake anyway. We all make careless mistakes (yes, even the experts); over 3.5 hours, it's not reasonable to assume that you can completely avoid making careless mistakes. Your goal is to learn how to *minimize* careless mistakes as much as possible.

Content Errors

"Content" is the actual knowledge you need to know in order to answer a question. What's the formula for the area of a circle? What are the rules for noun modifiers? Content errors typically come in two forms: knowledge you did know but forgot, and knowledge that you didn't know, or didn't know well enough, in the first place.

Technique Errors

Beyond the content itself, you can typically work through any Quant or Sentence Correction problem in multiple ways; the particular method you choose to use is the technique. For Reading Comprehension and Critical Reasoning, of course, all you have is technique; no actual knowledge is being tested on these question types. You also need to employ timing techniques, in terms of both individual questions and the overall section.

The Error Log

Your first step is to create an error log. You can do this in a notebook or an electronic file, but be sure to have one consistent place where you can record your errors. I typically record careless mistakes separately from all other mistakes, but you can organize things however you want, as long as the organization is consistent. Then, you can use the error log to learn from your errors.

For each problem you get wrong, keep track of this data:

1. The basics: Where the problem can be found again in your materials, the question type to which the problem belongs (as specifically as possible), the content category being tested (if applicable), the time you spent, and the current date.

2. The error: Describe the error in specific detail; if applicable, actually copy into your file the part of the work where you made the error. (Note: One problem could have multiple mistakes; include them all.)

3. The reason: Figure out *why* you made this error and write that down; if there are multiple reasons, note them all. The next step hinges on this step, so make sure you really dig deep to figure out why. If you can't figure out why, then you can't figure out how to fix the problem. (See more on this, below.)

4. To do: Figure out what habits you need to make or break in order to minimize the chances of making that particular mistake again. For example, you might:

    • Create flash cards to help you memorize some content or technique that you didn't know or messed up.
    • Re-write your work for this problem in its entirety and try the problem again in a week.
    • Do several problems of the same type, or drill certain skills, in order to build a new, good habit.
    • Decide that whenever you see a certain type of hard and relatively infrequent problem, you're just going to make an educated guess and move on—so learn how to make an educated guess and practice moving on!

    Whatever it is, do the necessary work to create good habits and destroy bad ones.

5. Review and reinforce: At least once a week, review your log. Are there certain types of mistakes you tend to make repeatedly? Are you continuing to make mistakes that you've made in the past and already tried to fix? Go back to steps 3 and 4 again.

The simple fact that you're now aware of your tendencies will allow you to notice when those kinds of problems pop up on the test. When you're already aware, then it's easier for you to double-check the parts of your work where you're most likely to make a mistake—or, if necessary, to let the problem go.

WHY did I make that mistake?

Let's talk more about figuring out why you made a mistake. Careless mistakes will usually be pretty obvious. When you're looking through your work, something will jump right out at you. You added when you should have subtracted. You thought something out in your head instead of writing it down. You calculated area instead of circumference. You missed the word "not," which negated the entire answer choice.

Quant content errors also tend to be more straightforward, but Quant technique errors can sometimes be tricky to fix. Don't assume that the first technique you tried is the one you have to use. Read the explanation, check out some online forums, and try to find different, better ways of tackling the problem.

Verbal errors can be even trickier to understand. Whenever you pick a wrong answer (or you guessed and got lucky), ask yourself several things:

- Why did I pick the wrong answer? Something about it looked good; something about it made me think it was right. What was that thing (or those things)? Now I know those aren't good reasons to choose an answer.
- Why did I eliminate the right answer? Something about it looked wrong. What was that thing (or those things)? Now I know those aren't good reasons to eliminate an answer.
- Why is each wrong answer wrong? (As specifically as possible!) Why is the right answer right? (Sometimes, the answer to that is: it's the only one left!)

There's one type of careless error I want to address specifically: when we meant to choose one answer (the right one!) but accidentally chose another. It's especially disheartening when this happens, and it often happens because of sloppy scrap paper technique.

On Quant, it is *critical* to write down what the problem asks for you to solve. On Problem Solving questions, I leave a little space for me to do the work, and then I write what I want to find and circle it. Then I go back and do the work in the space I left above. When I'm done with the work, I run right into my "$x =$ ___?" circle and I'm much less likely to, for example, pick the answer that actually represents y. On Data Sufficiency questions, I write the question at the top and the two statements below, and I've made it a habit to check the question after each step.

On Verbal, it is critical to keep track of your thinking for every answer choice. First, write down "ABCDE" *vertically*, just as the answer bubbles appear on the screen. Next, you need three consistent symbols. One means "definitely wrong," one means "maybe..." and one means "right!" As you think through each answer, make the corresponding symbol on your scratch paper. You can use any symbols you want, as long as you always use the same symbol for each category. When you're ready to choose an answer, circle that letter on your scrap paper, then immediately look up and select the corresponding bubble on the screen.

Okay, you're ready to learn from your mistakes. Go start that error log right now!

Why Flash Cards?

Congratulations: You've mastered new GMAT content! We're sorry to tell you, though, that mastering a new concept today is far from a guarantee that your GMAT score will improve 2+ months from now. The GMAT is like a college class where everything depends on the comprehensive final: there are no quizzes, labs, papers, or projects along the way to buffer your grade from the final's impact. On the day that you go in to take the GMAT, you need to make sure that you have all your months of studying at the forefront of your brain, ready to be called on at a moment's notice. But you know this already. The real question is *how?* The answer is *review*, and the secret weapon is *flash cards*.

If you follow this strategy to construct your flash card deck, you will have all of the math content (and GMAT tricks) that you learned over a prolonged period in one handy place, easily transportable and ready for review during those five minutes you have commuting on the train, waiting for your lunch date, or even trying to fall asleep at night (much more productive than counting sheep).

The goal is to make a flash card out of every quantitative GMAT-type problem that taught you something distinct that you want to remember on test day. They should *not* be problems that you found so difficult that you did not even understand the solution when you went through it. Likewise, they should *not* be the problems that you would have gotten right without a careless error. Sometimes they *can* be the problems, though, that you got right, but only after much serious contemplation and much more than two minutes.

> **TIP**
>
> Consider making your flash cards on 5" by 7" index cards to ensure that you have enough room for everything you want to remember about a problem.

What's the basic point? *Don't dilute your deck.* Overall, your flash card deck should grow to between 50 and 100 cards. A deck with over 100 cards is cumbersome to review each week. Don't forget that this is review of content you have already covered; you still need to be spending the majority of your time learning new content.

You can pull flash card problems from the *Official Guide* (OG), from your CAT tests, from problems discussed in a prep course, and from the online Question Banks. The best problems, of course, are the ones from the OG, because they are retired, authentic GMAT questions.

We know what you're thinking: *Doesn't MGMAT already have downloadable flash cards on their website?* Yes, we do. And they're good, but they weren't made with *you* in mind. Making your own flash card deck is like getting a personal training session instead of going to a class at your gym… except a lot cheaper. Yes, the flash cards do take time to make, but even the process of consciously choosing which problems to add to your deck, thinking through how to explain the problem to your future self, and writing your explanations on your index cards will help you master the content, and is valuable study time well-spent.

Quant Flash Cards

Front

The front of a flash card is the easy part. Write down the problem exactly as it would appear on the test. Here is an example:

Which expression is equivalent to $\dfrac{20^5 5^{10} 8^2}{10^5}$?

(A) $2^8 5^{20} 10^5$

(B) $2^{16} 3^{10} 10^8$

(C) $2^{16} 5^{15}$

(D) $2^{60} 5^{50}$

(E) $2^{11} 5^{10}$

Back

First, in the top left-hand corner, **categorize** the problem. The easiest way to categorize the problem is to identify it by the Strategy Guide (topic) and chapter (subtopic) in which its content can be found. Often, GMAT problems—especially tougher ones—can incorporate features of multiple different content areas. When this happens, categorize the problem as you see fit, and consider listing all of the features that the problem contains. For instance, our example problem could be categorized as:

Exponents, Fractions, and Factoring

Categorizing problems is valuable because the GMAT doesn't say, "Hey! Here's a rate problem! Can you solve it?" Instead, part of your two minutes per problem has to be spent understanding the content that the problem is testing. The faster you can do this, the more time you will have left to actually solve.

After you have categorized the problem, write down how you **solved** it—not just the *math*, but also the *thinking* that helped you to arrive at the math. Using the UPS framework discussed in Chapter 4 is highly recommended. If you recognize (either independently or after perusing the solution) that the question can be solved in multiple ways, make sure to show each way on your card—and discuss the pros and cons of each if appropriate.

The perfect place to discuss the pros and cons of each approach—and everything else you learned from the problem—is in a takeaways box at the bottom of the card (or anywhere else that you have room for it). If you cannot think of a takeaway for a problem, that's a big clue that the problem may not merit a flash card!

Below is one way that the back of a flash card on our example problem could look. Remember, though, making flash cards is an art, not a science—there is no *one* right way!

Exponents, Fractions, and Factoring

<u>U:</u>   G: exps., fraction, 2s & 5s, no fracs. in ACs

         N: simplify the exponent/fraction

<u>P1:</u> prime factors, combine & cancel

<u>S1:</u> $20^5 = 2^5 \times 2^5 \times 5^5$; $8^2 = 2^6$; and $10^5 = 2^5 \times 5^5$

$$\frac{2^5 \times 2^5 \times 5^5 \times 5^{10} \times 2^6}{2^5 \times 5^5}$$

No 3s: ABCDE

$$\frac{\cancel{2^5} \times 2^5 \times \cancel{5^5} \times 5^{10} \times 2^6}{\cancel{2^5} \times \cancel{5^5}}$$

$2^5 \times 5^{10} \times 2^6 \longrightarrow 2^{11} \times 5^{10} \longrightarrow \mathbf{E}$

<u>P2:</u> $10^5 \times 2^5 \longrightarrow$ to cancel denom.

<u>S2:</u> $20^5 = 10^5 \times 2^5$

$$\frac{10^5 \times 2^5 \times 5^{10} \times 2^6}{10^5}$$

$$\frac{\cancel{10^5} \times 2^5 \times 5^{10} \times 2^6}{\cancel{10^5}}$$

$2^5 \times 5^{10} \times 2^6 \longrightarrow 2^{11} \times 5^{10} \longrightarrow \mathbf{E}$

Takeaways:
  1. To mult. exps. with same base, add the exps.
  2. Using primes ensure no common factors missed.
  3. Matching num. to denom. can save time.

Verbal Flash Cards

Yes, we agree: it would be impossible to hand write an entire Critical Reasoning problem, let alone a Reading Comprehension passage, on the front of an index card! Here is what we suggest for Verbal flash cards.

Front

Instead of writing the entire problem as given on the front of the flash card, write the problem number. Unfortunately, this means that you will have to have your OG with you when you review your flash cards. For Sentence Correction and Critical Reasoning problems, you can also photocopy the problem from the OG and tape it onto the front of your flash card.

Back

For Sentence Correction problems, write a list of the key splits in the answer choices, which split option is correct, why, and which answer choices can be eliminated as a result. For Reading Comprehension and Critical Reasoning problems, complete a wrong answer choice analysis: write down what makes each wrong answer choice wrong. Regardless of the problem type, make sure to label the top left corner with key problem categories and to include take aways. Remember: For a problem to be worth a flash card, it has to offer a helpful take away!

Here are two examples of backs of Verbal flash cards, one for a Sentence Correction problem and one for a Critical Reasoning problem.

> **TIP**
>
> Verbal questions are most often solved through a process of elimination. See Instructor Stacey Koprince's article on "How to Make Educated Guesses on Verbal" in Chapter 5 for more on this.

Sentence Correction Sample Back

S/V, Pronouns, Parallelism	
is/(are) – b/c subj. is archeologists (pl.)	ABCD~~E~~
those / (artifacts) – b/c pronoun ambiguity	AB~~CD~~E
(to build) vs. building – parallelism w/to offer	AB~~C~~D~~E~~
Takeaways:	
1. Nouns that follow prepositions can't be subject.	
2. Identify the core of the sentence first when checking structure.	

Critical Reasoning Sample Back

Assumption
A – irrelevant
B – correct
C – uses same language as arg., but w/ diff. meaning
D – goes from relative to absolute
E – breaks a homogenous group in arg. into subgroups
Takeaways:
1. Same language may have a different meaning. Read carefully!
2. Don't break the arg.'s groupings into smaller subgroups.

What Mastery Is

Mastery isn't just getting it right. Mastery is identifying the general knowledge that the problem was designed to test and knowing *why* you got it right, what the different options are for solving, and what the traps in the problem are (if any). To achieve mastery, you have to do enough problems to have seen all of the basic content areas that the GMAT tests. Even more importantly, you build mastery through analysis (otherwise known as problem and practice test review) to understand where in your solving process you tend to go astray.

A famous psychology study evaluated dermatologists' diagnostic accuracy when they were given pictures of affected skin and a list of symptoms. The study discovered that the best predictor of diagnostic performance was not years in practice but rather the size of the dermatologist's slide collection. Flash cards are your slide collection: they are the different cases that you have seen and can compare to when you are trying to figure out which technique to use on a difficult problem. You need to have a flash card "database" of a certain size, and you need to periodically go back and review it. If you do not review, you will forget.

Question "Layering" – Chris Ryan

Instructor Insights

We all know that the GMAT is a computer adaptive test, and computer adaptive tests give you questions based on the difficulty level that you "earn" as you take the test. How do the test writers at ACT (the organization that writes the GMAT questions for GMAC) determine which questions are harder than others?

First, ACT engages in a process called "normalization," wherein all freshly written questions are tested by actual test-takers to determine what percentage answer the questions correctly (we know these questions as "experimental" questions). If too many people answer correctly, the question may need to be toughened up. If too few people answer correctly, the question may need to be dumbed down. ACT is looking to assemble a pool of questions that covers a range of difficulty, from cakewalk to mind-bending, and the test-takers help them do so.

How does ACT find these test-takers? Easy. Everyone who takes the GMAT will end up answering up to 10 unscored "experimental" math questions and up to 10 unscored "experimental" Verbal questions. These questions are interspersed with the actual, scored questions with no way to identify them as experimental.

Second, the writers at ACT have a general sense of what makes a 50th percentile question, or a 75th percentile question, or a 90th percentile question. Because each test is designed to evaluate proficiency in the same range of topics, the writers have to come up with ways to test the same concepts at different levels of difficulty. That's where "layering" comes in.

In a nutshell, a simple problem is made increasingly complex by adding information to obscure the core issues. As you progress in difficulty, ACT is less interested in whether you can perform basic calculations and more interested in whether you can peel away the layers to get to the core.

What follows are examples of layering in Data Sufficiency and Sentence Correction problems.

Layering in Data Sufficiency Questions

What is the value of x?

You have no way of knowing the value of x because (so far!) you have been given no information about it. In Data Sufficiency problems, you are given two pieces of information (called "statements") and asked to determine whether the statements (either individually or together) provide enough information to answer the question.

In order to answer the question (What is the value of x?), the test writers could provide you with a very straightforward statement. For example:

$$x = 2$$

This would be absurdly easy, so the test writers have to somehow tell you that $x = 2$ without stating it outright. What if you had the following statement:

$$x = \sqrt{4}$$

A little harder, but not much. What about:

$$x^2 - 4x + 4 = 0$$

This statement can be factored into $(x - 2)(x - 2) = 0$, which tells you that the value of x must be 2. This is a little tougher to decipher, but it is still not at an especially high level of GMAT difficulty. (Though there is a potential trap here: if you don't try to factor, you might assume that a quadratic equation will give you two different answers and so you might think it's insufficient.)

What if you were given the following statement:

$x^y = y^x$, where x is prime and y is even.

Try to figure this one out on your own before you continue reading!

If y is even, then y^x must be even as well. Because $x^y = y^x$, it must be true that x^y is also even. If x^y is even, x itself must be even. Since x is both even and prime, it must be true that $x = 2$, because 2 is the only even prime.

MANHATTAN
GMAT

Compare the statement $x^y = y^x$, where x is prime and y is even, to the statement $x = 2$. The statements provide the same information in the end, but one is unquestionably more difficult than the other.

In Data Sufficiency, the level of difficulty is not wholly dependent on the difficulty of the concept; it depends in part on the skill with which the test writer conceals the necessary information. As you study, you should note any questions where the information was cleverly hidden and work backwards through the levels to see how the writers were able to mislead you. Many of their tricks appear over and over in questions in the *Official Guide*. If you learn to spot them, you will have an enormous advantage over other test-takers.

Layering in Sentence Correction Questions

> *The dog are friendly.*

It does not take much effort to see that this sentence is flawed: the noun ("dog") is singular but the verb ("are") is plural. This would be much too easy for the GMAT, so the test writers must camouflage the error. One simple way to do so is to insert a lot of unnecessary verbiage between the noun and verb. We call this verbiage the "middleman." For example:

> *The dog, which was one of two puppies rescued from the shelter, are friendly.*

The subject-verb flaw is a little harder to see now, but still fairly apparent on a first read. If you take out the "middleman" (the intervening clause), you are back to the original sentence ("The dog are friendly"). Notice, however, that the writers have inserted a plural noun ("puppies") in the new clause so that you have plurality on the brain when you read "are friendly." If you are already thinking in plural terms, you are much less likely to spot the error. Even on a visual level, the subject of the sentence ("dog") is so far removed from the verb ("are") that the eye quickly alights on "puppies" as a possible subject for the plural "are." As tricky as this may already seem, the writers can put yet another kink in the rope:

> *Two puppies were rescued from the shelter, but neither of them are friendly.*

The error in this sentence is significantly less apparent than those in the previous examples, though it is still the same error: subject-verb disagreement. Here the subject is "neither (of them)," which is singular (think of it as "neither one of them"). The verb, however, is still plural ("are"). The saga of the mismatched subject and verb goes on. Can the writers make the problem even harder to spot? Sure! Let's take a look at the following example:

> *Neither of the two puppies that were rescued from the shelter are friendly.*

If you compare this sentence with the previous examples, the error is almost completely camouflaged. You can see that the subject is "neither (one)," which is singular, but the verb "are" is still plural. The core is simply "neither (one) are friendly." The test writers have managed to layer enough "junk" into the middle of the sentence to make it very difficult to spot the error. That junk, though, is just extra information about the subject: "Neither (one) <of the two puppies that were rescued from the shelter> are friendly." Only those who really know the rules backwards and forwards are going to be able to avoid this trap.

We have gone from "The dog are friendly" to "Neither of the two puppies that were rescued from the shelter are friendly" in a few steps, obscuring the central subject-verb issue along the way. Breaking sentences down into their component parts and analyzing their relationships is the key to success in Sentence Correction.

Takeaways

1. When reviewing a problem, try to figure out how the author "layered" the question stem or statement to make it more difficult. Can you write out the progression, from original language all the way to the simplest version? How did the author make this information so tricky?

2. If you can strip out the layers of a problem and get yourself to the simplest representation, then you won't be as likely to fall into a trap on a "layered" problem. On Sentence Correction problems, this means splitting out the core and understanding how the different pieces of "extra" info fit into the core. (You still might fall into a trap—but you will have a much better chance of avoiding it!)

Becoming a More Adaptable Problem Solver: Making the Best Use of Ottomans – Liz Ghini Moliski

Instructor Insights

As you become more familiar with GMAT problems and start to recognize patterns based on their wording, problem content, and answer choices, you will naturally start to categorize them based on these patterns (just as you categorize everyday objects, such as sofas and coffee tables). When you recognize a problem as belonging to a category, you can also remember how you approached prior problems from that category, making it easier for you to figure out how to tackle the problem at hand. Solving a categorized problem with a well-associated solution technique is typically fast because you are adapting an existing solution technique (or techniques) to the problem rather than thinking through a complete "from the ground up" approach to it.

Since categories are so helpful, why is there no definitive list of all GMAT problem categories? And why do some problems seem so hard to definitively categorize? Catego-

MANHATTAN
GMAT

ries are not perfect boxes. Just like a large ottoman in your living room can be both a place to put a tray of hors d'oeuvres, like a coffee table, and a form of padded seating, like a sofa, a GMAT problem can have features of multiple categories. Most Sentence Correction problems, for example, are ottomans, because multiple grammar rules are typically tested within a single sentence. Creating enough categories to accommodate every type of problem, such as a Sentence Correction parallelism and subject-verb, is not useful because there would simply be too many categories. The more categories you have to remember, the harder they are to remember. Finding the right level of granularity is a delicate balancing act: you want enough specialization so that the category really does help you quickly choose the correct approach and not so much that you are overwhelmed by the sheer number of categories to remember.

While at first it may be a challenge to figure out where to start with an ottoman problem because its different aspects call for different solution techniques, completing practice ottoman problems is helpful because they train you to become a more adaptive problem solver. To get the most learning from each ottoman problem, make sure to list out all the categories that the problem can fit into when working to understand the problem. Include the characteristics of the answer choices as well. For example, consider the following problem:

> **TIP**
>
> Choose descriptive names for categories, such as "answer choices increase by x10" or "CR Find the Assumption," because categories with meaningful names are easier to remember. Also use flash cards to drill yourself on both the categories and the solving techniques that you should associate with each type of problem in order to speed up your association of categories with their various possible solution techniques.

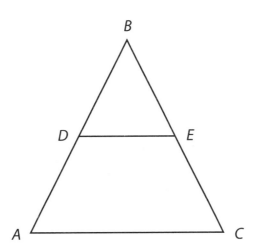

If *DE* is parallel to *AC*, and point *D* is halfway between points *A* and *B*, what is the ratio of the area of triangle *DBE* to the area of triangle *ABC*?

(A) 2 : 3
(B) 1 : 2
(C) 1 : 3
(D) 1 : 4
(E) 1 : 5

Since this is a geometry problem, looking at the diagram is a very important part of understanding the problem. This is clearly a triangle problem, and you might decide to solve it using triangle rules. You would write down what you know so far:

- DE and AC are parallel.
- D is halfway between A and B, so DB is half the length of AB.
- The formula for the area of a triangle is (1/2) × base × height.
- So the ratio of the area of the smaller triangle to the area of the larger triangle

must be $\dfrac{0.5 \times \text{base}_1 \times \text{height}_1}{0.5 \times \text{base}_2 \times \text{height}_2} = \dfrac{\text{base}_1 \times \text{height}_1}{\text{base}_2 \times \text{height}_2}$.

When you start to try to plan your solution to this problem, you realize that you don't know the lengths of the two bases or heights. You would have to introduce variables. But how many variables? If you introduce four variables (one for each base and one for each height), you will make the problem very complicated and might not be able to solve it.

You continue to think, looking back at the problem and every-thing that you've written down about it.... *Wait! If DE and AC are parallel, and D bisects AB, then E must bisect BC.... This means that the ratio of BD to BA is the same as the ratio of BE to BC. This makes ADE and ABC similar triangles! There must be a reason for the similar triangles aspect of the problem...what is it?*

TIP

Your choice of what to do first will depend on what most strikes you about the problem. While there is only one correct solution to this problem, the beauty of math is that there are typically many ways to get there, and nowhere is this so clear as in working on an ottoman problem.

At this point, you may have an "aha!" moment and realize that, since you are dealing with similar triangles, the bases and the heights must also be in the same 2 : 1 ratio.

If so, you would solve and the math would look like this:

$$\frac{0.5 \times \text{base}_1 \times \text{height}_1}{0.5 \times \text{base}_2 \times \text{height}_2} = \frac{\text{base}_1 \times \text{height}_1}{\text{base}_2 \times \text{height}_2}$$

$$= \frac{\text{base}_1 \times \text{height}_1}{2\left(\text{base}_1\right) \times 2\left(\text{height}_1\right)} \quad \text{because base}_2 = 2 \times \text{base}_1$$

$$= \frac{1}{2 \times 2} \qquad\qquad \text{cancel the bases and heights}$$

$$= \frac{1}{4}$$

You would then have used your knowledge of both the triangle category of problems and the ratio category of problems to successfully solve this problem.

If you didn't have an "aha!" moment, you could have gotten stuck at this point. The so-lution to this dilemma lies in noticing that the question asks about ratios and that the answer choices are all ratios (i.e., fractions), not absolute quantities, and realizing that in addition to being a triangle problem, this is also a fraction problem with no amounts given. This means that you can plug in Smart Numbers. Since the question demands that the ratio be true for any triangle, you can freely choose to plug in any number that will be convenient. *Hmmm... the easiest triangle to work with is a right triangle...a 45–45–90 right triangle!* You redraw the triangle to look like a right triangle. The problem tells you that point *D* is halfway between points *A* and *B*, so you decide to start by picking 2 for the length of *AB*, making *AD* and *DB* both of length 1.

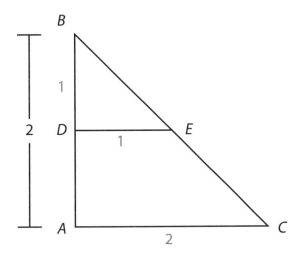

Now that you know the bases and heights for each triangle, you can use your formulas:

$$\frac{0.5 \times \text{base}_1 \times \text{height}_1}{0.5 \times \text{base}_2 \times \text{height}_2} = \frac{\text{base}_1 \times \text{height}_1}{\text{base}_2 \times \text{height}_2}$$

$$= \frac{1}{2 \times 2} \qquad \text{Plug the numbers we picked into the formula.}$$

$$= \frac{1}{4}$$

Using this approach was less theoretical. You used the geometry solving technique of redrawing diagrams and the fraction solving technique of plugging in numbers to solve this problem.

You might, however, not be sure how to approach the algebra at all and decide to use the general geometry problem backup technique, which is to reason about the answer choices by drawing as accurate a picture as possible and looking at the picture to estimate. The smaller triangle accounts for less than half of the big triangle's total volume so answers (A) and (B) must not be correct. Trying to narrow down the choices a little further, you might draw a line down the center of the lower

> **TIP**
>
> Planning a problem solution for an ottoman tends to be iterative, repeatedly returning for deeper understanding throughout the problem solving process. This is because multiple aspects of the problem need to be considered.

half of the big triangle to help you see that the smaller one looks like it is less than 1/3 of the size of the bigger triangle, so (C) cannot be correct either. You would then pick either answer (D) or (E) and move on.

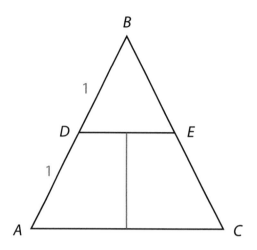

(A) 2 : 3

(B) 1 : 2

(C) 1 : 3

(D) 1 : 4

(E) 1 : 5

After solving or attempting to solve any difficult problem, take the time to review it and figure out if it is an ottoman. Would recognizing more of the categories that it fell into have helped you solve it more efficiently? Usually the answer to this question is yes, because ottomans typically require that you combine multiple solution techniques. As such, they are particularly good flash card problems because they remind you to be adaptive and flexible in your use of problem categories and approaches.

Online Resources

As you are working towards mastery, there are a number of additional, online resources available on the MGMAT website that may be of use. They are detailed below and can be found in the Student Center section of our website.

Online Resources	What They Are	When to Use Them
OG Archer	**The best way to do OG problems!** An online interface that lets you browse, input answers for, and review OG problems.	Whenever you complete OG problems!
Online Flash Cards	Flash cards for Quant and SC that train your recognition of key problem features.	When you need to build speed at problem pattern recognition.
Question Banks*	Sets of 25 GMAT-like questions ranging in difficulty from the 500s to the 700s. One bank is associated with each Strategy Guide.	When you need extra practice on the contents of a specific Strategy Guide.
Labs*	Practice-oriented drills focusing on specific test-taking issues. The PS Strategic Speed Guessing and DS labs are student favorites.	When you need extensive step-by-step practice on a particular process.
The Challenge Problem ShowDown and Archive*	If you solve the challenge problem of the week correctly, you get entered into a lottery for a free t-shirt or book (archive available).	If you are very good at Quant and need a break from what you are supposed to be studying (e.g., Verbal).
Prerecorded Class Sessions*	Generic, pre-recorded streaming video (like a YouTube video) of each class. Note: These *cannot* be downloaded.	When you miss one of your live class sessions and can't attend a makeup OR when you want to see a different approach to class content.
Recordings of YOUR Class (online students only)*	A streaming video (like a YouTube video) of YOUR class session. Note: These *cannot* be downloaded.	When you miss your online class OR when you want to use "replay" on your instructor.
Forums	Online community asking and answering each other's questions about GMAT and b-school topics.	See instructor Stacey Koprince's article "How Best to Learn from the Forums" on page 154.
Thursdays with Ron	Hour-long online study halls with veteran instructor Ron Purewal, detailing a different topic each week (archive available).	When one of the topics sounds relevant OR When you need some GMAT humor and a little kick in the pants.
Office Hours*	½ hour 1-on-1 phone calls with an instructor. Use or lose your 30 minutes weekly.	When you need a mini tutoring session.
GMATPrep	2 CATs made by the GMAC using authentic, retired GMAT questions.	When you have been through the MGMAT curriculum and want the best snapshot possible of where you are.

*These items are available for purchase from Manhattan GMAT, either individually or as part of a course package.

7

How Best to Learn from the Forums
– Stacey Koprince

Instructor Insights

Lately, as I've been discussing test questions with people on the forums, I've realized that a lot of students aren't using the forums in the optimal way. I'm defining the "optimal way" to mean the way in which students will best learn in order to boost their scores. I'll go out on a limb and assume that most people do have a goal of learning in the way that boosts their scores the most.

There isn't a one-size-fits-all approach in terms of the best way to learn; different things work best for different people. But there are certain principles that are universal—and you can use those principles to devise a "best practice" method for using the forums to maximize your learning.

How SHOULDN'T you use forums to learn?

First, let's talk about how you should NOT use the forums. You shouldn't use the forums as a starting point to learn all about some particular topic or question type. That's what your books (physical or electronic), classes, or tutors (or some combination of the above) are for. First, try to learn what you can, and then test yourself using practice questions. Those practice questions, again, don't typically come from the forums. They come from books or online banks of questions provided either by the official test makers or by test prep companies (like us!).

Some students do use the forums to find practice questions; I actually think that's a bad use. I have that opinion because of what I've witnessed over the past few years, as I've been discussing practice questions on various forums. First, if the source is not cited, it's difficult to judge whether the question is valid—there are a lot of bad practice questions floating around out there. (To be accurate, it's not terribly hard for *me* to judge; I've been teaching the GMAT for 15 years. But it's very hard for my students to judge.) Second, even if the source is a valid one, whoever typed it in might have transcribed the question incorrectly. I've seen this happen too many times to count, and then students are going crazy trying to learn from a GMATPrep question, for example, only to find out that the right answer is B, not A, or that what was typed for right answer A wasn't actually what the test itself said! Third, if you "troll" for practice questions on the forums, you may expose yourself to practice CAT questions before you take the CAT yourself. (I just spoke with a Beat the GMAT & Manhattan GMAT student yesterday who has been doing this. When he took his next MGMAT CAT, he saw questions that he'd seen already on the forums!)

Finally, I want to address the most common way in which I see people misuse the forums. They post a problem by itself, with minimal or no commentary or discussion of their own, and ask others to comment. This is exactly the *opposite* of what you want to do! (For more on why, read the next section.)

How SHOULD you best use the forums?

The forums are great for getting strategic advice from experts—validation on your study plan, a discussion of what to do about strengths and weaknesses, how to fix timing problems, and so on. I'm not going to discuss those kinds of uses in today's article, though.

The other great use of the forums is to discuss problems that you've already done. Let's say you just did 10 *Official Guide* (OG) problems. You read the explanations, you understand the basics, but you want more. Maybe you don't understand the right answer. Maybe you do understand it, but you want an easier way to do the problem. Maybe you want to know how to make an educated guess. Maybe you got the right answer and think you understand it, but you want to check your reasoning. Now, you go to the forums.

First, do a search to see whether that problem has already been posted before. If so, read the existing discussion. If not, post the problem yourself. (Note: If you post the problem yourself, PROOF the problem before you submit it. Make sure that every last word and punctuation mark is exactly correct!)

Next, post your own dissection of the problem. Write out what you thought when you first read it, how you did any work associated with the problem, what your reasoning was, what difficulties you had (if any), how you tried (or would try) to make an educated guess, and so on. Summarize whatever you were able to do or figure out, and formulate very explicit questions about anything you want to discuss. Try to push yourself to go as far as you can with the problem before you ask for help, and prove it to yourself by posting your analysis and your very specific questions about the problem.

An expert will respond and answer only the very explicit questions that you asked— and, even then, it's possible they won't answer fully. Ideally, an instructor would give you just enough information to "get over the hump" of whatever issue is giving you trouble, allowing you to continue forward and figure out the rest on your own.

Why is it so important for you to push yourself to do as much of the hard thinking as possible? Because your goal here is *not* to learn how to do this one particular problem in the way that the expert would choose to do it. You are not going to see this one particular problem on the test. The way some expert might choose to do it is not necessarily the best way for *you* to do it. And, of course, the instructor is not going to be sitting next to you while you take the test. Your goal is to learn *how to think about new* GMAT problems, ones that you've never seen before, in the way that works best for you. Your goal is to Train Your Brain!

Why is it so important for you to explain your thinking for the things that you did understand? Because it's important to validate your thinking. You eliminated (A). You had a reason for eliminating (A). You check the solution and (A) is, in fact, an incorrect answer. So you're done with that one, right? Wrong! Did you actually use valid reasoning, something that you could reuse on another, similar question in the future? If you're even the slightest bit unsure, then you'd better check your reasoning. (And there's even a bonus effect: you're not only helping yourself, you're also helping your fellow students when you post a thorough dissection of a problem!)

Let's try that again. You did the calculation and you came up with (C) as the answer. You check the solution and (C) is, in fact, the correct answer. Did you do the problem in a valid way? (Sometimes we get lucky!) If you're not 100% positive, check with an instructor. Or, if you know you made a mistake with the calculation, but you don't know why, don't just ask someone else to show you how to do it. Show them what you did and *ask where you went wrong*. Then, try to correct the mistake yourself.

Takeaways

*   So, if you haven't been doing what I describe above already (and most people aren't, from what I see on the forums), make a new resolution today to start using the forums in the best way. If you haven't been using the forums at all, now would be a good time to take advantage of a free resource! Make a resolution to Train Your Brain.

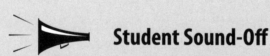

Student Sound-Off

MGMAT online forums: There is a lot of information in these forums. I used these forums extensively while reviewing my MGMAT practice tests. You will get a lot of information there.

Anoop 760
(V44, Q49)

MANHATTAN
GMAT

Chapter Takeaways

1. Prioritize review of the questions you answered incorrectly even though you understand the basic content (i.e., you are able to follow the solution and understand the right answer after reading it).

2. Keep an error log so you can learn not to repeat past mistakes.

3. *Build speed* by using flash cards to work on pattern recognition of Quant problem types, sentence structures, wrong answer analysis, and argument structures.

4. Getting a high score requires content mastery, which does not come from doing problems unless you also *review* and *analyze* your work afterwards.

5. Hard problems test the same concepts as easy problems, often just with layering. Rephrasing in DS and ignoring middlemen in SC are examples of techniques used to "peel away" the layers that make hard questions hard.

6. Many GMAT problems are hybrids that are hard to categorize as a single type. Solving hybrid problems can help you to become a more flexible problem solver and are often particularly flash card worthy.

7. There are a lot of resources available to students on Manhattan GMAT's website. Spend some time becoming familiar with them.

7

Chapter 8

Preparing for Your 2nd CAT

In This Chapter...

Chapter 8:

Preparing for Your 2nd CAT

Dear Jen,

I'm just not smart enough to do this. Every once in awhile, I get a really hard problem right and I feel like a genius, but I can't do that in two minutes, 37 times in a row on the Quant section. Other people who succeed at this must just be smarter.

Doubting in Detroit

Dear Doubting,

I know that feeling—sometimes you get a really hard problem and you do something super-smart (sometimes you can't even remember later what it was!) and it works out. But, yes, you can't do that all the time, and you can't just "get smarter."

Fortunately, all of the problems on the GMAT are solvable in two minutes, and most of them—while they can be cloaked in lengthy stories and difficult wording—fall into recognizable categories, and can be attacked with strategies that simply need to be learned and practiced.

While the "crazy genius" feeling is kind of a good one, that's actually not the feeling you want. You want to solve GMAT problems with the same feeling you'd have if I asked you what $6 + 5 + 9$ is. (Go ahead, answer that question.)

There's a reason I just wrote that example and not $2 + 2$. You know what $2 + 2$ is instantaneously. When you saw $6 + 5 + 9$, you actually had to add, and you might have done some kind of mental check, or done it twice, to make sure you were correct. But you knew *what* to do immediately (add two numbers and then add the third one), and you knew that you *could* do it. *That's* the feeling that you're shooting for on the GMAT. Realistically, you'd be lucky to feel that way half the time. But that's the goal:

calm, capable, confident, sometimes even a little bored that you're seeing the same kind of thing you've seen a dozen times before and could do in your sleep.

When you do a problem in a "genius" way, don't get too happy. You're not done. You need to either work back through and systematize your solution so that you could do it again, in two minutes, comfortably, on a "similar but different" problem, or else you need to find a better way to do it (such as by reading the answer explanation in the *Official Guide* or in the CATs). Make a flash card. Review the problem later. You're not shooting for genius. You're shooting for speedy problem recognition and efficient application of appropriate strategies.

"Speedy problem recognition and efficient application of appropriate strategies" sounds a lot less cool than "genius," but it's a lot easier to do 37 or 41 times in a row on the GMAT.

Jennifer Dziura, MGMAT Instructor, New York

Everything You Need to Know about Time Management

Time management is an essential GMAT skill. You need the ability to pace yourself. There are significant penalties both for not finishing the test and for getting several in a row wrong.

Make trade-offs on the problems that would be really hard for you to get right in two minutes. Identifying these problems quickly allows you to quickly guess and move on, saving precious extra time for problems where an extra 10–30 seconds can mean the difference between a correct and an incorrect answer.

There's no bonus for finishing early. If you leave time on the table, you are likely leaving points on the table as well. Unless you are earning a 99th percentile score, think of how you could have used that time—even just to check for careless errors.

Understand How the Scoring Works

If you don't understand how the scoring works, you cannot have an informed time management strategy. Here are the basics:

(1) Everyone gets a lot of questions wrong, no matter the scoring level; that's just how the test works. Pretend you're playing tennis. You don't expect to win every point, right? That'd be silly. You just want to win more points than your opponent (the computer)!

(2) Getting an easier question wrong hurts your score more than getting a harder question wrong. In fact, the easier the question (relative to your overall score at that point), the more

damage to your score if you get the question wrong. It is still very possible to get the score you want even if you make mistakes on a *few* of the easier questions.

(3) Missing three or four questions in a row hurts your score more, on a per-question basis, than getting the same number of questions wrong but having them interspersed with correct answers. Of course, if you are running behind on time for most of the test and then try to catch up toward the end, you're likely to end up with a string of wrong answers in a row.

(4) The largest penalty of all is reserved for not finishing the test—another possible consequence of maintaining a negative time position.

Analyze Your Data

Using OG Archer and CAT analysis reports, you can see aggregate data on your per question timing. Regularly checking in on your statistics will make you aware of your average per-problem pacing for each question type and will encourage you to consider time as you work through GMAT problems. Determine the question types that are generally costing you more than your average per question time. Note whether you're getting these "expensive" questions right or wrong (across the various categories— for example, Rate problems or Modifier SCs). For those that you're answering correctly, the primary question is: How can I become more efficient when answering questions of this type? For those that you're answering incorrectly, the initial question is simply: How can I get this wrong faster? (You're getting it wrong anyway—so if you can get it wrong faster, which shouldn't be that hard to do, then at least you won't be hurting yourself on other questions in the same section.)

How do you get things wrong faster? Quickly recognize problems that fall into categories that you do not yet solve very well, either because you have not studied them yet or because you just don't really "get them" yet. On the test, you need to make an educated guess—or a random guess if you just don't understand what the question's asking. Longer term, you may then decide to study that particular area or topic more closely in order to try to get better at it. Alternatively, there may be a couple of question types (such as Combinatorics or Advanced Divisibility) that you decide just don't come up frequently enough to be worth the time they would take to master. Plan to always quickly guess on questions that fall into these categories. Interestingly, the hardest problems to solve are often the easiest to rule out some answer choices on, based on commonsense reasoning about the possible answer range.

Also notice the question types that are buying you time (those that consistently take you less than the allotted time). First, make sure that you are not making many careless mistakes with these; working quickly is not a positive thing if you sacrifice a question that you were capable of answering correctly. You may actually need to *slow down* on some of these in order to minimize your careless mistakes. The goal is not to minimize the time spent, but rather to *maximize the number of correct answers per time spent*.

If you do find areas that are *both* highly accurate and quickly solved, excellent; these are your strengths; stay very aware of these while taking the test. If you find yourself running behind on time, still take your normal amount of time to answer any "strength" questions; don't sacrifice the ones you can answer

8

correctly! Instead, make a random guess on the next "weakness" question that you see in order to get yourself back to a neutral position.

Transition to Benchmarks

You probably noted that you might finish one "2-minute" question in only 1.5 minutes, and another in 2.5 minutes. This makes sense and can be advantageous as long as you are spending long enough to minimize careless mistakes and yet not so long (more than 2.5 minutes) that you fall behind. This is why it is better to use benchmarks than to time each problem on either a timed set or a full test.

> **TIP**
>
> Read about timed sets and Watertight Quant Timing later in this chapter!

Know How to Recover from Bad Timing

Everything discussed so far has focused on what you *do* want to do. What about if things get off track? There are two levels to this: what to do immediately during an actual testing/timed situation, and what to do during your study afterward, before you take another test.

What to Do During a Test

The only way to recover is to notice early that your timing is off before the problem becomes severe. This is why you need to use benchmarks. As soon as you notice a timing problem, you need to start dealing with it. Don't ignore it and assume it will get better later; almost certainly, it will only get worse.

You are going to need to sacrifice something in order to get back on track; you don't have a choice about that. You do have a choice about *what* you sacrifice. Don't sacrifice problems in your fast and accurate areas. Don't tell yourself that you'll do this question 30 seconds faster because you already know how to do it, so you can just speed up. You're risking a careless mistake on a question that you know how to get right, plus you're going to have to do that on several questions to make up the two minutes that you're behind, so you're really giving yourself a chance to miss multiple questions that you know how to do.

Instead, the very next time you see a question that you know is a weakness of yours, skip it. Make an immediate, random guess and move on. There—you've only sacrificed one question, and it was a weakness anyway. Depending upon the question type and how quickly you moved on, you saved anywhere from a little under one minute to a little under two minutes. If that's enough to catch back up, great. If not, repeat this behavior until you are caught back up. On average, don't skip more than one question out of every five. Don't worry if you see two "big weakness" questions in a row, though. Maybe you got lucky and got that first one right. Maybe one is an experimental. Even if they both count, getting two wrong in a row won't kill your score—you can recover because you still have more questions to come—and you're unlikely to have gotten them right anyway.

> **TIP**
>
> Reminder: Read more about developing a 1-minute sense in Chapter 6!

What about going too quickly? In this case, you do need to slow down a bit, because you might be making careless mistakes simply due to speed. Make sure you're writing everything down. Check your work on the questions that you know you know how to do. (On the ones you absolutely don't know how to do, though, just go ahead and move on—you don't need to spend more time on those.) Use your 1-minute sense! If you're ready to move on before it's been about a minute (and you think you got it right), now would be a great time to check your work.

What if the test is over and you realize that you messed up the timing? Go all the way back to the beginning of this article and start practicing all of the things we discussed until you're better able to balance your timing throughout a test section. Note that this can take weeks and even months, depending upon how severe your timing problems are and whether they are also related to holes in your content knowledge and skills.

Takeaways

- Understand how the scoring works.
- Analyze your data.
- Use benchmarks.
- Know how to recover from bad timing.

What Santa's Elves Have to Teach Us about GMAT Timing – Liz Ghini Moliski and Abby Pelcyger

Instructor Insights

8

Imagine, just for a moment, that you are one of Santa's elves. You are a new elf, an elf-in-training, if you will. You have just received your first list of children and the corresponding gifts that they have requested. Eager to show Santa how competent you are, you quickly get down to the business of making toys.

Then, you get to Jenny. Jenny has requested a very complicated, hard-to-make toy. You have never made this toy before, and aren't sure how to. However, you are confident in your toy-making prowess and believe that, if given enough time, you could do a great job making this senior-elf-level toy. "Wouldn't that impress Santa?" you wonder.

The problem is that you are on a tight schedule. Kids need their toys by December 25th, and you have a long list of kids whose toys you are responsible for making. If you spend the time it would take to make Jenny's toy as specified, you won't have time to make Mary's toy, or Joanne's, not to mention Bob's and Liz's. What should you do?

You realize that, while making Jenny's toy might impress Santa initially, he'll quickly become very disappointed in you when he realizes that you did not finish your list and left other children without their toys. You briefly consider making shoddy toys for all of the other children so that you can focus on Jenny's challenge. You realize, though, that it's not fair to give the other children toys that will quickly break.

You decide to make Jenny a simpler version of the toy she requested, the best you can do in the time you have to allot to each child. When Santa sees your toys on December 24th, he may not be "wowed" by Jenny's toy, but he will know that you are a solid elf that he can count on.

What does this have to do with the GMAT? Like one of Santa's elves, you have a long list to accomplish in a very short time. You just have problems to solve instead of toys to build. Also, like an elf-in-training, you have more asked of you in the time given than you are capable of accomplishing. During the GMAT you will constantly have to make time allocation decisions. You can spend a little more on one problem if there's a second one that you can finish faster. Your score will suffer significantly, though, if you run out of time on the test, leaving problems at the end unattempted. Likewise, if you rush through several problems that you know how to solve efficiently, you will likely make a slew of careless errors and take a hit on your score. This risk is not worth taking to spend more time on a single problem that you are unlikely to get right anyway.

So, if you recognize a "Jenny's Present" on a test, make an educated guess, and move on!

8

Student Sound-Off

I improved my score 80 points from a 530 to a 610 after taking the online MGMAT class. Unfortunately, the admissions staff at my top choice, Cornell, was not impressed with my score. My score needed to be at or close to a 700 to demonstrate that I could compete with other top applicants. This task seemed daunting and unattainable but it was one that I was unwilling to give up on.

I took the GMAT 3 more times, but was unable to score above a 610, so I hired a MGMAT tutor. My tutor and I isolated timing (especially on the Quantitative section) as a pivotal issue: I was spending inordinate amounts of time on problems I would never answer correctly and spending too little time on problems that were difficult to me but still solvable. It was challenging for me to just let problems defeat me, I felt guilty if I did not try to solve every question—even if it meant spending several minutes and placing myself in a dire position to complete the Quantitative section.

My tutor gave me an article on an NBA player, Shane Battier, which was written by Michael Lewis, the author of "Money Ball." The article highlighted that Shane used statistics and probability in every game he played at the professional level. Shane forced players to spots on the court where field goal percentage was dismal, he placed himself in optimal positions for rebounds, and used every statistical data point he could to maximize his effectiveness on the court.

I sought to apply Shane's example in my pursuit of a top score on the GMAT. When I reached problems that I knew intuitively would take too long to solve, I would silently say "ballin'" to myself and skip the problem. A question that I knew I couldn't solve regardless of how much time I spent on it was called a "freebie" and it was imperative that I guess and move on, preserving precious time for those questions that I could solve. I gave myself 7 freebies within the Quantitative section, which provided the freedom to move on from problems that were sabotaging my score. I took the GMAT one final time, 6 months after being placed on the wait-list at Cornell and less than a week before the class would be finalized. With the "freebie" framework, my score jumped to a 680 and earned me admission to two of the three schools I applied to with scholarship, and within a week Cornell also reached out with favorable news: I was accepted!

The biggest takeaway from my experience is that one of the most challenging aspects of the GMAT is getting comfortable with the fact that you are not going to answer every problem correctly. In fact, even top scorers only answer a slightly more than 50% of their questions correctly. The key is recognizing problems that are out of your league, skipping them, and focusing on accurately answering all the questions in your wheelhouse. It's correctly answering every question that you are capable of answering correctly that will earn you a great score and place you on track for a remarkable two-year experience at a business school of your choice.

Justin
680 (47Q, 35V)

Watertight Quant Timing
– Tom Rose

Instructor Insights

Indications: For students who continue to fall behind during the Quantitative portion of the GMAT and are looking for an alternate timing approach. (Advanced Quant Timing is also useful for helping students avoid the temptation to "speed up.")

Background: Most students work best at a natural speed or cadence. Disrupting this cadence by attempting to "speed up" can drastically reduce accuracy. The tendency to "speed up" must be avoided.

Challenge: If a student's natural work speed in the Quantitative section of the GMAT does not allow them to complete problems in an average time of 2 minutes or less, then time must be saved somewhere to avoid the need for guessing at the end of the section. (The Quantitative section allots an average time of 2 minutes and 1.6 seconds per problem.) How can the student execute the Quantitative section of the GMAT faster without "speeding up"?

Solution: Use watertight timing compartments and forced guessing.

How to Execute: Divide the Quantitative portion of the GMAT into 10-minute compartments. Memorize what problem you "should" be on for each timing benchmark. When taking the exam, answer problems at a normal speed and cadence. Do not rush! If you reach a timing benchmark and are not on the associated problem, guess immediately until you are back on schedule. (The benchmarks should be interpreted strictly.) Then, resume answering problems at a normal cadence.

Time Remaining	Problems Finished
65	5
55	10
45	15
35	20
25	25
15	30
5	35

Why This Works: This technique helps improve several conditions: (1) it helps reduce the effects of rushing, which lowers accuracy; (2) it helps students access higher levels of creative thought, which they can only access when solving problems at their natural rhythm; and (3) the GMAT penalizes strings of wrong answers in sequence. Watertight timing compartments help distribute guesses throughout the exam, reducing the risk of guessing incorrectly several times in a row.

Advanced Concepts: Hopefully, as the student becomes more in tune with her natural work speed, she can begin to calibrate herself so that she knows approximately how many questions she will need to guess on during the Quantitative section of the GMAT. Once the student begins to anticipate the need for guessing early, she can begin to pick her guesses strategically instead of simply guessing at the end of a slow time compartment. This will further increase accuracy by allowing the student to guess on questions that are above her difficulty level that she might answer incorrectly anyway. As the student masters watertight timing compartments, the strictness of the compartments can be relaxed to allow some wiggle room at the boundaries to allow for questions that are almost complete. Be careful not to backslide into old habits!

 Student Sound-Off

Even after practicing this "diligent timing" on ~10 tests, I STILL screwed up my timing in the actual test (it's super stressful and my nerves were all over the place) and I thought for some reason that Math had 41 problems instead of 37, so I guessed (I guessed wrong I figured later) on the last two problems when I had 4 minutes left thinking I had 4 more problems—but actually it was the end of the test! Woops! Talk about freaking out afterwards—got me super upset. Nerves do funny things sometimes—I had taken about a million practice tests so I can't imagine what I was thinking!! Also, I ran out of time on Verbal after stupidly spending ~5 min on a Critical Reasoning test—forcing me to rush through the last 4 problems and guessing on 3/4 of them—so I probably could have bumped up both my math and Verbal score about a point each if I had been stricter with timing—which means I would have had an even HIGHER score. SO, final WORDS OF WISDOM ON THIS: Practice the actual test taking scenario a lot (although I did this) and try to really be diligent about sticking to your benchmarks—it can really hurt you if you go off that too much. Luckily, in my case, it didn't hurt me too bad, but I probably could have scored even higher had I been more strict about only spending 2.5 minutes EVER on a problem. And as much as you can give yourself the "real situation" when taking the test, do it, because nerves do funny things sometimes (like seeing #37 on math and thinking you have 4 questions left? What?).

Amanda
730 (49Q, 40V)

8

Timing Considerations on the Verbal Section

Verbal timing is "looser" than Quant timing because it has to account for variance in problem types. For instance, if you get eight Sentence Correction problems in a row, it shouldn't take as long as if you had gotten two Reading Passages back-to-back.

In Verbal, check the time after every eighth problem. Here's what the timing chart looks like:

Problem #	Time remaining
8	60
16	45
24	30
32	15

While most students struggle to complete a Quant section in time, a sizable number finish the Verbal section with significant time left over. If you are more than two minutes ahead, slow down and spend more time on Reading Comprehension and Critical Reasoning problems. Ways to do that?

(1) Make sure that you carefully read the full text of each answer choice. *Every* word is important. Wrong answers are often wrong due to a single word.

(2) On Reading Comprehension detail and inference questions, make sure to find your proof in the passage. Often, wrong answers echo language from the passage but actually say something different.

(3) Don't spend your extra time on Sentence Correction. Students tend to second-guess themselves. If you followed a good process, you identified the splits and either you knew the rule or you didn't.

If you are struggling to complete the Verbal section in time, apply watertight Quant timing to the Verbal section, but using the timing chart provided above. If you have an extreme timing problem on the Verbal section and are not aiming for a 700+ score, it is okay to skip one entire Reading Comprehension passage. Try to pick a shorter passage in a topic area that you find difficult. The shorter passages usually have only three associated questions, not four. If you have a minor timing problem (i.e., fewer than five problems left undone or rushed on), you are better off skipping an occasional Critical Reasoning problem. Critical Reasoning problems tend to be more difficult for most people.

> **TIP**
>
> If you are a non-native speaker struggling with the Verbal section, check out Appendix A of this book.

Strats. for Scraps

As trivial as it may sound, even the way you set up your scrap paper can impact your GMAT score. If your notes are not logically organized on your scrap paper, it will be more difficult for you to check your work or branch off into a different solving strategy if the first one doesn't pan out. You are more likely to miss a critical relationship if all of the information that you know about a problem is not laid out in an organized fashion. In addition, you need a way to quickly check your progress against the watertight timing benchmarks without disturbing your workflow. Here's what we recommend (largely based on strategies that our students have reported to work for them):

TIP

Don't worry! The scrap paper they give you is gridded so all you have to do is write in the numbers. Also, if you take extensive notes on Verbal, record fewer problems per page than shown here. If you fall into this category, try eight problems per page, and use the time tracking system of writing the start time for each page as shown below for the Quant section.

For Verbal

First Page

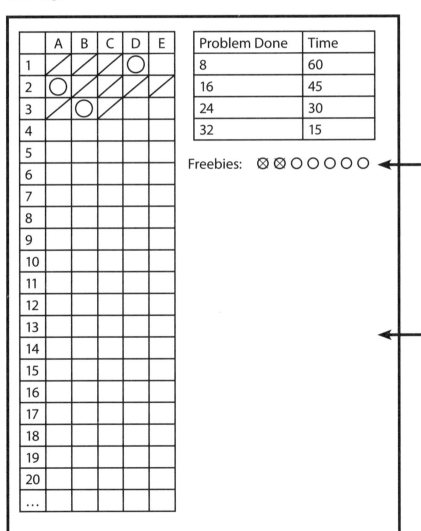

Problem Done	Time
8	60
16	45
24	30
32	15

Cross off one freebie box each time you guess on a problem in under one minute.

Use this space to diagram ONLY Reading Comprehension passages—this will help you to keep track of how many passages you have already seen. (Diagram for Critical Reasoning on the following pages as needed.)

8

For Quant

Second page

Start Time: 65 min	9
6 $x + 2y = 17$ $-(x - y = 5)$ $3y = 12$ $y = 4$ $x = 9$	(table with N−3, N, N+2 / A A−3, A, A+2 / B B−3, B, B+2)

At the top of each page, write the watertight timing time to start each new set of five problems. This will remind you to time check each time you turn a new scrap paper page.

7
$$\frac{170 \cancel{(9)} \cancel{(8)}}{\cancel{(15)} \cancel{(24)}}$$
  5   3

10

Each question gets its own area in order to keep notes organized and to make sure you can get through the entire Quant section with a single scrap pad.

8

$$\frac{170}{5} = 34$$

Extra room, if needed. Perfect for side calculations and for keeping track of how many freebies you have left!

Freebies: 5̶ 4

Why Use Timed Sets?

When you're training for a marathon, you may run four days a week, but you'll only have a long run on one of those days. The other days, you'll often be completing just three to five miles. These short runs are important for two reasons:

(1) They keep your body in fit running condition so that you can do the long run once a week.

(2) They provide running practice in small bursts that help you to improve your speed.

Timed sets are the short runs on the GMAT marathon. Unlike a marathon runner, you should not be taking CAT tests weekly, unless studying the GMAT is your full-time job... and perhaps not even then. Timed sets do the following:

(1) They provide review of all the problem types you've covered to date, keeping your brain fit and all already-studied content types fresh.

(2) They also build your speed by helping you to recognize problem type patterns, associate appropriate solution strategies, and execute quickly. In addition, they teach your brain how to change gears every two minutes, quickly jumping between content areas.

How to Do a Timed Set

Now that you have learned a significant amount of content, you have enough knowledge to complete timed sets. This is what you have been saving the OG supplement guides for. They will provide you with OG problems that you have not seen before to practice your skills on.

The initial goal is to complete five Quant problems or six Verbal in 10 minutes. Not every problem will take you exactly two minutes on the dot. The goal is to learn how to make time trade-offs between problems. Timed sets provide an opportunity to practice your comprehensive time management strategy, including "freebies" and educated guessing.

Freebies are problems that you look at for about 30 seconds, realize that you cannot solve, and decide to randomly guess on.

It is common to find, at the beginning of your timed-set work, that problems will take you a bit longer than you are used to. This is because, up to this point, when you solved an OG problem, you knew ahead of time what content area it covered and, therefore, which solution techniques you would likely employ. Now, you need to learn to recognize problem content areas based on clues in the problem's wording and in the answer choices.

Plan to spend 20 minutes reviewing the problem solutions after you have completed the entire set. Remember: it takes twice as long to review a problem as it does to complete it. In addition to the problem-by-problem review discussed in Chapter 6, you now need to also evaluate the timing decisions that you made:

> **TIP**
>
> Refer back to the UPS article in Chapter 4 and the Breaking Down Two Minutes article in Chapter 6 for guidelines on the amount of time to spend on each problem-solving stage, including content recognition.

- Did you spend too long on a single problem?
- Did you rush on a problem that you should have been able to solve?
- Did you appropriately select the problems to guess and move on from?
- Did you successfully maximize the number of problems that you were able to get right within the time constraint?

When you are consistently able to finish the timed set within the 10 minutes and are confident with your timing decisions, it is time to move up to longer sets. The chart below details how to create your timed sets of various lengths.

Quant Timed Sets

10 minutes	3 Problem Solving problems, 2 Data Sufficiency problems
20 minutes	6 Problem Solving problems, 4 Data Sufficiency problems
30 minutes	9 Problem Solving problems, 6 Data Sufficiency problems

Once you are able to excel at a 30-minute timed set of Quant problems, you will likely find GMAT Focus helpful. GMAT Focus is a product that you can purchase relatively inexpensively from GMAC at www.mba.com. Each GMAT Focus is a computer-based, adaptive set of 24 authentic, retired Quant GMAT problems. It's like a mini-math CAT (a kitten?). Give yourself 50 minutes to complete one, and plan for approximately two hours of review.

Verbal Timed Sets

20-Minute Timed Sets

15 minutes	1 Reading Comprehension passage with 3 questions, 2 Critical Reasoning problems, 3 Sentence Correction problems
30 minutes	2 Reading Comprehension passage, one with 3 questions and one with 4 questions, 4 Critical Reasoning problems, 5 Sentence Correction problems

Yes, we know, Reading Comprehension passages in the OG usually have more than four questions each. This is because, even within a single passage, the GMAT is adaptive. The test has to be prepared to ask you different questions within a passage depending on your performance. When completing timed sets, just randomly choose three or four problems in the passage to complete. Afterwards, you can come back and finish the other questions, giving yourself about one minute per question.

8

> **TIP**
>
> We have found it very helpful to use Post-it document flags to mark the problem that you intend to start in each OG problem section. This way, you will not lose time when you need to switch from one problem type to the other.

MANHATTAN
GMAT

Student Sound-Off

MGMAT CAT: 640 (Q43/V34)

I hit my ceiling. I've completed the course and it didn't seem like I'm going to get past that 700 mark. But my teacher suggested that I chill out and just keep practicing OG problems. I used MGMAT's OG Tracker spreadsheet and set it up to guide me to do an equal number of questions every day of varying difficulties. (Following the MGMAT curriculum, you do about 1/3 of the OG problems over the course. This leaves the majority of the problems to practice on with everything you learned.)

MGMAT CAT: 710 (Q46/V41)

This is basically my highest ever Quant and Verbal scores so far combined. Around the 4th day of starting the OG problems, I began to get comfortable with the structural makeup of GMAT problems. By day 6 or 7, I began to be able to pinpoint what kind of problem it was going to be and how to be mentally prepared for the calculations that would be needed. I can start to predict what they're going to ask before I finish reading the problem. By day 9 or 10, I understand how to shift my thought processes so that I can solve the problems within two minutes. I focus on speed and educated guessing. Also, I realize that I'm making a lot of stupid mistakes: misreading problems and/or answer choices, making absolutely asinine calculation errors, "adding" my own information when it's not given in the stem, etc.

MGMAT CAT: 720 (Q46/V42)

I have completed every single problem in all three OG books—each is timed and error logged using MGMAT's error log spreadsheet. I reviewed each one I got wrong and made sure I understood it fully. Occasionally, I'd run into a problem that was way over my head, in which case, I just let it go because I didn't really care about being able to know how to do a 750+ problem when I could focus on a 700 level problem.

Helen
750 (Q48/V46)

8

So What about the Essays?

The essays are not incorporated into your 200–800 score. They are graded on a separate 0–6 rating.

It is true that a computer grades your essays, but so does a human being. As long as the human grader and the computer's scores are within one point of each other, their ratings are averaged to give you your score. If their ratings differ by more than a point, though, your essay is read by a second person, the computer's rating is thrown out, and the two humans' ratings are averaged together.

You can think of the E-rater as an advanced version of Microsoft Word's spelling and grammar check. The computer is also programmed to check for essay organization. That means it's a really good idea to use transition words such as "first," "next," and "in conclusion." In addition, the E-rater assesses your writing acumen by ensuring that you are using multiple sentence structures and sentences of varying lengths.

The following exercise is designed to make your writing more engaging for the reader and more attuned to the E-rater criteria. You can try it using an essay you have already completed. First, draw the following grid on a piece of scratch paper:

#	Sentence Opening	Verbs Used	Words
1			
2			
3			
4			
5			

Fill in the grid using the essay you have just written. Under "Sentence Opening," write the first few words of each sentence. Under "Verbs Used," write all the verbs in each sentence. Under "Words," count and write the number of words in each sentence.

Your goal is to vary the contents of each column, and to eliminate as many "to be" verbs as possible. If you often start sentences the same way, tend to use the same verbs, or write many sentences of the same length, try rewriting the essay to fix these problems. While you won't have time to do Essay Grids on the actual GMAT, using this grid in practice will help you start to think about these issues as you write.

8

Excelling on the essays will *not* help you get into business school. Business schools view a 5 on the essay just as favorably as they view a 6. The essays are just there to ensure that the person who was carefully ID-ed on the way into the GMAT testing room is conceivably the same person who wrote those exquisite, flawless application essays. While business schools admissions officers do have access to your GMAT essay responses, they're busy people. The only times that we have heard of b-schools actually reading GMAT essays were in cases of non-native English speakers about whose English fluency they were particularly concerned.

If you skip the essays altogether (i.e., write nothing) or write on some other topic, not answering the question, then you get a 0. That would definitely raise an eyebrow at the schools—they'd wonder why you did that, especially if you had no good reason to. We don't have any way of knowing exactly how schools would react, but it wouldn't be worth testing the waters. Even on retakes, students should do the essays. Another reason is that even putting in minimum effort on the essays will probably be sufficient for most folks to get a decent enough score. So why not make that minimum of effort? (This is another reason why skipping the essays altogether would raise an eyebrow: if we were admissions officers, it would make us wonder about the person's general effort level.)

So what's the bottom line? Trying your hardest on the essays is like going to a wedding and getting filled up at the cocktail hour. Don't do it: there's a whole sit-down dinner about to be served. Aim for a five, not a six! However, the essays are important to take into consideration because taking a three-and-a-half hour test is harder than taking a two-and-a-half hour test. You need to make sure that you have, or build up, the stamina to get all the way through the test without running out of steam on the Verbal section. Taking your practice tests with the essays will give you good stamina practice and ensure that your practice exam scores are accurate representations of your test-day abilities.

> **TIP**
>
> Don't just skip the essays on your actual GMAT. If you do not complete the essay section of the test, b-schools will notice... and know that your score is artificially inflated.

If you're a Manhattan GMAT student, Lab 6 in your Student Center contains a prompt for each essay type that will be graded by the GMAC's essay-grading software. If you need extra practice (and an additional round of grading), GMAC sells GMAT Write, which is a web-based tool that provides authentic GMAT essay prompts and real-time essay grading. We recommend that you complete the essays in Lab 6 as the essay portion of your second CAT. This will help you to determine whether the essays are an area that you need to invest any time in. Before you do so, though, make sure to read the words of advice below from sage instructor Stacey Koprince.

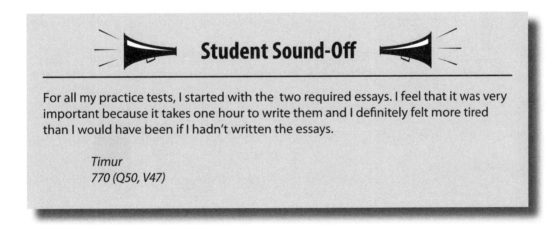

Student Sound-Off

For all my practice tests, I started with the two required essays. I feel that it was very important because it takes one hour to write them and I definitely felt more tired than I would have been if I hadn't written the essays.

Timur
770 (Q50, V47)

8

Ace the Essays? No, Thanks!
– Stacey Koprince

Instructor Insights

We all know that the essays on the GMAT are scored separately and that the schools don't care as much about the essay scores. We also know you have to write the essays first, before you get to the more important Quant and Verbal sections, so you don't want to use up too much brainpower on the essays. Still, you can't just bomb the essay section; the schools do care about the essays *somewhat*. So how do you do a good enough job on the essays without expending so much energy that you're negatively affected during the multiple-choice portion of the test?

You need to develop a template, an organizational framework on which to "hang" your writing. The template will not, of course, tell you exactly what to write. For that, you need the actual essay prompt, which you won't see until you take the test. You can, however, determine how to organize the information ahead of time, as well as the general kinds of messages you need to convey at various points throughout.

The template should tell you:

- How many paragraphs to use.
- The primary purpose of each of those paragraphs.
- The kinds of information that need to be conveyed in each paragraph.

The template will vary a little bit from person to person; the important thing is to have a consistent template for yourself that you've worked out *in advance of the official test.* In addition, you will need slightly different templates for the two different kinds of essays, so take note of the differences below.

> **TIP**
>
> Read the sample essays in Chapter 10 of the OG. Note that the longer essays received higher scores.

As a general rule, essays should have either four or five paragraphs total. The first paragraph is always the introduction, the last paragraph is always the conclusion, and the body (middle) paragraphs are for the examples you choose to use.

Each paragraph should contain certain things; these are listed in the sections below. The information does not need to be presented in the order given below, though; just make sure that each paragraph does contain the necessary information in some sort of clear and logical order. In addition, the information listed below is the minimum necessary info—you can certainly add more where appropriate.

First Paragraph

- Summarize the issue
- State a thesis
- Acknowledge that the other side does have some merit
- Introduce your examples

The first paragraph should contain a brief summary of the issue at hand *in your own words* (don't just repeat what the essay prompt said). For an Argument essay, briefly summarize the conclusion of the given argument. For the Issue essay, briefly summarize the issue upon which the prompt has asked you to convey your opinion. For either, you don't need more than a one- to two-sentence summary.

The first paragraph should also contain a thesis statement. The thesis is typically one sentence that conveys to the reader your overall message or point for the essay that you wrote. For the Argument essay, you can write most of your thesis sentence before you get to the test! You already know that the Argument will contain flaws, and that you will be discussing how those flaws hurt the author's conclusion. Guess what? That's your thesis!

> *"While the argument does have some merit, there are several serious flaws that serve to undermine the validity of the author's conclusion that XYZ."*

DON'T USE THAT EXACT SENTENCE. They're going to get suspicious if hundreds of people use the same sentence. (Besides, that's my sentence. Come up with your own!)

Note the opening clause: "While the argument does have some merit." This is what's called "acknowledging the other side." You shouldn't say, "Hey, your argument is completely terrible! There's nothing good about it at all!" Instead, acknowledge that some parts may be okay, or some people may feel differently, but your position is that the flaws are the most important issue (that is, your thesis is the most important thing).

On the Issue essay, you won't be able to write your thesis statement ahead of time, but you do know that in it you'll have to do two things: (1) establish one clear position for yourself, and (2) acknowledge the other side. ("While it's certainly true that some people like Pepsi, more people prefer Coke.")

Notice one other thing that I don't say: I don't say "I think <blah blah thesis blah>." I state my thesis as though it is fact and reasonable people *surely* agree with me. That's a hallmark of a persuasive essay.

Finally, the first paragraph needs to introduce whatever examples you're going to use in the body paragraphs below. Don't launch into the examples fully; that will come later.

Body Paragraphs

You can choose to use either two or three body paragraphs. (I use two body paragraphs, personally. Remember, we just need to be "good enough!")

Argument essay:

- Introduce one flaw.
- Explain why it is a flaw.
- Suggest ways to fix the flaw.

Issue essay:

- Introduce one real-world example.
- Give enough detail for reader to understand relevance of example.
- Show how the example supports your thesis.

The body of an essay is where you support your thesis statement. For the Argument essay, your support will come from the prompt itself: brainstorm several flaws from the argument (try to find the biggest, most glaring flaws). Each flaw gets its own paragraph, so you'll need either two or three, depending upon how many body paragraphs you want to write. Explicitly explain why each flaw makes the conclusion less valid in some way, and then discuss how the author might fix that flaw.

For example, let's say that an argument claims that firing half of a company's employees will help the company to reduce costs and therefore become more profitable. While it's certainly true that chopping half of your payroll will reduce costs, it doesn't necessarily follow that the company will become more profitable. That loss of personnel may reduce productivity, hurt the morale of the remaining employees, and so on. The author of such an argument could bolster the claim by, for example, showing evidence that half of the employees are fully redundant and firing them wouldn't affect the company adversely (if such evidence actually exists, of course!).

For the Issue essay, your support will come from your brain: you'll have to brainstorm some real-life example (*something that actually happened in the past*) in order to support your thesis. That example could be something from your own life (work history, school, friend of a friend) or from the broader world (business, history, and so on). Stating that Coke's market share is higher than Pepsi's, for example, would bolster your claim that more people prefer Coke.

There is no inherent advantage to a personal example versus a broader world example, but if you use a personal example, be sure to provide enough detail that the reader can understand the relevance. When you use real-world examples that the readers are likely to know, you don't have to worry about, for example, explaining what Coke and Pepsi are.

> **TIP**
>
> The essay graders are explicitly told NOT to mark anyone down for getting a fact wrong—they can't fact-check everything, so they are explicitly told to fact-check nothing in order to make sure there's a level playing field. However, that being said, you don't want to say obviously untrue things.

Finally, make sure to tie your example specifically back to your original thesis. Don't make the reader connect the dots—tell him or her exactly how this example supports your thesis.

Conclusion Paragraph

- Restate your thesis (using new words).
- Reacknowledge the other side (using new words).
- Briefly summarize how your examples supported your thesis (using new words).
- Minimum three sentences; ideally four to five.

Are you noticing a theme within the above bullet points? Basically, the conclusion paragraph isn't going to contain much new information. It's a conclusion; the major points should already have been made earlier in the essay. What you're doing now is tying everything together in one neat package: yes, the "other side" has some merit, but here's my point-of-view and, by the way, I proved my case using these examples.

Before you go into the real test, you should have a fully developed template, so that all you have to do is come up with your two examples and your thesis statement, and then "hang" your words on your framework. Practice with the above as a starting point until you develop something with which you're comfortable.

> **TIP**
>
> Don't forget to leave some time to proof your essay; it's okay to have a few typos, but systemic errors will lower your score.

  Student Sound-Off

I wrote AWA essays on alternate MGMAT exams, and on every official practice test. This is not to improve my AWA score but to test my endurance levels and build exam stamina. That extra one hour of thinking and writing essays will take a small toll on your stamina.

Gova
740 (Q49/V41)

Chapter Takeaways

1. The best test time management uses timing benchmarks rather than a rigid two minutes per problem approach.

2. Doing timed sets will teach you to transition to benchmarks in ways that other homework can't.

3. Good scrap paper management can help you reduce your timing stress as well as the number of careless errors that you make.

4. Take at least one practice CAT with the essays, because the essays can drain your energy if you don't have a good plan for them.

5. Use the Manhattan GMAT essay template to complete the essays with a minimum amount of stress. Save your energy for the main event.

8

Assessing Your Progress

In This Chapter...

My Score Dropped! Figuring Out What Went Wrong

Analyzing Your Practice Tests

Chapter 9:

Assessing Your Progress

Dear Jen,

My second CAT didn't go up! All this work for nothing!

Down in DC

Dear Down,

It's very common that students take a first practice test and get a horrible score (say, in the 400s). Most people don't read too much into that; if you've never seen a GMAT before, of course the first test is going to be pretty bad.

But then, lots of people take the second test and get another score in the 400s, and are just crushed; they feel like they haven't accomplished anything and it's hopeless. That is absolutely not the case!

Here's what's usually happening. On the first test, there were all kinds of things you had no idea how to do, so you just guessed and moved on. You may have even finished with time left over due to having skipped problems. On the second test, after studying, attending classes, etc., you then knew enough to attempt *everything*. But you weren't fast enough at any of it yet, so you ran out of time, either cutting off many individual problems before you could really solve them, or else running out of time and randomly guessing through a long string of problems at the end or even timing out completely and not finishing. Your overall score comes out the same.

Please know that this is very common. What I always tell people is that it's not about the overall score (yet). Imagine that someone had videotaped you taking the first exam. You're just looking baffled, messing around, and clicking "C" a lot, aren't you? Now watch the video of your second exam—oh look, you set that one up right and then got stuck… and on the next one, you almost got there but saw that you had taken more than two minutes so you guessed… and on the next one you realized you had an over-

TIP

It can be *very* helpful to create a question analysis spreadsheet for your CAT. To do so, review each question and determine which question analysis category you got stuck on (to read more on question analysis, see Chapter 7). If one category label keeps showing up over and over again, you know that this is the bottleneck in your problem-solving process.

lapping sets problem and made an appropriate chart but then couldn't figure out how to fill it in…. In other words, on the first exam, you got 0% of the way there on a lot of problems, and on the second exam, you got 50–80% of the way there on a lot of similar problems. Your overall score might be the same, but that video of your *process* looks really, really different.

This usually works itself out around the third or fourth CAT. Of course, to cause this to happen, you can't just take CAT after CAT, doing the same thing. After taking a practice test, go back over *all* of the problems. Actually *do* them again, don't just look at them. Go back and study any topics that gave you trouble. Even on the ones you got right, could you have done them more efficiently, thus freeing up time for other problems? Reviewing a test should take you longer than the actual test would.

Stay positive, and keep moving forward.

Jennifer Dziura, MGMAT Instructor, New York

My Score Dropped! Figuring Out What Went Wrong – Stacey Koprince

Instructor Insights

It's always disheartening to have a score drop, whether it happens on a practice test or (worst case scenario) on the real test. If this happens to you, the most important thing to do next is to figure out why this happened. If you can figure out why, then you may be able to do something to prevent a score drop from happening again.

Take a look at the most common reasons for a score decrease and ask yourself if any of them apply to you.

1. Official Test Conditions

Did you take your practice tests under official test conditions? Did you:

- Do both essays?
- Take only two 8-minute breaks (the first between essays and Quant, the second between Quant and Verbal)?
- Complete the test in one sitting (e.g., you didn't do the Verbal section later that evening or the next day)?
- Pause the test, look at books or notes, eat and drink during the test, or do anything else that wouldn't be allowed on test day?

If you did *not* take your practice tests under official testing conditions, then your practice scores were likely inflated—possibly just a little or possibly a lot, depending upon how far you were from official test conditions. If your practice test scores were inflated, then the bad news is your scoring level wasn't as good as you thought it was, and your official test didn't represent as much of a drop as you first thought (and, possibly, the official test didn't represent any drop at all).

While this is not great news, it is crucial to know, because it tells you what the problem is. You need to figure out in which areas you're falling short and do what you need to do (math, grammar, problem-solving skills) in order to improve. (And don't forget to take tests under official conditions in the future, so that you get a true picture of your current scoring level.)

2. Stamina

Did you prepare yourself adequately for the stamina required to perform at a high mental level for more than 3.5 hours? Did you:

- Take the tests under official conditions (including essays and breaks—see section 1)?
- Take the practice tests at the same time of day as you took (or plan to take) the real test?
- Avoid taking a second test (practice or official) within three days of taking another practice test?
- Eat good "energy" food before the test and during the breaks, drink liquids to stay hydrated, and stretch or do light exercise to loosen up and get your blood flowing?

This is a long test; stamina is critical to our ability to perform well. Don't tire yourself out in the days before the official test (don't study too much, don't take a practice test within a few days of the real thing, etc.). And experiment with food and liquid until you find a combination that gives you good energy without making you overly stimulated (too much caffeine is a bad thing).

In addition, many people skip the essays on practice tests and then see a substantial drop on the Verbal section of the official test. People are surprised when this happens, but if you use your Critical Reasoning skills, it shouldn't be that surprising! If you don't take the essays, then you're only spending about 2.5 hours on your practice tests. The real thing, with the essays, will take a bit more than 3.5 hours. Your brain is, quite simply, not prepared to last for that entire 3.5 hour period… and Verbal is the last section. So, the Verbal score drops.

That's why, although nobody cares about the essay *scores*, I still tell my students to do the essays on their practice tests. Your mental stamina is going to affect your Quant

9

and Verbal scores, and you do care (very much!) about those scores, so you have to make sure you're prepared to function at a high level for the entire 3.5-hour length of the test.

3. Timing

Mismanaged timing can cause a lot of variability in test scores. If your scores keep jumping up and down on practice tests and you're not sure why, your timing may be the culprit. Whenever I talk to a student who experiences more than a 100-point drop on a test, timing is almost always a factor.

Timing is so crucial because of certain consequences that can kill your score. Test-takers tend to make more careless mistakes when they're rushing. They may get multiple questions wrong in a row or they may run out of time entirely before the section is over. All of these things will have a negative impact on the scoring.

There are two major categories for mismanaged timing: too slow and too fast. Some testers will run out of time before the section is over; others will finish with lots of time left. Many testers mismanage the time badly, yet actually do finish the test on time. *Just because you finished the test on time does **not** mean that you managed your time well throughout the sections.*

The vast majority of students who mismanage time badly enough to experience a big score drop will do so by going too slowly at some point on the test, and consequently forcing themselves to move too quickly at other points. Alternatively, people sometimes do move too quickly throughout an entire section because of general test anxiety; if you finish with more than five minutes left, you definitely moved too quickly through that section, and likely made careless mistakes as a result.

The common factor in either scenario: having to go too quickly at some point. When you go too quickly, you make careless mistakes. You also tend to choose to go too quickly on problems you think are easy (or, at least, easier than others). So going too quickly basically equates to giving yourself lots of chances to miss lower-level problems.

The "death spiral" (otherwise known as "my score dropped in a big way!") occurs when you start to get a lot of lower-level problems wrong that you knew how to get right—if only you weren't rushing and making mistakes.

(By the way, think about the other side of things: the problems on which you would go too slowly. You're going to do this on the really hard problems, right? Well, the chances aren't very good that you'll get those problems right, even by spending extra time— precisely because the problems are really hard!)

4. Anxiety

The test is a nerve-wracking situation for everyone, but some people experience anxiety symptoms that are strong enough to interfere with rational thinking and the ability to perform. If you are experiencing physical symptoms (nausea, rapid heart rate, difficulty breathing), you should consult a medical professional. Also, read Chapter 10 of this book on managing test stress.

The Most Important Thing to Remember

If you can figure out what went wrong, then you can do something to prevent another score drop in the future—so please take the time to think through everything that happened. Also, use the Manhattan GMAT and the Beat the GMAT forum communities to help—your fellow students and the GMAT experts can be great resources in helping you figure out what went wrong and what to do next.

Reaching the GMAT finish line is like running a marathon. You need to maintain motivation—and a lot of it—over an extended period of time. Motivation can be thought of as the combination of your *desire* to and your belief that you *can* accomplish your goal. There are many strategies you can use to help stay motivated, but running into the proverbial wall sometimes happens to the best of us. The important thing to remember is to just not give up. Even if your study plan falls through one day, picking it up again the following day is the only way to ensure that you reach your GMAT finish line.

Analyzing Your Practice Tests

Practice tests are an invaluable component of any test-taker's study plan, but the most valuable thing is actually *not* the act of taking the practice test. Just taking a test doesn't help you to improve all that much. While taking a test, you are concentrating on *doing* (using everything you've learned up to that point); as a result, you're not really *learning* much.

The most valuable thing is *actually* the data that you can extract once you've *finished* a test; that's how you learn to get better and know what to study before you take another practice test.

By analyzing your practice test, you can ascertain whether you've learned what you have been trying to learn and diagnose your strengths and weaknesses so that you can revise your study plan accordingly going forward.

First, look at the score. Also note whether you did the essays (if you didn't, assume the score is a little inflated) and whether you used the pause button, took extra time, or did anything else that wouldn't be allowed under official testing guidelines. Any of these actions could inflate your score.

TIP

It takes about 45–60 minutes to do this analysis, not counting any time spent analyzing individual problems.

9

Problem Lists

Next, look at the problem lists for the Quant and Verbal sections; the problem lists show each question, in the order it was given to you, as well as various data about those questions. The primary value of analyzing the data lists is to assess your time management.

First, scan down the "Correct / Incorrect" column to see whether you had any strings of four or more answers wrong. If so, look at the time spent; perhaps you were running out of time and had to rush. Also, look at the difficulty levels, because sometimes the difficulty level is high for the first problem or two, and the timing is also way too long. Then, on the later questions, the difficulty level may be lower, but the timing is also too fast. This happens when you have a sense that you spent too much time on a couple of hard questions, so you speed up… and then you not only get the hard questions wrong but you also get the easier questions wrong because you were rushing.

Next, scan down the "Cumulative Time" (how much time you've spent cumulatively on the test) and "Target Cumulative Time" (how much time you should have spent cumulatively) columns. Specifically look for periods when you were more than two minutes off of the Target time. When you see that you were too fast or too slow, try to figure out what happened: Where were you spending too much time? Where were you rushing? What happened on those problems?

Then, scan down the "Time" column, which lists the time spent per question. Even if you managed to stay on time cumulatively, you still might exhibit "up and down" timing—spending too long on some problems and then rushing on others to catch up.

Look for patterns. How many times did you fall more than three minutes behind or spend way too much time on a single problem, and how many times did you move too quickly? What was the cumulative outcome of these statistics?

> **TIP**
>
> For per-question timing guidelines, refer to Chapter 6. Also, remember that the first Reading Comprehension question of any passage will include the time used for the initial read through of that passage.

If such instances occurred more than a few times (regardless of whether the questions were answered right or wrong), you have a timing problem. It isn't (necessarily) okay to spend too much time on a question just because the question was answered correctly. Any time you spend on a question above the allotted per-question time is time that you are taking away from a different problem. For example, if you had four questions over three minutes each, then we can practically guarantee you that you missed other questions elsewhere simply due to speed—that extra time had to come from *somewhere*. You know those times when you realized you made an error on something that you knew how to do? If you were also moving quickly on that problem, your timing was at least partially a cause of that error.

Alternatively, if you have even a single problem that is very far over the "way too slow" mark, you have a timing problem. For instance, if you have a Quant question on which you spent 4.5 minutes, you might let yourself do this on more questions on the real test—and there goes your score. (By the way, the only potentially acceptable reason is: I was at the end of the section and knew I had extra time, so I used it. And our next question would be: Why did you have so much extra time?)

If a timing problem seems to exist, try to figure out roughly how bad the problem is. How many problems fit into the different categories? Approximately how much total time was spent on the "way too slow" problems? How many "too fast" questions did that cost you? You may also want to examine the problems themselves to locate careless errors. How many of your careless errors occurred on problems when you were rushing?

Be flexible with the assessment. For instance, if you answered a Quant question incorrectly in 45 seconds, but you knew that you had no idea how to do the question, so you chose to guess and move on, that was a good decision. You don't need to count that "against" you in your analysis.

Finally, see whether there are any patterns in terms of the content area (e.g., perhaps 80% of the "too slow" Quant problems were Problem Solving problems or two of the "too slow" SC problems were Modifier problems). Run the assessment reports next in order to dive deep into this content data, but do try to get a high-level sense of any obvious patterns.

All of the above will allow you to quantify just how bad any timing problems are. Seeing the data can help you start to get over that mental hurdle ("I can get this right if I just spend some more time!") and start balancing your time better. Plus, the stats on question type and content area will help you to be more aware of where you tend to get sucked in—half the battle is being aware of when and where you tend to spend too much time.

Assessment Reports

In the Manhattan GMAT system, click on the link "Generate Assessment Reports." For now, run your first report based solely on the one test that you just did; later, you can aggregate data from your last two or three tests.

The first report produced is the Assessment Summary. This report provides the percentages correct for the five main question types, as well as average timing and difficulty levels. Problem areas are indicated by:

- Percentages correct below approximately 50%, especially when coupled with lower average difficulty levels (though I'm *not* worried if I see, say, 48% correct with an average difficulty level of 730—that's a *good* result unless you're trying to score 760).

- Average timing that is 30 seconds (or more) higher or lower than the expected average.

- A big discrepancy (more than 30 seconds) in average time for correct vs. incorrect questions of the same type; it's normal to spend a little extra time on incorrect questions (because those are probably the harder ones!), but not a ton—that just means you're being stubborn.

9

If you think there is or might be a timing problem, next look at the second and third reports (by Question Format and Difficulty). These two reports (one each for Quant and Verbal) tell you your performance based upon the difficulty levels of the questions.

In these two reports, there are two important trends to note:

1. Average timing that is 30 seconds (or more) higher or lower than the expected average, and whether that is happening on correct or incorrect questions (or both)

2. Lower percentages correct on lower-level questions than on higher-level questions

In particular, these two things might appear together. If that happens, you might be spending too much time on incorrect higher-level questions and not enough time on lower-level questions, which you are then getting wrong as a result.

The timing averages for Reading Comprehension can be misleading because the first question for each passage includes the time to read the passage itself. For RC, you need to dive back into the problem list to look at each problem individually in order to get a true picture of what happened.

> **TIP**
>
> If you choose to look at the data from only one test for these last two categories, be aware that your analysis may need to be flexible for those sub-categories with only 1 question. If you get 0% of 1 question right, that doesn't mean that area is a big weakness!

Finally, look at the fourth and fifth reports (Quant by Content Area and Topic, Verbal by Verbal Type and Topic). Before you do this, though, you may decide to run the reports based on your last two or three tests rather than just your last test. You're diving deep into the details with these final two reports, so there will be lots of categories with only one or two questions unless you add more data to the report.

The fourth and fifth reports show all of the questions broken out by question type and subtype or subtopic. In general, you should split each content area sub-topic into one of five categories:

Group 1. You got these right roughly within the expected time frame (>50% right and neither way too slow nor way too fast).

These are your strengths. Going forward, they're not high on your priority list, but there may still be things you can learn, such as: faster ways to do the problem; ways to make educated guesses (so that you can use the thought process on harder problems of the same type); and how to quickly recognize future problems of the same type. Also, make sure that you actually knew what you were doing for each problem and didn't just get lucky! Finally, you may want to move on to more advanced material in these areas.

Group 2. You got these wrong roughly within the expected timef rame (<50% right and neither way too slow nor way too fast).

These indicate a possible weakness in content or methodology, but check the difficulty levels—perhaps you just happened to get a couple of really hard ones in the same category.

First, you need to figure out why you got each question wrong. If it was 700+, you got another lower-ranked question of the same type right, and you were fine with these on your last test, then your fundamentals may be good, and it may be time to lift yourself into the toughest areas for this particular question type or content area.

Alternatively, maybe you did know the material but you made careless mistakes.

Finally, something in this category may indicate a fundamental weakness. Is the material something you already studied or something you should know? Return to it. Have you not studied it yet? Time to start. Is the material commonly or rarely tested? Prioritize the commonly tested material first. As needed, return to the relevant sections of your Strategy Guides.

Group 3: You got these wrong way too quickly (more than 30 seconds faster than expected).

Are these really weaknesses or were you just going too fast (and making more careless mistakes)? Why were you going too fast on these?

If you chose to rush because you knew you didn't know what to do (in other words, you made a guess and moved on), that's fine. Decide now whether you want to study this area further.

If you chose to rush because you thought it was easy and then you made a careless mistake, remind yourself not to sacrifice a correct answer just to save 30 seconds!

Alternatively, if you sped up because you were worried about time, then you need to fix your timing problems elsewhere in the section.

Group 4: You got these right way too slowly (more than 30 seconds slower than expected).

These are still weaknesses; it doesn't matter that you're getting them right! They're costing you points elsewhere in the section—possibly more points than you earned by getting the too-slow ones right.

Figure out why the timing is higher and how you can do these more efficiently. If the timing is just a little bit too high on one problem of that type, that may be okay—perhaps the problem is extra hard and long. If you're consistently going long, however, then perhaps you struggle to recognize this problem type, struggle to associate this problem type with appropriate and/or efficient solving techniques, or both. Also realize that, sometimes, the "solution" is simply to guess faster and move on. Sometimes, it's better to get something wrong in two minutes than right in four minutes.

Don't forget to make sure that you really did know what you were doing on the ones you got right; if you got lucky, then move questions from this group to group 5.

9

Group 5: I get these wrong way too slowly (more than 30 seconds slower than expected).

These are the biggest weaknesses, obviously. Get them wrong faster! Seriously—you're getting them wrong anyway, so start by just taking less time to get them wrong! Use that time on questions from one of the other groups, where additional time is more likely to make a difference.

What is slowing you down? Figuring that out will tell you what to do next. You may need to review the material from your books, do more practice with problems of this type, find more efficient ways to solve, learn better how to recognize questions of this type, or more quickly make an educated guess and move on.

For all of the above, don't forget to think about the frequency with which the material is tested. If something is a great weakness of yours but is not frequently tested, then make that a lower priority than something that is a medium weakness but is really tested a lot. (If you're not sure what is more or less frequently tested, get onto the forums and ask.)

Takeaways

(1) It's critically important to evaluate your performance across all three main axes at once—percentage correct, timing, and difficulty. It's not enough to look only at percentage correct. A timing weakness is as much of a problem as an accuracy problem—perhaps more. If your timing is bad enough, it can kill your accuracy.

(2) Split out the data into the 5 major groups described above. Groups 2, 3, and 4 typically represent your biggest opportunities to improve (though that doesn't mean you should ignore groups 1 and 5).

(3) Use the forums! When you discover certain weaknesses, present the data on the forums and ask instructors for their advice about how to remedy those weaknesses. Post specific problems, discuss what you did, and ask for advice about how to solve (or how to solve more efficiently), how to guess more effectively, or whatever is relevant for you.

9

> **TIP**
> For advice on how to improve your identified weaknesses, refer to Chapters 6 and 7.

Student Sound-Offs

The "generate assessment report" tool on the MGMAT website: I think that this tool is brilliant. Once you start scoring above a certain level, you will notice that your performance has reached a "plateau" and then you can score higher only if you can pinpoint your weaknesses and eliminate them one by one. The "assessment report" is a nifty little tool from MGMAT that helped me find out topics or question types where I was "wrong" as well as "slow." I would then take the *Official Guide* and work on questions from that area and try to do better the next time.

> *Anoop*
> *760 (Q49, V44)*

Initially, I used to think that my SC was weak but then I realized looking at the score report that the average difficulty of questions I got wrong was less for CR & RC and then focused on CR & RC. Also the categorization of every question by level of difficulty let me know where I was lacking.

The most important point about GMAT is that if you are not getting 600–700-level questions right, you'll not reach the 700–800 level, hence, there is no use in practicing the toughest questions if you are not getting the easier questions right.

> *Abhishek*
> *730 (Q50, V38)*

I can suggest several things for review based on my experience.

1. For math, study the questions that you got wrong and questions you got right but were not exactly sure about. Make sure you can answer the questions correctly after reviewing them and can also answer similar questions. It's especially easy to modify a Combinatorics problem yourself and see whether you can solve it. For Data Sufficiency questions, definitely make sure you know what general topic is being tested and what "trick" the authors used to make a particular question more difficult. The GMAT guides have whole chapters on paraphrasing DS questions but I didn't really read them because I was already good at math.

I did, however, have to come back to the GMAT math study guides to review certain topics and redo some of the end of chapter exercises. When I was working on the exercises I had done before, I only picked the ones that seemed difficult on first read so the review was pretty subjective.

Also, official GMAT prep software has an excellent review of math concepts–I did not know about it at first, but it's very thorough.

2. Most importantly for me, Verbal was the problem. I had the most trouble with Sentence Correction and with Critical Reasoning. I had trouble with Critical Reasoning not because I was somehow dumber than I am now, but because I didn't realize how subtle each question is. In some of the questions, one word, even one article ("a" vs. "'the"), can make an answer choice wrong.

9

Once again, I would suggest studying all the incorrectly answered questions from the practice exams. Make sure that you know what type of question each question is, strengthen/weaken conclusion, etc. Then re-read the relevant chapters in the GMAT guides, making any notes that would help you answer those particular questions correctly next time.

For Sentence Correction, which was the hardest portion of the exam for me, I reviewed each question I got wrong and made my own notes under each relevant topic: idioms, subject/verb agreement, parallelism, etc. I also made my own list of idioms based on SC guide's list and any other idioms I wasn't sure about from practice exams. I suggest being very honest with yourself here and writing down any less familiar idioms even if you got the corresponding practice questions right.

In some cases, the preparation was fairly easy. For example, I was making mistakes on "if" vs. "whether" usage, so I just looked in the guide and made sure I understood what's going on. Occasionally, the SC guide's explanation was not good enough and I "googled" the web for additional explanations of a particular topic, but one has to be careful using the internet because there is a lot of questionable information out there.

For Verbal, the official GMAT prep software and the OG/Verbal guides do have some review of Verbal concepts. Although the reviews are insufficient, they are the best, so make sure to read them.

At the end of my preparation, I knew most of the rules but was still not applying them efficiently, so I practiced as much as I could and was finally able to recognize the question types almost immediately. I also found that on some very hard questions, I got lost because I was looking for mistakes that weren't there. Eventually I was able to trust my instincts without making up nonexistent mistakes, but it took a lot of practice using the Verbal OG guide and the GMAT Verbal forum. Of course, it helps that I've lived in the U.S. for 15 years.

Timur
770 (Q50, V47)

Chapter Takeaways

1.   Don't be unduly alarmed if your second CAT goes down. Complete a thorough review to identify your weaknesses along content, problem solving process, and time management axes. Then, work to correct them.

2.   Focus your attention most on your weak areas that frequently come into play on the test. Don't forget that problem-solving process and time management are relevant to *every* problem.

Chapter 10 *of*

Managing Test Stress

In This Chapter...

Chapter 10:

Managing Test Stress

Dear Jen,

I know it's class 8 and we have a practice test assigned for next week, but I just don't feel ready. I'd like to wait longer and study more.

Waiting in Washington

Note: Many students are crippled by perfectionism and are afraid to take practice tests or otherwise dive in. This question was from a student in our 9-week course. She had done all of the homework, attended all of the classes, and often volunteered correct answers and insightful explanations. She puts very high demands on herself.

Dear Waiting,

I think I know what's happening here. You really don't want to even take a practice test unless you're sure the score will be good. But you've been studying diligently for two entire months since your last practice exam! It's definitely time for another one. I'm sure you'll see the test differently now. However, I think you're right about one thing—your score won't be pleasant this time around. And that's okay. Many people take a second CAT and fail to see a score increase because they've learned a lot of new skills, but they haven't really learned to execute those skills fast enough yet.

How do you get faster? Practice, practice, practice. That includes timed problems from the *Official Guide* and also—you guessed it—taking CATs.

After many years of perfectionism in school and in college, it can be hard to let go for something like the GMAT, where nearly everyone misses nearly half of the problems. So, here is an assignment: you are going to take a CAT, and there are goals I want you to achieve by doing the CAT, but those goals are not related to the score. Your goals for this CAT are:

- To get more comfortable taking CAT exams.
- To try out the strategies you've learned so far under pressure.
- To keep an eye on the clock and not fall behind.
- To go over the exam afterwards and learn as much as possible by reviewing missed problems and becoming more efficient at the problems that were correct.

Are those achievable goals for your next exam? Of course they are—they don't depend on luck, but on hard work.

Feel free to devise your own goals for future practice exams and even for the real test. It is not helpful to go into the exam thinking "700, 700, 700" in your head. Instead, think: "My goals are to keep an eye on the clock and not fall behind, to quickly recognize problems that fall into certain categories where I can apply strategies I am good at executing, and, when that doesn't happen, not to get too hung up on any one problem."

When I start a section on the real GMAT, I don't think about the score; I think: "I am going to nail 37 math problems!" or "I am going to destroy 41 Verbal problems!"

For now, your goals can be smaller than that. It's totally okay to have intermediate goals related to the test-taking process.

Jennifer Dziura, MGMAT Instructor, New York

What Is Anxiety, Anyway?

Managing stress is something we talk about with *many* of our students. It makes sense to feel somewhat anxious about the GMAT, and that in and of itself is not a bad thing. It would be weird not to feel anxious. Your goal should simply be to prevent that anxiety from taking control.

Adaptive exams can be particularly stressful because you may not be accustomed to adaptive test taking. It can feel awful to be repeatedly faced with hard questions; your training tells you that you must not have really learned the content and that you're doing poorly.

Physiologically, anxiety is excessively heightened arousal. Most students don't have trouble getting to the aroused-enough-to-not-fall-asleep-during-the-test level. However, many students' arousal levels get too high, which gets in the way of their performance.

How Does Stress Affect Performance on the GMAT?

To see the relationship more clearly, consider the extremes:

- **Let's say that you're super-relaxed.** Well, if you're *too* relaxed, you won't maintain concentration throughout the entire test. You might take your time throughout, maybe too much time. Note: Being too relaxed is *not* a problem for most GMAT test-takers!

- **What if you're very stressed?** If you have too much stress, then you might become anxious over time constraints, and rush to finish problems. Your concentration will not be properly focused on the questions at hand, and your accuracy will suffer.

- **There is a point where you're focused but not too stressed.** This is ideal!

So, in Goldilocks terms, the relationship would look something like this:

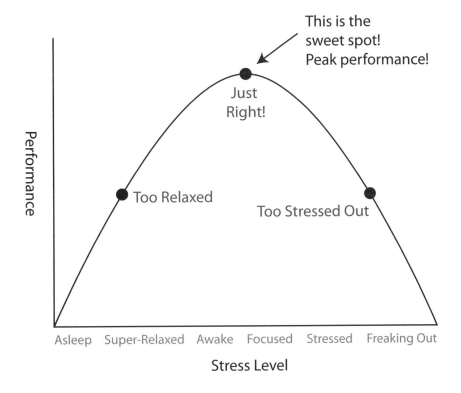

The "just right" level of arousal differs based on the difficulty of the task. When faced with a task perceived as easy, you are most effective with a relatively higher level of arousal. Alternatively, when faced with a task that you find hard, you'll do your best with a relatively lower level of arousal.

This means that you need to be especially careful when working on simpler problems (do the work cleanly, and double-check), and you need to calm yourself down on the most complex problems, to puzzle them out. This is often the opposite of your instinctual urges. Learning to listen to your brain instead of to your urges adds to the mental challenge of the GMAT.

10

How Do You Know If Stress Might Be a Factor in Your Performance?

Anxiety affects many of us. In fact, stress may be the largest factor in explaining the difference between expected and actual performance on test day. Sometimes, test-takers who have prepared are more stressed than those who have not because they have higher expectations of their performance. You create the stress with your expectations.

You may know explicitly that you're experiencing anxiety. Or you may be experiencing mental blanking or insomnia, which could be symptoms stemming from anxiety. It doesn't have to manifest obviously.

Why Does Stress Affect Our Performance?

To understand why stress affects performance, you need to understand something about how memory works. In order to perform complex tasks that involve comprehension and reasoning, such as solving GMAT problems, you need the capacity to actively hold information in your mind. This capacity is called working memory. *Working memory stores what you are thinking about.* For example, it will store a sentence's subject, so that you can link that subject up with the appropriate verb. You can think of it as a scratch pad or the "RAM" on a computer. The really interesting thing is that working memory capacity is actually surprisingly small; cognitive psychologists and neuroscientists agree that most people can hold no more than seven items, plus or minus two, in their working memory at any given time.

Now, when you are stressed, your working memory capacity shrinks, so you can hold less active information in your mind and you become a much slower thinker, like a computer that struggles because it simply does not have enough RAM. To make matters worse, working memory capacity is very closely linked to the ability to pay attention to the information that is relevant and ignore other information, such as distracting thoughts about not doing well on the test, so you also lose the ability to focus on the limited amount of information that you can still hold on to. The overall result is that, under acute stress, you tend to choke and lose the ability to perform to your full potential.

To learn more about choking, check out either Sian Beilock's book *Choke: What the Secrets of the Brain Reveal about Getting It Right When You Have To* or Malcolm Gladwell's article "The Art of Failure," available on www.gladwell.com.

So What Should You Do If You suffer from Working Memory–Killing Test Stress?

There are two fundamental approaches to minimizing the effects of stress on your testing:

1.   Minimize the test stress
2.   Minimize the effects of test stress on your performance

Minimizing Test Stress

The instructor articles in this chapter address how to get test stress under control. Instructor Jon Schneider discusses techniques you can work on by yourself to reduce your stress. Instructor Jamie Nelson discusses medical options for cases when you cannot contain the stress by yourself. You have to decide: is your stress manageable to a point where you are able to reduce your stress independently, or has your stress become uncontrollable and reached a level where it makes sense to seek professional advice?

Minimizing the Effects of Test Stress on Your Performance

A key to reducing the likelihood of choking is to attain true "expert" status. As you become expert at manipulating a certain type of data, you learn to "chunk" it, so that although you are still only thinking about a few things, each one has more meaning. For example, a young child just learning to read might "chunk" squiggles on a page into letters and, with effort, sound out words, whereas an older child might "chunk" the same squiggles into whole words without having to consciously think about individual letters. So even if an expert's working memory capacity is diminished by stress, it still holds more than a novice's does because each "chunk" of information is bigger.

Experts typically also have both explicit step-by-step process knowledge and rich mental databases of previous similar cases, so if high-level analysis fails due to diminished working memory capacity, they can fall back on step-by-step solving and lower-level thinking to keep going. More recently acquired cognitive skills are usually more vulnerable to stress than practiced ones, so the ability to solve a math problem with a clever trick because you recognize a pattern is likely to be more vulnerable to stress than the ability to write down variables and work step-by-step through algebra the way you did in high school.

Using step-by-step reasoning alone is slower than combining it with high-level pattern recognition, but at least it lets you keep going. Don't forget that *anxiety is excessive arousal*. If you have the scaffold of step-by-step thinking to fall back on, part of your brain (at least) starts working on the problem. That takes some of your focus off of thinking about being anxious, reducing the arousal, and allowing you to relax enough to use your working memory again. It starts a positive test stress recovery spiral!

So what do we recommend for anxious students? Train, train, train! How do you do this on the GMAT? We recommend flash cards. Creating flash cards forces you to think through the step-by-step approach to a problem. In addition, flash cards enable the kind of repeated practice that helps you move your knowledge to your long-term memory, which is less vulnerable to stress than working memory but takes a lot of effort to build.

A complementary technique is to work on your time management. Anxiety and certainty are inversely related: the highest level of stress usually occurs at the start of a new GMAT problem. You start a problem with uncertainty—all the methods for that section (math or Verbal) are open to you. As you read the problem, you winnow out large numbers of methods. Finally, when you've successfully recognized the problem and decided on the best method, your certainty level has risen, causing your anxiety level to fall. If you can decrease the time that you spend feeling uncertain, your anxiety level will decrease

10

as well. Using flash cards can help speed up your recognition process. In addition, learn to make use of answer choice elimination strategies. Eliminating answer choices along the way increases the certainty level for remaining answer choices, thus reducing stress. Finally, learn to be comfortable using "free-bies": if you look at a problem and quickly realize (in less than a minute) that you will be unable to suc-cessfully even narrow down answer choices within the per-problem time guidelines, you should guess and move on. It is very possible to use multiple freebies per section (Quant and Verbal) and still earn a 700+ score on the GMAT. Just make sure that your freebies are well spaced out.

Self-Help for Test Anxiety
– Jon Schneider

Test anxiety is real. Not everyone experiences test anxiety, but most people do, to some extent. But what is test anxiety exactly, and what can you do to overcome it?

In order to beat test anxiety, we first must understand it. It turns out that test anxiety is a form of social anxiety: we fear being evaluated. This fear causes us to think more about being evaluated than about the test itself. We start to worry about what people will think if we get a low test score, or worse, what we will think of ourselves. We remember times when we performed poorly on tests in the past, and we begin to think that we are almost guaranteed to fail. This pattern of thought becomes so overwhelm-ing that it can become self-fulfilling: if we can't concentrate on the actual test, we probably *will* fail.

The GMAT is particularly tough on test anxiety. Even if you never experienced test anxiety in school, you may face it here. This is because, as an adaptive exam, the GMAT regularly gives you questions that you don't know how to answer quickly.

Fortunately, you can overcome test anxiety. There is a significant amount of psychol-ogy research that says so, and I've seen it myself with lots of my students. Now, the "cure" for test anxiety isn't easy—it requires practice—but it is available. I'll do my best to describe it here.

First, let's come back to the point that the GMAT is particularly tough on the nerves. This is true regardless of your ability level. If you're a very strong quant person, you're going to be mostly getting high-level Quant questions, many of which will be too hard for you to crack in two minutes. If you are used to doing well on math tests, this may feel very nerve-racking.

Think back to your years in school. How many tests have you taken in your life? If you're like me, the number may be in the hundreds, perhaps even over a thousand. Now ask yourself: how many of those tests were adaptive? Probably very few, maybe even none. Most likely, the tests that you took in school were paper tests, and the way to get a top score was to get as many questions right as possible. If you couldn't answer the questions on a paper test, your score would drop. So it's reasonable to presume that we all have a learned reaction to getting stuff wrong: it makes us worry. So what if the GMAT causes you to feel this on almost every other question? Well, now it's likely that you'll worry a lot!

But here's the good news: getting stuff wrong is just part of the GMAT. It doesn't mean that you're doing poorly. You know that old quote that "the only thing to fear is fear itself"? Well, that applies here. If you feel that you're unable to answer a question, don't worry! That's just part of the test. And if a negative voice pops up in your head and tells you to start worrying, that you're doing poorly, that you're going to fail, etc., just smile and know that that voice is there because it learned to be there… on paper tests. The voice doesn't know that you're taking an adaptive test. It only knows that the test feels hard. So don't worry. Let the voice go, and continue smiling as you move to the next question.

OK, so a bit more about test anxiety. Basically, it has two components: physiological and cognitive. The physiological part is easier to notice. When we feel stressed, our heart rate increases. We sweat. We hold our breath, and this spikes our adrenaline levels so that we feel even more stressed. This is all a good thing, in a way, but it's really more effective if you're in immediate danger. If a rabid dog is chasing you, your body needs a way to kick into overdrive, releasing a huge surge of adrenaline. But such increased physical stress can spiral and affect thought processes. Cognitively, things are a bit more complex. The heightened physical response limits our mental flexibility, making it tough to really sit with and break apart a difficult question; we are more likely to see one thing and either try that approach immediately or else stare, frozen, at the screen. The other cognitive aspect of test anxiety is often called "negative self-talk." This basically means that we start to have a negative inner voice, saying things like "I'm failing this right now," "I can't do this," "I'm going to run out of time," etc. Such negative thoughts also spiral, and they interrupt our cognition, so that we cannot use our mental powers for the task at hand.

So, let's be honest: test anxiety is a tough thing to overcome! But, at the same time, it's not…

A lot of psychological research (mostly done at U.S. universities in the '70s and '80s) shows that test anxiety can be overcome. Personally, I'm amazed that this stuff is not taught regularly in schools. I had to find it by digging through a lot of old articles on the subject.

Basically, you have two lines of defense against test anxiety: relaxation techniques to combat physiological symptoms, and the use of "positive self-talk" to combat negative self-talk. The simplest, and most effective, relaxation technique is deep breathing. Try it, right now. Sit up straight, shut your eyes for a second, and take a deep breath. Deep

10

breathing adds oxygen to the blood stream. Remember how we said that holding your breath spikes adrenaline levels? Well, deep breathing does the opposite—it relaxes you. The thing is, most people actually don't know this, or they've heard it but don't know the effectiveness of simply taking a deep breath. But deep breathing works. Now, you can't sit in the test center with your eyes closed the whole time and expect to get a good score on the test. But you can take a deep breath whenever you start to feel physically tight or anxious.

As for "positive self-talk," it works like this: when negative voices start to pop up (or even before they do), counteract them with positive ones. If your negative inner voice says "You're not prepared; you're going to fail," hear the voice but let it go. Then say to yourself something like, "I can do this test; I'm prepared and I can balance my timing." The effect is to get yourself back into game mode, so that you can focus on the actual problem before you, rather than on a cycle of self-doubt.

Admittedly, both of the above tools sound pretty New Age-y. But that doesn't mean they don't work. In fact, with practice, they work quite well. One major study showed that, after six one-hour sessions practicing the above skills, a group of incoming college freshmen showed significant and lasting improvement on tests versus control groups. In fact, by senior year, the group that had undergone this training had a significantly higher average GPA. Think about that. Six one-hour sessions. That's not that much practice for a set of tools that can help you for years.

But how do you practice? Well, the first thing is that you can actually practice this stuff anywhere. I live in New York City, and I can tell you that I use the above skills daily. Crowded sidewalks, missed subways, slow elevators—there are lots of mini stresses that we all face during an average day. And it is in just these instances that I try to take a deep breath and monitor my inner voice, to make sure that I am not giving too much credence to negative self-talk.

For starters, you may need to actually sit and gain more awareness of your breath and inner voice. Don't worry if you've never done this stuff before. It's pretty simple. Just sit somewhere comfortable and quiet, and take slow deep breaths. At first, just work on taking deep, even breaths; then, as you gain comfort with this, pay attention to your inner voice. Try saying positive things to yourself. Not fantastic things ("I'm going to win the lottery tomorrow") but things you can believe in (start with "I can overcome test anxiety"). Continue to practice this until you feel that you can turn these skills on in the moment, whenever you need them. It may help to begin each study session with 5–10 minutes of this practice.

The long-term goal is to be able to counteract the symptoms of test anxiety as soon as they come up. That is, as soon as you start to feel tightness in your chest or find yourself holding your breath, you'll take a deep breath. And when you start hearing that negative inner voice pop up, you'll smile and let it go or counteract it with a positive

10

voice. This takes practice (you need to get to the point where you can use these skills without focusing on them 100% of the time), but it's very, very doable, and it's easier than you might think.

Finally, a couple of quick tips for additional ways to overcome test anxiety. First, don't tell anyone your test date. If no one knows that you're taking the GMAT, then you don't have to tell anyone how it went, so no one will be checking in on your score. If it goes well, call people up to tell them the good news! If not, no worries; fortunately, you can retake this test! Second, make sure that you don't study too hard in the final week. You need to be mentally fresh on test day. I normally tell my students to eat a healthy meal and watch guilty-pleasure movies the night before the test.

Happy test-taking!

> Dear Jen,
>
> I suffer from terrible test anxiety. I'm miserable. I just hate standardized tests, and I've never performed well under pressure. My anxiety is really holding me back. Help!
>
> *Anxious in Albuquerque*

Dear Anxious,

I have three suggestions that you might enjoy.

First, realize that everyone on the GMAT, even top scorers, misses nearly half of his or her problems. Imagine that you're back in college taking an exam—whatever kind you did well on—but now, 60% correct is an awesome score! Really imagine that. The GMAT is a bit like that. Of course your overall score on a CAT is not based on what percent you get correct but on what score level you're functioning at for most of the test. Still, the idea that you're simply going to miss a lot of problems and that it's just fine is a very important one to come to terms with. Adjust your feelings.

Second, don't go into the test thinking about extrinsic (outside) motivators such as: your overall score, business school, or your future career with an MBA. Ignore all that. Olympic athletes are in the moment. They are thinking about the performance, not about the parade their hometown will throw for them if they win. You are about to do 37 math problems and 41 Verbal problems. That's it. You are going to play 78 little contests today! Don't let your thoughts wander from that.

Finally—and this is my favorite tip—there have to be parts of this that you enjoy (at least relative to other parts—work with me here). When you open the *Official Guide* to do a practice set, I'll bet sometimes you don't start with the very first problem you see—instead, you sort of skip over a few problems to start with one that seems more… attractive? What's attractive about it? It's short? It has a diagram? It's just numbers, not a word problem? It's a Critical Reasoning or Reading Comprehsnsion problem about a topic that's actually kind of interesting? Make a little list of things you enjoy about GMAT problems.

For instance, I *love* when I'm doing a problem with a bunch of fractions and then they all just cancel out perfectly and I get a really simple answer! I also love canceling out factorials—once you expand the top and bottom, you can cross out practically every-thing. So cool. And I love when a Sentence Correction problem has a really obvious split right in the first word of each answer choice—oh, so I can get rid of two or three of the answers right away just by deciding whether the subject of the sentence goes with "differ" or "differs." Thanks, GMAT!

Make your own list, and talk yourself up before practice tests and the real test: I can't wait to cancel some fractions! Oh, I hope they give me some rates to put into a Rate, Time, and Distance chart! I wonder what I'll get to read about in Reading Comp today! Exciting!

It's hard to feel too much anxiety about something you're really looking forward to!

Jennifer Dziura, MGMAT Instructor, New York

 Student Sound-Off

For me, one of my biggest problems is psyching myself out. I've had friends and family both say, "You know this is your biggest enemy, so just don't let it get the best of you." Right, like if I say, "Okay heart, stop beating so fast" it will miraculously obey. But find out what works for you. For me, it was the reminder that even if I didn't do well, I still had other options.

I think what really helped was my approach to studying, which was a lot less intense this go-around. When I was studying for the GMAT the first time, I felt like every free moment needed to be devoted to studying and felt guilty otherwise. This time I studied, but I still went out and partied, still did my hobbies, still went on Saturday morning runs. Mentally I placed a lot less emphasis on the test—I went in more with an attitude of "just try again and see what happens, it's not the end of the world." During this time I also got a new job that I like a lot more than my old one, so I felt like even if I didn't do well, I still had a lot of other options. Don't get me wrong, I was still nervous that morning.

Hope this helps. Now, onto burning my flash cards....

Annie
740

10

Professional Help for Test Anxiety
— Jamie Nelson

One of the aspects I love most about teaching the GMAT is celebrating the success of my students. There is nothing more wonderful than receiving word that a student has attained a score he or she is pleased with, and then getting a later message that the student has been admitted to a desired business school and will be enrolling soon.

On the other hand, one of the most difficult and frustrating situations for instructors and students alike occurs when a student should be able to achieve a great score, yet, for whatever reason, appears unable to do so. It's such a terrible blow to students to have consistent diagnostic scores in the target range, yet take the actual test and perform much worse. However, a thorough investigation of the reasons for this underperformance may yield a surprising cause and provide hope for resolution and a better outcome on a future test.

I recently worked with a student I'll call Kim (not her real name, but she gave me her blessing to tell her story as she wants to help other students). Kim is a wonderful person and student; she's bright, motivated, diligent, and organized. A graduate of an outstanding university, Kim holds a business position of great responsibility, speaks four languages, and devotes herself to considerable community and charitable activities. A top business school should regard Kim as a highly desirable candidate.

Kim's only possible hindrance to admission was her GMAT score; she had scored a 620 on the official test. Kim knew that her odds would improve if she could raise her score, so she decided to start private tutoring. We were paired together and Kim told me that her goal score was 700. After examining her diagnostic tests, I believed that Kim had a good chance to hit this goal, and we began tutoring in October.

Kim worked hard and in late November she scored a 700 on a diagnostic test. We were happy with this but decided to keep working to ensure that she could hit this score on a regular basis. After Kim took three more diagnostics and attained scores of 720, 740, and 740, we felt very confident that she was ready for prime time. She took the actual GMAT in February, and I waited eagerly to receive her text with the good news.

However, the news was not so good. Kim scored a 640 on the actual GMAT and was crushed. She had worked so long, so hard, yet had scored 100 points below her most recent diagnostic taken only two weeks earlier. What went wrong? How could this happen?

Kim and I talked about the test and the problem quickly became clear. Kim told me that after hitting a bad patch of questions in the Quant section she began to panic.

She started thinking that she could not recover from these questions, that she would not do well on the test, that she would never get into business school, and that her life was pretty much over. Understandably, these thoughts led her to be quite rattled on Verbal, causing serious timing issues, and she never felt that she was in a groove. Kim went on to say that she had been unable to sleep for two nights before the test as well as unable to eat the morning of the test. Furthermore, this was a long-standing pattern throughout her life: whenever she would have to take an important exam, she would feel overwhelmed with anxiety and thoughts of failure.

Bingo! We now knew what was going on. Kim is a classic case of a student suffering from test anxiety, which can range from mild to severe. A mild case can consist of a few "butterflies" before the test and have very little impact on a student's performance, but an extreme manifestation can completely derail the student's ability to perform.

Test anxiety symptoms are varied and can include physical signs such as dry mouth, sweating, shaking, rapid heartbeat, nausea, vomiting, and fainting. Psychological symptoms can include the experience of "blanking out"; students often tell me that they sat down to take the test and were so overwhelmed with anxiety that their minds went blank and they could not remember anything. Other students suffer such symptoms as racing thoughts, negative self-talk, and a process called "catastrophizing," which Kim experienced when she went from hitting a tough patch of questions to believing that her life was ruined. Obviously, it's pretty tough to concentrate after thinking that! At the most extreme end, a student with severe anxiety can experience panic attacks before or during the test.

Over time, a student suffering from severe test anxiety can experience depression and hopelessness. There seems to be no way to resolve the situation, and many students eventually give up on the test and their dreams of business school.

If this sounds painfully familiar, take heart! There are tremendous resources available to help you with this problem, and you should not give up until you have explored them. These options are not only effective but also tend to be cost-efficient and work relatively quickly.

The most proven method of treating test anxiety is cognitive-behavioral therapy. This therapy helps ease anxiety symptoms through a variety of methods. The therapist teaches the student to recognize the physiological symptoms of anxiety as well as relaxation techniques such as visualization or breathing exercises to allay these symptoms. The student practices thinking stress-inducing thoughts and then monitoring and controlling the physical response.

The therapist also works with the student to recognize dysfunctional thought patterns and replace them with more helpful thoughts. For example, rather than entertain the thought that "if I don't get a 700 today, I'll never get into business school," the thera-

10

pist teaches the student to substitute more realistic, helpful thoughts such as "if things don't go my way today I can always take the test again."

Several of my students have worked with cognitive-behavioral therapists and seen substantial improvements. This process typically requires four to six weekly sessions which tend to cost around $100–$150 each. Many therapists now use Skype and other technologies to connect with students in all locations; a student of mine on another continent recently worked with a therapist in my hometown of Houston over Skype and after four sessions was able to finally obtain his target score.

My student, Kim, had already tried cognitive-behavioral therapy for other issues in her life and wanted to try something different. In her case, I suggested that she try hypno-therapy.

To be clear, hypnotherapy is NOT what you see on television, in which people are "hypnotized" by watching a swinging pendulum and then believe that they are ballet dancers or NFL quarterbacks. Rather, hypnotherapy involves teaching people to enter a state of very deep relaxation during which suggestions are made to the subcon-scious mind. The individual is never fully "out" but is more receptive to suggestions and thoughts that will serve him or her well in test conditions. Hypnotherapy is well established for the treatment of smoking cessation, weight loss, and anxiety, and several hypnotherapists have undergone additional training for test anxiety.

Similar to cognitive-behavioral therapy, hypnotherapy typically requires about four to six sessions and has a similar cost. Between sessions, the student is asked to listen to a CD each day that contains a recording of the hypnotherapy session. Through this, the student not only practices relaxation but also continues to internalize the positive messages.

Kim had experienced so much trouble sleeping that we investigated a very light sleep-ing pill for her to take the few nights before the test. Kim spoke to her physician and obtained a prescription for a sleeping pill that would not impair her performance upon waking. She practiced taking this pill and then completing a diagnostic the next morn-ing to ensure that there was no "hangover" effect.

Finally, I asked Kim to do her best to eat a protein bar the morning of the test, and to take water and nutritious snacks such as nuts and yogurt to eat during the breaks. Kim agreed to do this and after a month of working with the therapist (while continuing to review her GMAT content about eight hours a week), she felt ready to attempt the GMAT again.

Approximately six weeks after she obtained the disappointing score, Kim headed back to the GMAT test center. She was rested and well nourished, and, most importantly,

10

was now in a relaxed state. The negative thoughts and feelings were mostly gone, and the few that popped up were like pesky flies that she could easily swat away.

Four hours later I received the text—Kim had scored a 720! She was thrilled and ready to move on to the school selection and application process.

Kim and many of my prior students have conquered test anxiety by seeking very short-term, focused help. If you relate to Kim's story and believe that test anxiety is holding you back from your best performance, please consider looking into these resources. Good sources for finding therapists include your state's chapter of the American Psychological Association (www.apa.org) and the National Guild of Hypnotists (www.ngh.net). Look for a practitioner with a specialty in anxiety and ask for a brief complimentary consultation to discuss your goals.

Test anxiety can be a discouraging and debilitating problem, but with proper intervention it need have no impact on your GMAT performance. As Kim and others have found, there is tremendous help and hope!

 Student Sound-Off

One often overlooked aspect of the test is test anxiety. A common misconception for dealing with test anxiety is that you simply have to "relax" and "think it away." Unfortunately, this advice simply does not work for people who suffer from extreme forms of anxiety. I am one of those people. The anxiety will come, and instead of going into denial, it is best to prepare for it as best and as honestly as you can.

I suffer from such extreme test anxiety, which is exacerbated by my demanding work schedule. It got to the point where I had panic attacks during practice tests and eventually had to seek professional help for treatment. It was probably the best thing I've ever done for myself. I have been on anti-anxiety medicine for the past 2 months and the medication has helped immensely to help calm me down so I can perform to my true ability. It was a very trying time for me and my family—I was ready to take the test months ago but I did not know how to get over the anxiety hump.

My advice is that if you are one of those people who suffer from extreme anxiety, it is perfectly fine to seek medical help to alleviate your nerves—there is absolutely nothing wrong with that. Clinical depression and test anxiety are very common and it is best to get them properly treated by a professional, if you decide that it would be helpful.

A couple other tricks that helped me to deal with anxiety outside of medication:

10

1. Give up, a lot. Get used to getting A LOT of questions wrong. This is part of the test. For me, I decided to give myself 3 "free passes" that are just throw-aways. No strategic guessing… no estimation… just pure pick an answer and go. This allows me to catch up when I am behind and focus my energy on questions that I know I can get right.

2. Redirect / relabel the anxiety. The anxiety will come, and you have to expect it. When it comes, try to harness it as an extra boost to your performance. Thats what professional athletes do… they also feel anxiety, but the great ones are able to get into a "zone." Try to envision yourself taking the test as much as you can… and get your body to start producing that adrenaline rush. Keep practicing this and once the test comes, you will not let the adrenaline rush overtake you.

3. Look away (if you have to). If you find yourself just spazzing out… just stop for 30 seconds. Use one of your free passes. Close your eyes, take deep breaths, then tackle the test again. I had to do this twice during the test and it worked wonders. It's better to do this and throw away some of the test rather than plowing forward and feeling worse as you go.

4. Overload yourself with happy thoughts. The test sucks—there is no other way to look at it. It's a stressful, hard, and demanding test. One thing I found helpful is to overload your memory with happy thoughts. When the adrenaline rush becomes too much to bear, overload your thoughts with happy memories (e.g., things that you are looking forward to doing after the test is over). This gives you the courage and the motivation to get through a 4-hour test.

5. Be prepared. The best way to alleviate test anxiety is to prepare, prepare, and prepare some more. There are no shortcuts to doing well on the test—you must know your content. Follow the MGMAT curriculum religiously and you will get the content down if you put in the time. Of course, be within reason—know when you hit a diminishing return on your studies. Go into the test feeling that you are going to ace it, and you will increase the probability that you will end up doing well.

6. It's just practice. No one wants to take the test more than they have to… but you should find relief that the option is there. If this is the first time you are taking the test… just pretend it's a dress rehearsal. You are simply there to check out what it's like to take the real thing without any investment put into the result. If you do well, superb, you won the lottery. If not, no biggie the second try will be your real try. I find that this mentally really helped me relax during the exam.

James
750 (Q49, V44)

10

Dear Jen,

I understand everything in the Strategy Guides and all of the *Official Guide* problems, but when I take a practice test, I get just one problem I can't do, and it freaks me out and messes me up for the whole test.

Phreaking Out in Philly

This question was from a private tutoring student who could do nearly any problem during tutoring sessions, but couldn't seem to put it all together when taking the CAT. His tutor felt that he should easily be scoring around 700, yet he took the real GMAT and scored 470, all due to anxiety and poor emotional management. (He ultimately retook the test and got a 700). Keep in mind that this advice does not apply to most students, only those who have mastered nearly the entire Official Guide.

Dear Phreaking Out,

Ah, yes, welcome to the joys of computer-adaptive testing.

I'm going to answer this question with a metaphor. Imagine that you're climbing a mountain, and at the top of the mountain is a temple containing an 800. Outside the temple is an old man whose job it is to keep people away from that 800. Now imagine that you're not only climbing a mountain, but doing so wearing a blindfold—you don't know how high up you are.

So, when you feel like you're doing pretty well and then you get hit with something really, really hard, don't feel bad, and don't freak out. There's a really good chance that you don't need that problem to succeed. What might be happening is that you're over the 700 mark—say you're at 730. And then you try to climb a little higher and the old man smacks you with a rock. That's him telling you that you can't have an 800. That's okay. You're back exactly where you need to be! Cool. And yet this keeps going on—you're at 700 something, you try to climb a little higher, the man on the mountain smacks you back down to 700 something. If you're going to walk out of the GMAT with a 700 something score, what I'm describing is what's going to happen for basically the entire length of the test.

10

A person who leaves the GMAT with a totally awesome 740 score is someone who spent half the test failing at 750- and 760-level problems. That's why he has a 740. It might feel weird while it's happening, but that's the reality of the CAT. Get used to it.

So, next time you get an impossible-seeming question, say to yourself, "Ha! That's nice, old man on the mountain—I don't need your 800. I'll give this a two-minute try, and if it doesn't work out, that's cool—I'm just fine sitting right here on my 700-something." And then, if you can't get it in two minutes, make an intelligent guess and move on. Top scorers do this all the time. It's not failure. It's necessary.

Jennifer Dziura, MGMAT Instructor, New York

Chapter Takeaways

1.   Test anxiety is more common—and has more impact on test performance—than you may realize. Most students suffer from it, at least to some degree.

2.   There are two techniques for reducing the impact of test stress on your performance. The first one is to minimize the amount of stress that you experience by using stress reduction techniques. The second one is to become a more robust, expert GMAT problem solver by practicing specific techniques that will allow you to continue solving problems even when your brain is stress impaired.

10

Chapter 11

of

GMAT Roadmap

Approaching Test Day

In This Chapter...

Chapter 11:
Approaching Test Day

You may be reading this when you have a lot of time left before your test day. If this is the case, you should still be in study mode—learning new content, practicing mixed sets, working on your timing, and building your test-taking stamina.

However, if you are reading this with two or fewer weeks left before your GMAT, this is the final stage of your test-taking journey. The time has come to wind down. You are done with learning new content. All you should be doing from here on in is reviewing problems you have solved before in order to remember, internalize, and truly master them. You should be working out those last kinks so that you don't make any preventable computation errors. You need to come to terms with your strengths and weaknesses—at least as they will stand for this test. Your goal at this point is not to increase your ability level, but rather to figure out how to consistently deliver your best performance given your current capabilities. You should be deciding now which difficult problem types are your strengths, so that on test day, you can invest time in them, and quickly move on from difficult problems in your weaker areas.

A week before your exam day, you need to stop taking practice tests. It's too late to reschedule, so go ahead and take the test, even if you decide to think of it as your dress rehearsal. Remember: most business schools only care about your highest score.

On the day of your test, arrive at the test center at least half an hour early. Turn your cell phone off. Your score may be canceled if you use it during a break; it is viewed as potential cheating. Also, be prepared for test center security. It is like going through the airport. Be prepared to have your palm print or finger print taken and to show appropriate and current identification (e.g., driver's license, passport, etc.). Outside of the U.S., call ahead of time to find out what the country you are in considers appropriate identification.

Final Words of Advice
– Abby Pelcyger

I end each of my GMAT courses with these final words of advice:

5. Do NOT waste any of your brain power wondering how you are doing on the test while you are in the midst of the GMAT—save it all for the problem in front of you. Think about it: if you were hiding in a foxhole at war and you saw an enemy soldier approaching you, you would have two options.

One option would be to think to yourself, "Hmmm. He looks like he's wearing ratty clothing. I wonder if this means that we're doing well in this war and guys like this are all they have left to send to attack us… Or… Wait! Oh no! Maybe it means that they think we're a joke and are only sending us their least trained soldiers because they think that even those guys can take us!" What's going to happen while you're having all of these thoughts? Yup, you guessed it: the enemy soldier is going to get you.

Your other option is to see the guy and immediately put all of your concentration into focusing on him and shooting. You win a war by focusing on individual battles one at a time, giving each one your all, and making strategic decisions as necessary. Like-wise, while taking the GMAT, the only thing that you can do at any point in time to improve your score is to give your all to the problem in front of you. Sometimes, giving your all will mean realizing that this is a problem that you cannot correctly answer in the allotted time, and then you need to feel comfortable making a guess and moving on. This is okay; sometimes you lose a battle to win the war. Just make sure that you are in control and choosing an intentional strategy for each question.

4. We have primarily been focused up until this point on how to prepare you for the GMAT intellectually. To do well on the GMAT, though, you must also be prepared physically and emotionally.

I had a GMAT student who scored a 750 on a CAT the week before his official GMAT. He did not listen to my advice about making sure to get on a regular sleep schedule, though. So, the night before the GMAT he found himself unable to fall asleep. What did he do? You guessed it: he drank a couple of night caps. These did not help him fall asleep, quite the opposite. He wound up getting two-and-a-half hours of sleep before his test. So what did he do? Yup, he drank a lot of coffee, something he did not do as a normal part of his routine. He started crashing near the end of his Quant section, but he was prepared. During the break before Verbal he ate a chocolate bar that he had brought and put in his locker specifically to infuse himself with some ad-ditional caffeine. He wound up with a 680. While that's a decent score, it is 70 points lower than his practice test the week before.

11

MANHATTAN
GMAT

The point is that if you do not allow your body to be in top physical shape when it takes the GMAT, your intellectual preparedness will not have the chance to shine. This means, at least a week before the test, start getting used to going to sleep and waking up at the same time each day—a time that will get you up and raring to go with plenty of time on test day. It also means that now is not the time to alter your normal morning routines. If you drink coffee every morning, drink coffee on test day. If you usually do not drink coffee, do not drink coffee on test day. If you smoke cigarettes, now is not the time to stop. Yes, you read right: I'm the only teacher who will ever tell you not to quit smoking—at least not until after your GMAT.

Emotional preparedness is just as important as physical preparedness. I had a student a few years ago who told me that he took the LSAT once, he didn't do well, and so he's not going to law school. He was going to take the GMAT once, and if he didn't do well, that was it, he wasn't going to business school. Now, first off, I don't think that this is a productive attitude to have. Lots of people take the GMAT more than once and get into the b-school of their dreams. Yet, this student insisted that he found taking the test so stressful that he would not put himself through the experience more than once.

Since the student's obstacle appeared to be emotional and not intellectual, I asked the student what made him feel peaceful, what helped him reach that feeling of "zen" or "being in the zone." For me, it's running. For others, it is yoga, reading a good book, or even calling a friend. For this student, it was gardening. So, I assigned him to garden for half an hour before each of his study sessions, and then, again, on the morning of his test. He did so, got a 720, and went off to business school, having conquered his emotional demons and never having to take the GMAT again.

3. Never forget that the GMAT is just a number. Yes, it can keep you from getting into b-school. Single-handedly, though, it cannot get you in. The GMAT is just a number, just a box to get checked off. B-schools are looking for interesting, intelligent, passionate, diverse individuals. One of my best friends scored a 770 on the GMAT after taking an MGMAT class. She did not even get an interview from Harvard or Stanford. (Luckily, she did get into a great school, where she is now thriving.)

2. The GMAT and business school are both means, not ends. On our last night together, I have my students go around and share why they want to go back to business school. It's incredibly inspirational and one of my favorite parts of teaching the GMAT. It's amazing how much more is shared than when I ask the same question on the first night of class. Don't lose sight of where you are trying to go. There are many paths up any mountain. If you are committed to getting there, you will develop the resiliency needed to find a path that will take you there.

1. Having this book in your hands means that you are incredibly lucky. I think it's easy for all of us to get caught up in thinking that the small piece of the world that inter-

11

acts with our lives is all that there is. I know it's easy for me to do. It's simply not true, though. When we take a step back from our own lives to consider all of the people out there and all of their circumstances, it's clear that simply holding this book means (relatively at least) we're all doing incredibly well. I urge you to continue to pursue your dreams of climbing higher up that mountain. I just hope you'll do so remembering to feel blessed and grateful.

Advice for Approaching Test Day

 Student Sound-Offs

I went through many levels of mental and emotional preparation throughout the entire 2+ months. I'm generally a pretty optimistic person, but I also put A LOT of pressure on myself, and I noticed that things really turned around when I reached this certain understanding:

I had been studying so much and had given up everything for this test. I knew that I was doing my ultimate best, and that there was nothing more I could humanly do. I wasn't going to beat myself up over anything because being in the GMAT cave is hard enough. This sudden realization resulted in some major shift and my practice scores started going up (passing the 700 mark), and I began to really get a grip on the problems. I started achieving insane laser focus, and best of all, I just wasn't afraid of the test anymore.

When this happens, you kind of become badass—in a good way. And I believe that this may have been one of the biggest factors that helped me break the 700 barrier.

> Helen
> 750 (Q48/V46)

There are three components that were important for me to achieve the results (from 630 to 730) I wanted on the GMAT:

1. Relearning the Quant content (THANK YOU, ABBY!). Although I work with numbers, relearning the algebraic concepts, shortcuts, and efficient utilization of fractions was crucial for time efficiency.

2. Learning to walk away from certain (700–800) problems in areas that were not my strengths. The epiphany that the huge time cost associated with these types of problems outweighs the gain of answering them correctly was one of the most important and difficult lessons to learn as a "perfectionist."

3. Not "overdoing" it and "psyching" myself out. The test is truly a mental marathon; you have to pace yourself, have confidence in yourself, and train for it appropriately. At first, my obsession in achieving the result led to overtraining by taking too many

practice tests, which then lead to mental fatigue during the test. This is a nasty circular trap to get into, because not only do you need to be fresh for the test, but you also need to be calm enough not to lose it when you hit a hard problem. Sure enough, overtrained as I was, when I inevitably got stuck on a problem, instead of calmly moving on, I "freaked out" about time, my score, etc. The end result was that my heart rate spiked, and I probably blew at least 7 problems just calming down, thereby sabotaging my score!

> *Patrick*
> *730*

Pick a test date! As soon as I got > 700 on a MGMAT test, I scheduled my test for a month from that date. This was truly critical in giving me a "light at the end of the tunnel" for all the weekends I spent in my room studying. I would definitely advise doing this, as I studied much more proactively/efficiently after setting this date.

> *Amanda*
> *730 (49Q, 40V)*

CAT 3 — Overall — 680 (90th Percentile), Q47, V35 — I took this exam at the end of my online class and this score was a huge disappointment to me. I only had two weeks before I was going to take the actual GMAT.

The best advice I can give anyone is to put more faith in your ability than your practice test scores. Despite my CAT 3 score, I stayed calm and stuck to my study plan. I finished up my final study guide the week after class, and spent the remaining week leading up to the actual GMAT reviewing the material and key topics. At this point I wasn't trying to learn anything new. I also decided I wasn't going to take any more practice tests, which would probably have been a huge distraction, especially if I had scored below a 700 again!

> *Jonathan*
> *760 (Q51,V42)*

I decided not to take any more practice tests. That is right. The last practice test that I took was two weeks before the GMAT. Taking a practice test was draining my energy and I couldn't get much done for the rest of the day.

For the final one week, I made sure that I started solving problems everyday exactly at 8am for an hour. I wanted to train my brain for that time of the day. I went to the test center one week before the test to make sure that I was familiar with the driving directions. I checked with the test center to make sure that my name was on the list. I did not want to leave anything to chance.

For the final week, I drastically reduced my study time. You read it right, I reduced, not increased. I made sure that I did not read continuously more than 45 minutes. The thing was, I was getting a little nervous thinking about the exam and could not concentrate. I relaxed as much as I could and got plenty of sleep and watched a lot of YouTube.

11

Speaking of sleep, it is essential that you get a good night of sleep not only before the test day but also for many days leading up to the test. I started going to bed at 10pm and getting up at 6am at least one month before the test to get into a rhythm.

I started reviewing one final time, even the topics that I was feeling good about. I did not learn any new things in this one week, rather, I reviewed all the content that I had studied so far. I reviewed all the notes that I had prepared, and reviewed all the mistakes that I had made so far. I read a few sample AWA essays once in a while to get a feel for what and how to present the ideas.

> *Gova*
> *740 (Q49, V41)*

For Quant this time as well as the last time, I didn't practice permutations/combinations or probability as I was very weak in these topics. So instead of wasting any time, I left them, as my other Quant topics were pretty strong.

> *Abishek*
> *730 (Q50, V38)*

Quant started out on a slightly bumpy note, but I think I kept my cool and managed to complete it on time. Practice making calls on questions. I had 3.5 minutes for the last two questions and the last but one was a paragraph long. I just glanced at it and clicked Next. I was able to comfortably answer the last question with 45 seconds in hand. Conversely, somewhere in the middle of the test I was faced with a screwy Geo problem. I was tempted to click Next, but I ended up solving it after devoting some time. So, knowing your strengths helps you make such calls.

> *Sridhar*
> *720 (Q49, V40)*

Do not put too much pressure on yourself; if something goes wrong, you can always take the test again.

> *Timur*
> *770 (Q50, V47)*

Advice on Snacks

There are two schools of thought on snacks. Some people go in to the test too amped up to eat. Others crash and burn halfway through if they don't eat. Most people can drink something. Know yourself: you have two eight-minutes breaks, one between the essays and the Quantitative section and the other between the Quantitative and Verbal sections. If you're worried about crashing and you can't eat, bring a sports drink or one of those gels that runners use. (After all, it's an intellectual marathon.) Whatever you do, though, make sure to bring water. The test center's water fountain could be broken, or the water could taste terrible! You also may need to get to the bathroom during a break, so be sure to locate it (and possibly use it) before you start the test.

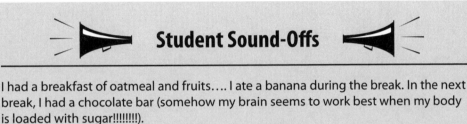

Student Sound-Offs

I had a breakfast of oatmeal and fruits.... I ate a banana during the break. In the next break, I had a chocolate bar (somehow my brain seems to work best when my body is loaded with sugar!!!!!!!!).

Arjun
750 (Q49, V42)

I took with me two bananas, a bottle of water, and some Tylenol, just in case I got a headache during the exam.

Gova
740 (Q49, V41)

During the breaks, I drank some water and ate part of an apple.

Timur
770 (Q50, V47)

Acai energy booster—works good for me without having any crash.

Soomodh
700 (Q46, V41)

11

Advice for the 24-Hour Countdown

 Student Sound-Offs

The night before the exam, I put away the study guides early and got a good night's sleep. You aren't going to master anything new the night before the exam. The morning of the exam, I had a good breakfast and made sure I got to the testing center early. The exam "felt" very similar to the CAT exams, and I think it really helped me to work all of my OG practice problems using the MGMAT laminated booklet and felt pen.

> *Jonathan*
> *760 (Q51,V42)*

Warm up your mind on the test day: I solved about ten questions on the morning of the GMAT day. That warmed up my brain and boosted my confidence. I recommend doing this if it helps you.

> *Anoop*
> *760 (Q49, V44)*

D-Day: I woke up too weak to be anxious. I figured that I could always take it again and know not to feel bad for myself because I know I worked really hard and re-learned what a factorial is. I told myself that this still has the possibility of being the first and last time I ever take the GMAT—I told myself that I will treat each problem with a melodramatic air of love and preemptive nostalgia because it may very well be the last GMAT problem of its kind that I will ever try to solve again for the rest of my life. This turned out to be true. I did a booty shaking dance in front of the security window. That footage is going to be worth some money one day.

> *Helen*
> *750 (Q48/V46)*

11

Chapter Takeaways

1. The GMAT is a mental marathon. You must be physically and emotionally, as well as intellectually, prepared in order to perform at your peak. Plan to eat well and sleep well in the week approaching the test.

2. Do not burn yourself out before the test. Practice tests in the final week are counter-productive. You do not have time to learn. The best case scenario is that they will tire you unnecessarily. The worst case scenario is that they will worry you.

3. Do *not* bring your cell phone into the test center.

4. Eat well the morning of the test and consider bringing an easy to consume snack, such as an energy bar, to eat during the break.

11

Chapter 12

of

GMAT Roadmap

After Your GMAT:
Next Steps

In This Chapter...

The GMAT's Value in Business School

Now What?

Chapter 12:

After Your GMAT: Next Steps

It is very common for students to decide to take the GMAT more than once in order to improve their score. If you choose to take this path, we highly recommend that you do not take a break between completing one official test and commencing study for the next one.

Taking a few days or a weekend off to recover and refresh may be a wise decision, but you don't want to take more than a week or so off because you will start to forget the things that you have worked hard to learn. Any skill, if not practiced regularly, will fade. You will be making your GMAT journey harder and longer than it has to be if you need to relearn a substantial amount of material between each test.

> **TIP**
>
> While we often think that our lives will be easier and less busy in the future, this is very seldom true—unless you're planning to take a sabbatical.

If you have finished the GMAT once and for all, the time has come to concentrate on the other aspects of your business school application, including choosing which schools to apply to, writing numerous essays, and obtaining letters of recommendation. While we are experts on the GMAT, we now hand you off to our sister company, mbaMission, for some expert advice on these topics. But first, a small celebration of how your GMAT success is beneficial to your business school endeavor (beyond the entrance exam)....

The GMAT's Value in Business School – Eric Caballero

Instructor Insights

Make no mistake about it: business schools love the GMAT. And despite admissions officers' statements that the GMAT score is "*only* one piece of your application," it is a *huge* piece. Since its inception in 1953, the Graduate Management Admission Council (GMAC)—creator of the GMAT—has studied the desires of business schools. In fact, GMAT content is refined by intelligence gathered from frequent surveys of MBA faculty around the world. Additionally, GMAC sets aside profits to fund management education research—since 2005, GMAC has awarded $1.3MM in grants and fellowships to business school faculty and PhD candidates.

Validity

Validity is the degree to which GMAT scores predict first-year MBA grades. It turns out that GMAT scores and first-year business school grades have an average correlation factor of 0.48 (where 1.0 indicates perfect accuracy of prediction). In contrast, the average correlation between undergraduate GPA and first-year business school grades is 0.28. Therefore, GMAT scores are generally better than undergraduate GPAs for predicting average grades in business school.

In 2009, INSEAD performed a survey of several years' worth of its MBA graduates. INSEAD confirmed that the closer one's GMAT score was to **800**, the higher his or her MBA GPA tended to be. However, before you assume that Manhattan GMAT drinks its own Kool-Aid, allow us to share this curveball: the INSEAD study also confirmed that the closer one's GMAT score was to **600**, the higher his or her post-MBA salary tended to be!

Proof Positive

If you desire evidence that GMAT concepts are directly relevant in business school, consider the following math problem adapted from **Wharton's official 2010 Mathematics Self-Assessment Test**©:

> *Let-it-Ride Lucas invests $100,000 in a bank. If he requires his investment to grow to $140,000 after six years, what nominal annual rate, compounded continuously, must he receive? What interest rate would Lucas have to receive if the money were compounded annually?*

And here is an actual GMAT problem:

> *Leona bought a 1-year, $10,000 certificate of deposit that paid interest at an annual rate of 8 percent compounded semiannually. What was the total amount of interest paid on this certificate at maturity?*

While the problems are not identical, both require the compound interest formula, namely $P_t = P_0(1 + r)^t$. There are many examples where GMAT know-how overlaps with business school concepts, so readers might be wise to resist burning their GMAT books after their exam is complete.

Intellectual Curiosity & True Grit

Okay, so we agree that you will witness content similarities between the GMAT and business school coursework. But perhaps the greatest justification for the GMAT's relevance to business school is the shared character traits required of both.

We posit that great business leaders who earn their rank do so by leveraging a blend of intellectual curiosity and true grit. In other words, business schools desire alumni who demonstrate an insatiable desire for learning and a relentless pursuit of victory.

The GMAT will push you to your limits in this regard. Most tough GMAT problems are so sophisticated that they require of you (A) an openness to "tug at a thread and see where it goes" and (B) the ability to power through several small steps before the silver lining begins to show. Both of these facets will test your intellectual curiosity and true grit.

Your GMAT journey may require more memorization than you wish to give. Your journey may necessitate more reading and note-taking than you can stomach. Your journey may require more problem solving and *repetitive* problem review than you have energy or patience to extend. Each of these stages will test the depth of your intellectual curiosity and true grit.

When you find yourself questioning how GMAT concepts—such as Geometry—will *ever* be used by a CEO and then wanting to throw in the towel, realize that it is your reserves of intellectual curiosity and true grit that are really being measured.

So, please! Stay the course, earn your MBA, and set the world on fire.

Now What?
– mbaMission

Congratulations—you've taken the GMAT! Now you can breathe a sigh of relief, congratulate yourself on the accomplishment… and turn your attention to all the other parts of your business school applications. Some candidates get so caught up in taking the GMAT that they forget the admissions committee will be looking beyond just that three-digit score. Even if you excelled on the GMAT, you will need to put an appropriate amount of effort into the other parts of your application. (In fact, an admissions officer at a top-10 school recently stated in an online chat, *"I joke sometimes that I relish nothing more than rejecting people that have a 780 on the GMAT, because they come with the 780 GMAT and think they're golden, and they don't have to worry about anything else on the application."*) Now is the time to take a step back and assess your candidacy as a whole, thinking not only about your strengths but also about the areas in which you can improve. We at mbaMission have several big-picture recommendations for candi-

12

dates to consider at this point in the application process, so they can be as competitive as possible.

Few candidates realize that *now is an ideal time to visit campuses* to learn about and establish interest in specific schools. Such visits are not just opportunities to "register" with the various admissions committees, but also—and more importantly—times for you to gain an intimate understanding of each school's academic methodology and social environment. In addition, these visits will certainly help you frame your thoughts about each program and write far more personal and connected essays for the school's application. After all, you can only learn so much about a school from its website. We advise candidates to complete their campus visits early; doing so will allow you to experience the true character of your preferred MBA programs, fully absorb the information, and effectively discuss your connection to each school in a profound way.

By *meeting with alumni or students now*, you can also gain a more intimate understanding of your schools of choice. Current students, in particular, will have an awareness of specific programs and classes that may not be prominently featured or fully explained on a school's website but that may be quite appealing to you. Knowing more about such offerings could help you strengthen your case for attending that particular school. Through these meetings, you can collect data points that will serve as a foundation for you to persuade the admissions committee that its school is ideally suited to you, in a way that few others will be able to do.

We at mbaMission also feel that after candidates have taken the GMAT, they should consider whether now is the time to *take on a leadership role in the community* (though, in many cases, it would be optimal if you have already been committed to an organization or cause). If your applications are not due for several more months, you have adequate time to create a track record with an organization and show that you are a substantive individual outside the office. Be sure, however, not to volunteer for activities just so you can check off a "community service" box on your profile, but instead seek out opportunities and groups that have meaning for you and where you will be most likely to gain profound experiences that you can later share and explore in your essays. If you are genuinely excited about the volunteer activity you choose, you will be more committed to it, enjoy a more meaningful experience, and ultimately have a far more authentic story to tell. Ideally, you will create a record of community service that will complement and/or supplement your profile. Your community activities can reveal a true passion for your field (complementary) or shift the committee's perspective (supplementary) on you and thus differentiate you from other applicants. For example, the accountant who volunteers with Junior Achievement is complementing his profile by showing a commitment to his professional path and the desire to give back in this area; the accountant who coaches youth soccer in his community is supplementing his profile by offering a new window into his personality and abilities.

12

Regardless of the organization you choose and the nature of your activities, if you can (to cart out a cliché) "make a difference" via your contributions and show true leadership in doing so, you should be able to add an entirely new—and positive—dimension to your application.

In addition, by *advancing your personal achievements*, you can effectively differentiate yourself from the otherwise indistinguishable masses. The likelihood that a number of candidates will have similar professional backgrounds and academic records—and even GMAT scores—is high, so your volunteer and personal accomplishments can be key to offering the admissions committees a far more diversified and remarkable picture of yourself.

To advance your personal achievements, focus on *accelerating the timeline of existing endeavors*. For example, if you have always intended to publish a certain article and have almost finished a final draft, put in the necessary effort to finish it soon. If you have always intended to earn your CFA and only have Level Three of the exam left, then take that final test this year—don't wait! If you can run 20 miles and have always dreamed of completing a marathon, sign up for a race that will take place in the near future. We are not suggesting, however, that if you have never run a mile in your life that you start training for a marathon—especially if such an endeavor has no special meaning or appeal for you—but if a goal is in sight and will otherwise be achieved after your applications are due, you should hasten your efforts toward it now to ensure that you have attained it before your application deadline.

Building up your personal and community profiles is obviously important, but equally important is *bolstering your academic profile through additional coursework*. Many candidates fret about their poor undergraduate performance and feel that they are powerless to change the admissions committees' perspective on their academic aptitude, but MBA programs are actually far more forgiving of previous academic problems than other graduate programs are. Many applicants' academic experiences are far in the past, and their GMAT score, references, and work experience are better indicators of their potential for success. This is not to suggest that poor grades do not matter, but rather that poor grades can be mitigated.

If your past academic performance is a concern, consider immediately enrolling in a course or two that would address the area(s) in which you do not feel confident. For example, if you did poorly in math courses in college (even if your overall GPA is quite high), an admissions committee may doubt your ability to manage a heavily quantitative workload. Thus, you should consider taking a calculus or statistics course. Furthermore, to demonstrate an aptitude for management studies, you might enroll in an accounting, economics, or corporate finance class. Of course, you would need to earn A's in any such courses to show that you have a capacity for this kind of work and that you take academics quite seriously.

Additional coursework is not solely for the "academically challenged," however. Even candidates who performed quite well in their undergraduate classes could certainly benefit from taking supplementary courses. Liberal arts majors with 4.0 GPAs but no quantitative background could benefit from earning two additional A grades—one in a math discipline and one in a management discipline—which would entitle them to make strong statements about their competency in these areas.

As we noted earlier, our advice here has largely consisted of "big-picture" recommendations, but candidates can also take some smaller steps at this point that will help make the application process less stressful. For one, spend time right now doing your homework on potential recommenders, and as you do so, *take time to reconnect with previous supervisors* who could be strong recommenders, but with whom you may have fallen out of touch. You do not want to find yourself in a position where you are contacting a former supervisor for the first time in a year or more and asking him or her for a large chunk of their time on a tight timeline. If you know you will need to call on a former supervisor for a recommendation, make contact with him or her now and keep the relationship warm for the next few months. If you do, you will be far better off when the letter-writing process begins.

Virtually every MBA program requires that candidates write an essay that details their short- and long-term career goals, so having a solid understanding of where you see yourself after business school is extremely important. If you aspire to enter a competitive field, such as banking or consulting—or, more importantly, if you are unsure about what industry you may want to enter because of a lack of exposure to your options—now is the perfect time to *conduct informational interviews with or even job shadow individuals* who work in positions or areas that appeal to you. MBA admissions committees frown on vague goal statements or generic claims that fail to demonstrate a profound personal connection to a position and therefore lack credibility. The more firsthand knowledge you can gain about your target industry and/or role, the more sincere and better articulated your interest will be in your essays (and possibly your interview), and this can make all the difference for you in the admissions committee's eyes.

12

Sendoff

We began this book with the recognition that the GMAT is a challenging and difficult exam, but we also told you that with the right information, the right strategies, and the right attitude, you would be able to excel. We hope that, to some degree, *The GMAT Roadmap* has provided you with those resources and given you the foundation you need for GMAT success.

If you are looking for further direction or guidance, visit our website at **www.manhattangmat.com** and see whether any of our products or services can help you achieve your GMAT goals.

Chapter Takeaways

1. If you decide to retake the GMAT, do not wait too long.

2. Your GMAT prep has sharpened your intellectual skills and tested your perseverance. Being good at analysis and persistent will serve you well in business school.

3. Think about getting started on your applications. You took this test for a reason!

Appendix A
of

GMAT Roadmap

Advice for
Non-Native Speakers

In This Chapter...

Advice for Non-Native Speakers

Mi ingles no es muy bueno

Advice for Non-Native Speakers

It can be intimidating to approach the GMAT as a non-native speaker of American English. Although there are a few little wrinkles in the language of math, for the most part, the issues are in the Verbal section of the test. Here are some tips that can really help:

Tip #1: If you learned English in India, we recommend that you read Manhattan GMAT's *Foundations of GMAT Verbal* Appendix: Helpful Hints for Indian Speakers of English. This material is actually useful for anyone who learned any variant of British English. The GMAT tests American English, and there are some significant differences in idioms and even verb usage that you should be aware of.

Tip #2: Even if you scored above the 40th percentile on your Verbal pre-test, the reading practice recommended in Chapter 3 of this book is strongly recommended for all non-native speakers.

Tip #3: If your pre-test Verbal score was particularly low (below the 25th percentile), start your reading program even sooner than recommended in Chapter 2. We have seen non-native students who committed to the reading program make huge progress in Verbal—however, it usually takes those students extra time to build their reading fluency.

Tip #4: A very helpful thing to do during your reading program is to make flash cards of the words that you read in the articles that you do not know. Sometimes the biggest problem words are not the scientific and technical terms, but rather the academic words (e.g., moreover, henceforth, and thusly) that are important for determining the passage structure but that are not used much in everyday speech.

Above all, do not avoid studying Verbal and hope to make it all up by doing well on math. This is *not* a good strategy. There is nothing magic to Verbal content—it can be mastered just as any other GMAT content can be mastered. You have already mastered a tremendous amount of American English if you are reading this book, and all that is really necessary is refinement.

Non-native speakers can and do achieve excellent Verbal scores on the GMAT. One of our most beloved 99th percentile scoring instructors, Horacio Quiroga, is not a native English speaker. Read his words that follow for some encouragement and suggestions.

Mi ingles no es muy bueno.
– Horacio Quiroga

Instructor Insights

If you think that because you are not a native English speaker you cannot ace the Verbal part of the GMAT, or the full test for that matter, think again; I hold a 99th percentile GMAT score and am not an English native-speaker. What's more, my Verbal score is higher than my quantitative one. How did I do it? No easy answer for that, but I am sure that I can share a tip or two.

There is not just one type of test taker whose mother tongue is not English, but two. On the one hand, we have the guy like me, whose command of English approaches that of the native speaker in terms of oral fluency, listening comprehension, and writing and reading performance. On the other hand, we have those people whose spoken English is not that fluent and who have trouble quickly understanding a written passage.

I do not have that much to tell to people who fall into the first category—only that the fact that English is not your mother tongue will not at all be an obstacle to your acing the Verbal part of the test. In fact, I think that you will do better at Sentence Correction than a native speaker of English would, since English grammar was actually taught to you and you are used to analyzing sentences and finding errors. Ultimately, if your English is native-like you should just plan your studying as any native speaker would.

If you fall into the second category—your Reading Comprehension is not that good and your command of English grammar is quite flaky—then I can tell you a couple of things. First of all, most of your improvement will be in Sentence Correction, so do not expect miracles in Critical Reasoning or Reading Comprehension. Follow our *Sentence Correction* Strategy Guide and you will not believe how much your error-spotting skills will have improved. On the Reading Comprehension and Critical Reasoning side, what you should do is practice a little every day, by which I mean doing two Reading Comprehension passages and, say, six Critical Reasoning problems. If one day you do not have time or do not feel like studying, do one Reading Comprehension passage and three Critical Reasoning problems, but whatever you do, do not go one single day without practicing a little.

No matter which of the following categories mentioned above you fall into, the final message is simple: do not be put off by the task ahead, you can do it! I am living proof of it.

Student Sound-Offs

How to get a high score and how to use a language are different animals, which involve distinct strategies. In my view, there are not so many significant differences between native speakers and second-language learners when preparing for the GMAT. Though, as a typical ESL student who got a good GMAT score of 750 in a short period, I'd like to share my experiences here as others may encounter similar situations. I also want to formally thank Ron Purewal for his unconventional instruction and priceless encouragement.

The first thing, if not the only thing, is to make the best use of the *Official Guide*.

Make sure you know exactly what the GMAC wants to test first, and then try to squeeze as much juice from OG problems as you can. Do not leave a problem until you have gotten TAKEAWAY from that problem—a takeaway that you can APPLY TO OTHER PROBLEMS. Once you know how to utilize that TAKEAWAY, keep practicing until you get to that point of "déjà vu."

Good improvisation requires years of preparation, so namely, the best improvisation isn't improvisation at all. Instead, the actor has been in hundreds of similar situations before, and so has developed instincts that will guide him or her through the current situation smoothly.

> *Tina*
> *750 (51Q, 39V)*
> *Native Language : Chinese*

As an engineer, I see everything in numbers, formulas, mathematical relationships, and structures. When I first started studying for the GMAT, I was clueless about SC, I would waste too much time on RC reading every single letter, and I needed to improve my CR to beat the buzzer. The MGMAT SC book was a gate that connected the unfamiliar "English grammar and idioms" territory to my comfortable realm of formulas and structures.

At the beginning, I could not imagine that one day I could scan sentences and find the right answer through a formulated approach. However, after reading the book cover to cover, I started watching "free sessions with Ron," and that is when I was able to apply the information I had gained from the book to real problems using Ron's strategies. Although what Ron covers in every session exists in the books, his method of teaching and interactive sessions helped me understand when, where, and how I could apply my knowledge.

My end note to all GMATers is practice all the rules and tricks enough so that they come to you as second nature; under test conditions, with the clock ticking, there is no time for digging in memory and going through a trial-and-error process.

> *Hoss*
> *730 (51Q, 37V)*
> *Native Language: Farsi*

Appendix B
of GMAT Roadmap

Extended Time and
Other Accommodations

In This Chapter...

On Finding the GMAC Accommodating

On Finding the GMAC Accommodating
– Dmitry Farber, Liz Ghini Moliski, Ian Jorgeson, and Jon Schneider

Who gets special accommodations?

Most of this section focuses on what to do and how to study differently if you are granted the accommodation of extra time on the GMAT. However, extra time is not the only accommodation that we have seen students need or receive, and we'd like to take a moment to point out some of the other accommodations that are available. Keep in mind that the goal of accommodations is NOT to provide a test-taker with an advantage over other students. Instead, the aim is to provide test-takers with fair testing, so that they are in a situation in which they can perform as well as they would have if they did not suffer from a specific issue (as covered in the Americans with Disabilities Act).

For example, a student with moderate ADD might be given a private testing room so that she is not adversely affected by distractions. That student might not get any extra time on the test (as her disability does not affect her ability to finish the test in the allotted time), but might still be provided with an environment that will allow her to reach her full potential. (It's worth noting that, because it's pretty easy to find a doctor to diagnose a person as AD/HD, GMAC is leery about accepting such requests if they don't include a history of previous accommodations.)

When presented with an accommodations request, GMAC reviews each case individually, and over the years we have seen some decisions made that have surprised us. We have had diabetic students successfully petition to be allowed either longer breaks to test their blood sugar, or to bring their testing supplies and insulin with them into the room (which seems harder to get than the longer breaks). We've also seen partially blind students successfully petition for accommodations including larger screen font text. Note that these situations all resulted in being granted accommodations, but *not* extra time.

> **TIP**
>
> We have found that students who are easily distracted do best when they have a detailed study plan comprised of short, focused study sessions.

That's not to say that extra time is impossible to get. A student with specific processing issues that affect reading skills might be granted extra time, the rationale being that this student requires the extra time in order to perform to the level of their ability. Examples of such learning disabilities (LDs) include dyslexia as well as general processing disorders; a student with brain damage from an accident might be granted extra time, for instance, if the brain damage manifested in some sort of testable processing disorder.

Diagnosis of most LDs generally requires a number of neurological tests, and students who have LDs usually know about them because they would have been documented since grade school. Students who are granted extra time are often allowed time-and-a-half. This accommodation also includes an extra 8-minute break between the two essays. Students with a more extreme LD, however, are sometimes granted double time, which includes an hour break for lunch.

How do you get special accommodations?

To get extra time on the GMAT, you have to petition GMAC. Directions of how to do so are on their website at **www.mba.com**. Generally speaking, the easiest way to get testing accommodations is to provide documentary evidence of previously received accommodations along with medical documentation. GMAC generally seems to rubber stamp requests when the student can show that they received similar accommodations for the SAT, throughout high school, in college, and so on; they appear to trust that if a student has requested and received such accommodations over the course of many years, they honestly require such accommodations in order to be fairly tested. They take a dimmer view when the issue has been recently diagnosed.

Our advice to students who are requesting special accommodations is to start the request process early. While GMAC states that they decide on cases within three to four weeks, we have seen it take longer. Also, when accommodations are approved, students must undertake a separate registration process and cannot simply sign up for the test on the website. These students must submit three top choice test dates to GMAC and wait to be contacted with the date on which they are allowed to take the test.

How should you use extra time?

Most people with an LD struggle with the information uptake. In other words, they have difficulty—or take longer—decoding, interpreting, and processing what they read. Many students with LDs also have a difficult time understanding what to write on their scrap paper and how to organize it. Yet, once they understand the problem, these students are often able to solve it just as rapidly as other test takers. For this reason, we generally recommend that students with processing LDs spend their extra time in the first phase of the problem-solving process: making sure that they understand the problem.

It is important to realize that double time is *not* the panacea that many people think it is—you've just turned a three-and-a-half-hour test into an *eight* hour test (with the lunch break)! Talk about test fatigue! For this reason, students sometimes find it most useful to spend some of the extra time by taking extra breaks. The extra time does *not* need to be used to solve questions. It is fine to use the time (or part of it) for an extended break or for several short breaks.

MANHATTAN
GMAT

Finally, just because you are given extra time does not mean that you have to use all of it. You may need the extra time, for example, in one section but not the other, or you may use some of the extra time, but not all of it. You will find what works for you by experimenting.

Learning Techniques and Tips for Students with LDs

(1) *Extended Time GMAT Prep:* If you have been approved for extended time on the GMAT, call GMAC to request an extended time version of the GMATPrep CD. This CD exists, but is not available for download. The information needed to receive one of these CDs is emailed to students with extended time when they register; don't overlook it! The CD can take several weeks to receive by mail. We have also had students outside of the U.S. whose CD never arrived (seized by customs?), so if you live outside of the U.S., you may want to have the CD sent to a friend in the U.S., who can then repackage it and send it to you.

(2) *MGMAT CATs:* Our CATs can be set for different time restrictions per section. Make sure, when taking one of our CATs, to adjust the timing to match the length of time that you will actually receive on the GMAT.

(3) *Determine Your Problem-Solving Time Needs:* Work with a stopwatch to identify the timing needs that you have for each type of problem. A useful exercise is just to keep a clock running to see how long it takes to read and understand a problem (including taking notes or whatever else helps to understand it), then to see how long it takes to come up with a reasonable plan for how to solve that problem, etc.

> **TIP**
>
> If possible, get a doctor who is experienced with GMAT extended time documentation to be responsible for your paperwork.

(4) *Flash Cards and Mechanics Drills:* Flash cards are invaluable. Your association and recognition need to be as fast as possible. Also make sure to consistently use mechanics drills as part of your study process. We have found that, for students with LDs, review has to be more continuous. It's use it or lose it.

(5) *Drills on Skipping:* It is better to skip problems on a regular basis and to finish the test than it is to not finish the test. During a skip drill, give yourself five GMAT problems to solve in real test-condition timing, and make sure to pick one to skip. Under circumstances where timing is still an extreme barrier, remember that your score won't suffer a severe hit if you skip two out of every five problems.

(6) *Be Reasonable and Kind to Yourself:* Set score expectations that are a little lower than what you would normally expect given your ability level. It's simply very difficult to keep everything fresh and to manage the time. You likely have a more difficult feat to accomplish than the average GMAT test-taker, so focus on your weaker areas and don't try to do more than is reasonably possible.

Student Sound-Off

Being four years out of college and not having taken a standardized test in close to ten years, the notion of sitting down to study and take yet another such exam was extremely daunting. With the help of my MGMAT instructor and the related resources provided therein, however, I quickly became comfortable with a targeted plan of attack. Perhaps the most frustrating part of the process was taking the first practice GMAT without having studied. Though I initially questioned the value of what I viewed as a waste of an available practice CAT—as nearly all prep programs tout the total number they offer—this exercise proved invaluable to roadmapping an efficient course of study.

After reviewing the first practice exam, it was blatantly obvious that I needed a comprehensive math review. As a result, my instructor advised that I spend at least 80% of my review time going forward to focus solely on math. As someone with a learning disability, this adjustment to my point of focus was truly invaluable as I am a very slow reader. Originally setting out to boil the ocean in my review, I now had more focused marching orders, which included a comprehensive math review and very little Verbal review. My instructor accordingly gave me a specific roadmap of study topics to target the areas in which I needed the most improvement.

Beyond the initial planning process, I found that many of the old study habits I had practiced in the past helped me to sustain a rigid study routine. Studying at the same time of day for the same duration was a helpful way to build my routine. All in all, I am grateful for the disciplined routine that MGMAT helped me build in my pursuit of a 700.

Dan
710

MANHATTAN
GMAT

ALL TEST PREP IS NOT THE SAME

mbaMission